LANGUAG
AND
TRADITION
IN IRELAND

LANGUAGE
AND
TRADITION
IN IRELAND

· ·

CONTINUITIES AND
DISPLACEMENTS

· ·

Edited by

· ·

MARIA TYMOCZKO AND
COLIN IRELAND

UNIVERSITY OF MASSACHUSETTS PRESS
Amherst and Boston

Published in cooperation with the
AMERICAN CONFERENCE FOR IRISH STUDIES

Printed in the United States of America
LC 2003014559
ISBN 1-55849-426-X (cloth); 427-8 (paper)

Set in Sabon by Keystone Typesetting, Inc.
Printed and bound by The Maple-Vail Book Manufacturing Group

Library of Congress Cataloging-in-Publication Data

Language and tradition in Ireland : continuities and displacements /
edited by Maria Tymoczko and Colin Ireland.
p. cm.
"Published in cooperation with the American Conference for Irish Studies."
Includes bibliographical references and index.
ISBN 1-55849-426-X (lib. cloth : alk. paper) — ISBN 1-55849-427-8 (pbk. : alk. paper)
1. Ireland—Civilization. 2. Language and culture—Ireland. 3. Ireland—Literatures—
History and criticism. 4. Ireland—Languages. I. Tymoczko, Maria. II. Ireland, Colin A.,
1949–   III. American Conference for Irish Studies.
DA925 .L365 2003
306'.09415—dc21
2003014559

British Library Cataloguing in Publication
data are available.

Contents

Acknowledgments

It is always a pleasure to work on a project with people who are able to cross cultural and linguistic boundaries skillfully, especially when those boundaries encompass the realm of a culturally rich but waning minority. Such a pleasure has been ours in working on this volume, and many people deserve our gratitude. Members of the American Conference for Irish Studies (ACIS) publications committee — including John Harrington and Gary Owens — encouraged us early on to submit a proposal for this volume to the committee. The two presidents of ACIS during the period the volume was in preparation — Nancy J. Curtin and Michael Patrick Gillespie — assisted us in countless ways, granting us not only their imprimatur but also their helpful enthusiasm. Thomas Dillon Redshaw and Vera Kreilkamp made available to us their vast experience related to publishing in Irish studies in the early stages of this project. We owe a special debt to Maureen Murphy for her close and judicious reading of the manuscript and for her special ability to move back and forth across Ireland's cultural and linguistic boundaries effortlessly. Bruce Wilcox of the University of Massachusetts Press was from beginning to end supportive as well as cordial, efficient, patient, and professional, offering helpful counsel on many points and making our work with the press pleasant and productive. Thanks also to Carol Betsch, managing editor of the press, whose help was invaluable during the production of the volume.

This book began with a conversation between us about the need for more attention to Irish-language issues in Irish Studies. We were, thus, both pleased and surprised by the flood of responses — many coming from younger scholars — to our initial call for papers. The variety and quality of proposals were so good that it seemed worthwhile to attempt to publish a larger selection of essays than we could include here. The result is a companion volume to this ACIS publication, a special issue of *Éire-Ireland* entitled *Language and Identity in Twentieth-Century Irish Culture*, volume 38, numbers 1 and 2, published in spring/summer 2003. The two collections of essays are mutually complementary, developing similar themes and arguments that resonate both diachronically and synchronically across Ireland's complex culture and its languages. We are grateful to Vera Kreilkamp and James S. Donnelly, Jr., the editors of *Éire-Ireland,* for making the additional essays available to scholars as an integrated collection.

Finally, because this volume is coedited, we reserve for ourselves the right to express our appreciation for each other. If we all had such colleagues, we would have to drop the word *work* from our professional vocabularies. Most of all we thank our contributors, who were gracious and assiduous in responding to our suggestions, in meeting deadlines, and in working together to bring to fruition this joint project.

MARIA TYMOCZKO
COLIN IRELAND

Language and Tradition in Ireland: Prolegomena

IF LANGUAGE AND CULTURE are intimately connected — as linguists, ethnographers, and literary scholars agree — then cultures involving people who speak more than one language must have special characteristics, as well as particular social issues to negotiate. What are the challenges faced by a people with two or more languages as their heritage? How does that multiple heritage affect cultural forms, including literature and the arts? How does linguistic difference affect the conceptualization and writing of history? Is it in fact possible to be one people with a united culture, or is the community constantly in danger of falling apart along the divide of linguistic heritage? To what extent does language remain thematized within the polity or nation? And if the meeting of languages within a people has been polarized or agonistic, if it has involved contestation and power, how are these conflicts negotiated?

These questions are at the heart of the essays in this volume, for all must be asked of Ireland and Irish culture. Although the linguistic interface of Irish and English has dominated cultural negotiations in Ireland in the last five hundred years, Ireland has a long history of linguistic and cultural interface. Just as in England many linguistic and cultural groups came together, so too in Ireland we can chart a persistent history of linguistic mixing. From the pre-Celtic languages and the various dialects of the Celtic invaders to the integration of Latin after the conversion of the Irish to Christianity by British clerics, from the linguistic diversity encountered by Irish missionaries abroad to the assimilation of Scandinavian dialects introduced by the Vikings, the early history of Ireland is rich in multilingualism. The Anglo-Norman conquest brought still other languages to Ireland at the end of the twelfth century, with the armies and settlers speaking more than one dialect of French, Occitan, Welsh, Flemish, and English. Most of these early linguistic groups had turned to the Irish language by the start of the Tudor period, but it is important to mark them, because they remind us that Irish-language culture was not pure, essentialist, singular, isolated, or untouched by other languages and cultures before the time it began its serious negotiations with English.[1] Irish-language culture — like English-language culture — had already been mixed and hybridized through the course of time, changed by countless cultural contacts with people speaking many different languages.

Insofar as language and culture are intertwined, what do we mean by *tradition?* In this volume we are using the term in its earliest sense, that is, *tradition* as representing something handed over or handed down through time. This meaning is reflected in its etymology: *tradition* is an old word in English, coming from Middle English *tradicion,* 'a handing down, a surrender', which comes in turn from an Old French word of that meaning and ultimately from Latin *traditio,* a participle of *tradere,* 'to hand over', from *trans-*, 'over', and *dare,* 'to give'. Used in this well-established way, tradition can be discerned in written as well as oral cultures, in high culture as well as folk culture and popular culture; it can be traced in literature and other verbal arts, in conceptions of history, and in material culture. *Tradition* and *traditional* are words that have been much used in scholarship about Ireland in the last 150 years, because the presence of the past has been palpable in Irish life. Irish shares with English this common European vocabulary in the words *traidisiún*, 'tradition', and *traidisiúnta,* 'traditional'. The persistence of archaic lifeways, cultural forms, and oral verbal arts inherited from the depths of time has been notable in Ireland, particularly among the Irish-speaking populace, and the words *tradition* and *traidisiún* facilitate discourse about those features of Irish culture. Scholars from many different fields — folklore, music, oral epic, and anthropology, among others — have examined culture in Ireland, and all these disciplines use the terms *tradition* and *traditional,* as well as their Irish counterparts, to refer to cultural forms and products which have been inherited from the past and which have persisted through time.

Most scholars have attempted to use these terms — *tradition* and *traidisiún* — without prejudice: a major concern of many academic fields has been to define how culture works in relation to time in varied environments. The results of such investigations have often been startling. Despite disclaimers from respondents and performers who insist that they have changed nothing, scholars have found that change and adaptation are

---

1. Issues of Ireland's multilingual heritage are taken up at greater length in the essays in Cronin and Ó Cuilleanáin 2003.

basic features of "traditional" cultures and their art forms.[2] Moreover, despite the oral base of most "traditional" cultures, the impact of literacy is often obvious and must be taken into account, whether in the verbal arts or in music. Borrowings from other cultures and from other classes — including borrowings from "high art" — are ubiquitous even in seemingly isolated rural populations. Frequently it is also possible to identify and name specific individuals as originators of certain "traditions." What is traditional — what is handed down from the past — is, therefore, also subject to constant innovation and change.

Still, different peoples have different heritages, different inheritances from the past. Part of the concern in this volume is to investigate the intersection of multiple traditions, multiple inheritances from the past, as they occur in a society with a multilingual and multicultural foundation. The traditions of specific cultures — particularly when carried in different languages — will have their own proper characteristics. For example, English literary tradition cannot be fully separated from French literary tradition, because there has been so much interchange between the two languages and cultures for hundreds of years, yet each literary tradition has its own particular characteristics as well. Minutely expressed in linguistic forms, ritual, and gesture, traditions are manifest in allusion, intertextuality, and all the other elements that bind cultural forms together, making them self-reflexive and interdependent, even as they change and develop.

Irish culture as inherited by the twentieth century was arguably archaic in many ways. The archaism is seen not just in contrast to the industrial cultures of Europe but also in the preservation of lifeways showing filiation with neolithic material culture (Evans 1957) and with ancient Celtic ritual and religious patterns (Mac Neill 1962). Irish-language culture retained elements of literary richness documented in medieval manuscripts, with forms of some of the medieval stories continuing to circulate in oral storytelling (cf. Ó Súilleabháin 1970:588–99). These stories perpetuate the consciousness of an aristocratic past, even in the context of their peasant transmission. Not all this preservation of the past was of Gaelic Ireland's own choosing, for the Penal Laws of the eighteenth and nineteenth century, as well as the extreme poverty of the Irish-speaking population, blocked modernization for two hundred years in segments of the

2. The classic study of such changes and adaptations in oral literature is found in Lord 1960.

Irish population. It is remarkable, for instance, that the medieval tradition of manuscript production continued until the mid-nineteenth century in Gaelic Ireland — alone among Western European populations — to a large extent because printing in Irish was proscribed under English rule decade upon decade, right into the nineteenth century.

In virtue of its perceived archaism, Irish-language culture has been characterized by some as conservative in the literal sense of the word and by others as backward-looking.[3] There are perhaps reasons for both characterizations: until the seventeenth century, Irish-language culture had been in the hands of a strong learned class that maintained professional standards and institutions, including schools, modes of training, and "gatekeeping" benchmarks for competence, thus institutionalizing the preservation of cultural forms that were rooted in the Middle Ages. These institutions are documented from the seventh century in Ireland and mutatis mutandis persisted as long as the Gaelic Order lasted in Ireland. It is also relevant that early Irish culture had sustained no concerted external aggression for more than a thousand years between the coming of the Celts to Ireland in the third or second century B.C. and the first raid of the Vikings in 795. Thus, spared the conquest of Rome and Christianized by peaceful and accommodating means rather than by the church militant, Ireland never experienced a definitive rupture between present and past during this period, which facilitated the sense of a continuous heritage that tied the culture to the depths of time (cf. Richter 1999:16–20). In addition, the Irish people had been long dwelling in one place, a relatively small island, such that legends, customs, and rituals became localized and embedded in the constant landscape; in such circumstances memories of ancient things do not die easily.

But backward-looking is not necessarily backward. There is ample evidence of adaptation and innovation from the earliest period of Irish-language culture. Christianity was taken up relatively quickly throughout the island by the middle of the sixth century, and the peacefulness of that conversion was such that Ireland could claim no blood martyrs. With

---

3. Frank O'Connor promoted this idea in his 1967 volume *The Backward Look: A Survey of Irish Literature*. Minority and "low-prestige" languages, even in modern Europe, are often characterized as being conservative and backward-looking, particularly by speakers of majority and high-prestige languages. Such characterizations are especially evident in postcolonial contexts where the privilege and status attributed to high-prestige languages reflect the social status, political power, educational opportunities, technological advantages, economic well-being, and public standing of their speakers.

Christianity came literacy, Latin learning, and a Christian-Latin sense of history;[4] these too were rapidly appropriated by Irish culture, with the result that Ireland developed the first secular literate class among the vernacular cultures of Europe, making the immense transition from a purely oral culture to literacy in just a few generations, by the end of the sixth century. A bilingual learned culture in Irish and Latin quickly evolved with secular and ecclesiastically trained scholars cooperating in a society where oral and literate modes functioned side by side (Stevenson 1995; Ireland 1999:45–48). The literary result—to speak of only one cultural domain—was what is arguably the richest vernacular literature in medieval Western Europe. Thus, paradoxically, during the early Irish period, at the very time that we might expect stasis and constancy of culture—the period that cultural nationalists looked to for an essentialist baseline of native Irish culture—we see instead a rather free use of tradition, notable manipulation of cultural materials, and interrogation and reformation of attitudes, values, and norms inherited from the past.

The early Irish themselves were keenly aware of the workings of tradition, that is, the passing on of their lore. For example, in the introduction to an Old Irish compilation of law tracts known as *Senchas Már,* 'the great tradition', dating from 700–750, the Irish jurists show a remarkable prescience in their grasp of the interplay of orality and literacy. Using the Old Irish word *senchas* (Mod. Ir. *seanchas,* 'traditional lore, history', literally 'old things'), which designates the collection of law texts as a whole, the introduction begins:

> Senchas fer n-Érenn, cid conid-roíter? Comchuimne dá sen, tindnacol cluaise di arailiu, díchetal filed, tormach ó recht litre. . . .
>
> The traditional lore of the men of Ireland, what has preserved it? The concordant memory of two elders, transmission from one ear to another, the recitation of poets, augmentation by the law of the letter [i.e., Scripture]. . . .[5]

Here is a clear statement of both constancy and change, highlighting the oral transmission of lore in early societies, the exalted place of memory, and, in the case of Ireland, the central role of the poets, the native learned class. At the same time it adumbrates the role of literacy in passing on and

---

4. The impact of literacy on Irish cultural history is discussed in Stevenson 1989. Broader considerations of the differences between oral and literate cultures are taken up in Ong 1988 and Havelock 1963.

5. The text is normalized from the edition in Thurneysen 1927:175; our translation.

"augmenting" lore. *Recht litre,* 'law of the letter', refers to ecclesiastical law generally and Holy Scripture specifically, and it acknowledges the literacy of the clerics, both Latinate and vernacular, as a source for innovation and as a mechanism for the transmission of lore.

Genealogies stand as another example of the workings of tradition in early Irish culture. Conceived of as a means of reifying alliances and affiliations, genealogies were not treated as absolutes; instead, they were rearranged and reassigned, continually reedited to represent changing political needs and realities.[6] Similarly, the various annals were reedited at points early in Irish history, bringing the seemingly objective account of these historical documents into line with political orthodoxies of the day.[7] Similar manipulations of tradition can be seen in the earliest lives of the saints, notably those of St. Patrick. The first life written by Tírechán of Armagh and the second by Muirchú maccu Machthéni were both redacted in Latin in the late seventh century, probably within a decade of each other (ca. 680). Although both rely on evidence from the surviving writings of Patrick himself—his *Confession* and his *Letter to (the Soldiers of) Coroticus*—they are nonetheless full of invented material, much of it intended as propaganda for the ecclesiastical primacy of Armagh and the political prominence of the Uí Néill dynastic kindred. We can see the manipulation of evidence at work when we note that Tírechán has Patrick fail in his attempt to convert Lóegaire, the pagan king of Tara, whereas Muirchú has Patrick succeed in the conversion, though with great difficulty.[8]

If such basic documents of law, politics, and faith could be rewritten, reinterpreted, and even reinvented, it should be no surprise that the same is true of the legends and heroic narratives of the past. The stories of the Ulster heroes are not simply characterized by variants, as is to be expected in any materials that derive from an oral tradition, but also by thematic manipulations that indicate the earliest manuscript versions are rewritings

6. Traces of such manipulations and reeditings can be seen in the inconsistencies that pervade the large genealogical corpus preserved in early Irish manuscripts, examples of which are found in O'Brien 1962. Some of these variations in Irish materials can also probably be attributed to the homeostasis of oral culture, in which "the integrity of the past was subordinate to the integrity of the present" (Ong 1988:48), as well as to the conscious manipulations of the Irish literate learned classes.

7. Discussions of the shaping and editing of the annals are found in Hughes 1972:97–159 and Kelleher 1963, which originated as a paper read at the inaugural meeting of the American Committee for Irish Studies, held in conjunction with the annual meeting of the Modern Language Association in Chicago, 1961. See also Kelleher 2002.

8. See Bieler 1979:132 and 96–99, respectively.

of primary mythic material.[9] Some of these manipulations may have had political implications, which suggests that they were not neutral to their historical context.

Perhaps the single greatest example of invented tradition in Irish cultural history is found in the medieval creation of *Lebor Gabála Érenn* (Mod. Ir. *Leabhar Gabhála Éireann*), usually rendered as *The Book of Invasions*, literally 'the book of the taking of Ireland'.[10] *The Book of Invasions* contains the pseudohistory of Ireland: the "traditional" history of Ireland before A.D. 432, the conventional date for the coming of Patrick and the beginning of written history in Ireland. Its prototype was probably composed in the seventh century to supply a narrative for Ireland in late Roman "universal" histories, such as Eusebius's *World Chronicle,* which placed events of the Near East and the classical world in a historical framework based on the Bible. Originally restricted to the postdiluvian history of the Milesians, supposed ancestors of the Goidelic stock in Ireland, *The Book of Invasions* was elaborated for centuries, and many of the pseudohistorians who contributed to its evolution can be identified, including Máel Muru Othna (d. 887), Eochaid ua Flainn (d. 1004), Flann Mainistrech (d. 1056), and Gilla Cóemáin (fl. ca. 1072).[11] These writers invented the past in the absence of historical records (Scowcroft 1988:49), and the text eventually came to include many doublets of migration myths, as well as some remnants of Ireland's pre-Christian cosmogony and myth pertaining to the old gods, the Túatha Dé Danann. With narratives based principally on biblical patterns and archetypes, the temporal framework of *The Book of Invasions* provided a matrix for historicizing the rest of Irish literature, king lists, and genealogical materials, thus locating Ireland's oral heroic material in chronological time and giving it a more historical cast, in ways that were rather foreign to the original nature of the legends and hero tales. The framework became the rationale for salvaging many stories pertaining to Ireland's pre-Christian religious beliefs, as well as the greatest vector of distortion of those same materials.[12]

9. Tymoczko 1985–86 gives a specific example of this sort of rewriting.
10. The texts of *Lebor Gabála* are found in Macalister 1938–56; Scowcroft (1987, 1988) offers a critical discussion of the text.
11. Scowcroft (1987, 1988) provides particulars. Note that the involvement of the church in this enterprise is clear from the epithets of two of these pseudohistorians: Máel Muru Othna and Flann Mainistrech, associated respectively with the monasteries of Fahan in County Donegal and Monasterboice in County Louth.
12. All the later refractions of Irish history and literature look back to these early manip-

There is never a simple way to describe a culture or define the past. What is so startling about the early Irish evidence, however, is its seeming modernity. On the basis of surviving evidence, we cannot project backward a time in Ireland when the past was not reinterpreted and reformed in the service of the present, when tradition existed in a "pure" and "changeless" form. Looked at in a sinister way, the process can be likened to the treatment of history in Orwell's *1984*.[13] More soberly, one recognizes in the early Irish materials confirmation of postpositivist views: there is no way of achieving "objective" truth, no way of eliminating perspective, no way of separating the view from the viewer or evidence from the time and place it derives from. Thus, what is perceived as tradition and traditional — and what is in turn passed down as such — is constantly colored and refracted by the eye that sees and the mouth that speaks, shaped in turn by the moment and place of vision.

Not only can we chart the invention and manipulation of tradition for centuries in Irish culture, but Irish receptivity to outside influences and the uptake of cultural materials from other cultures is also palpable. Michael Richter argues that it was Ireland's openness to external models that made possible the unparalleled breadth and diversity of artistic and spiritual accomplishments during the seventh and eighth centuries (Richter 1988: 94–95). These factors are implicit in what has already been said: in the conversion to Christianity, in the adoption of literacy by the native learned classes, in the use of Christian and classical intellectual frameworks for native history, and so forth. They are seen tangibly in Irish accomplishments during the Middle Ages. By the late sixth and early seventh centuries, Irish missionary activity had begun in earnest, and for the next several centuries Irish clerics and scholars were at the center of learning throughout Europe. During the same period, in Ireland itself a rich secular literature of law tracts, poems, and prose narratives was being written down in the vernacular. Moreover, what the Irish learned abroad was often reflected at home. This blend of foreign and native, Latinate and

---

ulations of Irish traditional materials. They include the great seventeenth-century recastings, including the work of Seathrún Céitinn (Geoffrey Keating) known as *Foras Feasa ar Éirinn* (literally 'a basis for knowledge about Ireland'), as well as *Annála Ríoghachta Éireann, Annals of the Kingdom of Ireland*, better known as the *Annals of the Four Masters*. In turn, these early modern formulations became the basis of later patriotic histories and nationalist recastings.

13. Scowcroft (1988:49) cautions that the inventions and manipulations of Irish traditional materials were not propaganda per se, which involves deliberate falsification. Rather, the historians projected the status quo backward, reconstructing causes from known effects.

vernacular, can be seen in the texts attributed to scholars who are designated *sapiens,* 'the wise', in the early Irish chronicles (Ireland 1996). The Irish law tracts, for example, when dealing with native customs and institutions, at times cite biblical precedents to justify or explain practice. Conversely, Irish canon law, written in Latin, shows adaptations to the Irish community not found on the Continent, and specialized Latin vocabulary based on calques of Irish legal terms is also found. Similarly, the visual arts, including the illuminated manuscripts, display a blend of Mediterranean and native design features.

The permeability of Irish culture is also notable in the period between the Norman invasion of the twelfth century and the collapse of the Gaelic Order in the seventeenth century, the period when the greatest number of surviving Irish manuscripts was produced. Their contents reveal the wide interests of the Irish learned classes. The native narrative tales pertaining to the Ulster heroes, Finn mac Cumaill and his *fianna,* and the traditional kings are represented, of course, but there is also an abundance of translations, adaptations, and literary creations related to classical literature (including versions of the *Aeneid* and the *Odyssey*), Arthurian literature, and so forth. Other Continental sources, such as medical tracts and philosophical treatises, as well as devotional literature, are translated into contemporary Irish as well (see Williams and Ford 1992:119–45). At the same time, the genres of romance and the ballad become productive and popular in Irish, as they were throughout most of Europe. This uptake and adaptation of new cultural material suggest the long-standing innovative quality of Irish culture that continued to modern times.[14]

That there is no neutral way to describe a culture or a tradition is clearly demonstrated in the thematizations of culture since the eighteenth century in the West. For a variety of reasons — not least of which was dissatisfaction with modernization, as well as anxiety caused by the cultural erosions and uncertainties that modernization spawned — the past and the primitive became valorized in the eighteenth century in European culture. Such views about the past came to full flower in Romanticism, and the Celts became the focus of many of these projections. The construction of what it was to be "Celtic" was spurred to a considerable extent by James Macpherson's refractions of Scottish traditional stories,

---

14. Declan Kiberd has claimed that "far from being a backward-looking people, the Irish have for the past century and a half been one of the more future-oriented peoples of the world . . . one of the first countries to embrace modernity" (1998:12).

with Macpherson's portraits of early Celtic literature and culture initiating some of the discourses of Romanticism, as well as romantic views of the Celts. Such views have had a long life span, continuing actively into the modern period, reflected in the work of the writers associated with the Celtic Twilight at the turn of the last century, and continuing to color contemporary views of the Irish, not only in popular culture but in some scholarly quarters as well.

Thematization of culture intensified during the nineteenth century, for a tenet of European politics at the time was that national autonomy—nationhood—had as a necessary prerequisite the existence of a national language and a national culture. Thus, the nineteenth century was a period in which there was acute self-consciousness about the relationship of language to culture. Nationalists found themselves perforce engaged in the exploration of their national culture or—absent the recognized existence of such—engaged in the invention of cultural tradition and the definition of heritage.[15] Such impulses have continued since that time not only in political movements but also in popular culture; in Celtic spheres, for example, they are notable in the contemporary Cornish culture movement, manifestations of which have the potential to drive some scholars to distraction.[16] Because of the political values of culture and language, during the nineteenth century cultural identities hardened and even became oppositional. In part a function of European colonialism and enforced cultural dominance, cultural difference became politicized and entered into issues pertaining to power politics. To be Irish was in many ways not to be English. And vice versa, of course.

How was Irish culture constructed under these imperatives? Ironically, Ireland was faced with the task of constructing an autonomous culture just when the bulk of the Irish country people were giving up the Irish language in favor of English.[17] Thus, the constructions of Irishness proceeded largely in English, in tandem with the Irish-language movement spearheaded by the Gaelic League. In this context Ireland was celebrated as the island of saints and scholars, as the home of an archaic reflex of Indo-European culture, as a seat of nobility and heroism, as a druidical and mystical land, as an unspoiled, natural, and moral nation. Behind

15. Examples might include the "re-creation" of the *Kalevala* in Finland in the first half of the nineteenth century, as well as the reinstitutionalization of the *eisteddfod* in Wales.
16. See James 1999.
17. Cf. Kiberd 1998.

these summary descriptions we can hear echoes of ideologies, ideologies that are Catholic, Aryan, romantic, spiritualist, and anticolonialist in turn. Remnants of nineteenth-century constructions of Irish culture — from sectarian loyalties and secular faiths, to ideologies pertaining to nationalism and implicit theories of race — continue to color explorations of the role of language and the nature of tradition in Irish culture. They are aspects of the modern *doxa* surrounding the very subjects explored in this volume.

Throughout the nineteenth century and into the twentieth, these several definitions of Irish culture were articulated and developed. They were promulgated in political tracts, scholarly publications, literary works, artistic creations, and popular media, including newspapers, broadsides, and journals. Contradictions notwithstanding, they all contributed to the coalescence of cultural nationalism in Ireland, resulting in essentialist definitions of Irish culture, as well as oppositional ones. Contrary to current views of culture that stress variations and differences within cultures as much as differences between cultures, many earlier pronouncements presupposed views of culture that were monolithic or homogeneous. So Matthew Arnold could talk in all good conscience about Celtic melancholy — even as he was trying to argue that the greatness of English culture derived from its syncretic drawing together of Celtic, Germanic, and Romance elements and dispositions. The earlier easy give-and-take across language boundaries and between populations that is so clear in premodern Irish history was effaced from public consciousness, as was much of the variation within Irish traditions themselves. We see tangible traces of this homogenization in the treatment of medieval Irish literature in translation: particularly in nonscholarly refractions, most of the ancient variants and oral multiforms that characterize the medieval Irish manuscripts were suppressed in favor of a standardized and consistent version of each tale. The literary cycles, in turn, were also brought into "order," with the tales synchronized and contradictions between them rationalized or eliminated. Variations in tone that suggest alternate or self-reflexive views — say, the coexistence of humor and heroism in the same tale — were similarly often effaced.[18]

This recrudescence in the definition of culture — a phenomenon not peculiar to Ireland but widespread throughout Europe — proceeded dur-

18. Tymoczko 1999 offers a detailed discussion of the translations.

ing the second half of the nineteenth century at the same time that the Irish-speaking population was abandoning the Irish language in favor of English, as we have discussed. It was also the period when "English" (or, more properly, modern or metropolitan) customs and ways of life were becoming generalized throughout much of the population. To a large extent these immense cultural shifts were motivated by the devastations of the Great Famine of 1845–50, which struck the Irish-speaking population and the poorest classes disproportionately. The people took the lesson that English was a means of literal survival, not just of economic well-being, and began translating their children to English speakers, such that by 1911 only 12 percent of the population were Irish-speaking (Edwards 1973:229). In the second half of the nineteenth century as well, the Gaelic population shifted mores, shifts that include the "devotional revolution" (Larkin 1972). Thus, it was at this period, for example, that the rather robust attitudes toward sexuality in Irish-language culture were abandoned in favor of a sexual puritanism in which Victorian morality and Catholicism coincided (cf. Lee 1978:40). Ironically, acknowledgment of such cultural syncretism was made difficult by the political exigencies of cultural nationalism. In such a complex cultural context, it is perhaps not surprising that the Irish peasants became the essentialized embodiments of national culture in all its "integrity" and "authenticity."

These romantic and nationalist constructions of culture that can be charted since the eighteenth century take us to critiques of the concept of tradition, particularly those mounted by Eric Hobsbawm and those which see traditions as primarily exiguous constructions of nationalist movements. Hobsbawm has focused on "invented traditions," defined by him as "a set of practices, normally governed by overtly or tacitly accepted rules and of a ritual or symbolic nature, which seek to inculcate certain values and norms of behaviour by repetition, which automatically implies continuity with the past" (Hobsbawm 1983:1). He continues, "In fact, where possible, they normally attempt to establish continuity with a suitable historic past," thus suggesting that invented traditions actually are part of a process that defines and normalizes the past. Many instances of the invention of traditions in this sense can be documented in Ireland in the last 250 years, and the values and norms inculcated by such practices, as well as their ideological underpinnings, are of great interest. One need only think, for example, of the endeavor to shape the celebration of St. Patrick's Day in Ireland since the beginning of the nineteenth century, including the promotion of parades with political valences and the attempt to discourage inebriation; the ideological implications of these shifts are patent. Such modern inventions of tradition are preceded by the medieval manipulations and inventions of tradition in Irish-language culture that can be documented from the earliest period, as we have already discussed.

At the same time, Hobsbawm's definition of tradition has severe limitations. He focuses on practices with a ritual bent, limiting the applicability of his arguments and making it difficult to extend them to analyses of tradition in, for example, oral folklore, literature, and music, the "practices" with respect to which Irish scholars most often use the terms *tradition/traidisiún* and *traditional/traidisiúnta*. Moreover, in drawing the distinction between *custom* and *tradition*, Hobsbawm asserts that "the object and characteristic of 'traditions,' including invented ones, is invariance. The past, real or invented, to which they refer imposes fixed (normally formalized) practices, such as repetition" (1983:2). By contrast, as we have already seen, scholars of folklore, oral literature, music, and so forth are united in acknowledging the pervasive presence of variation and change in the domains they study in traditional cultures, and the same is true of, say, high-art literary traditions in nontraditional cultures. We are faced here with a problem of language: Hobsbawm is attempting to hijack standard, well-established, and useful terms for his own ends, bending ordinary language to arguments that manifestly do not apply to many of the domains he purports to address. In this regard it is perhaps not entirely innocently that he extends his claims for "invented traditions" to all traditions, and that he abbreviates his references to "invented traditions" by simply employing the term *tradition* to cover all cases. Although it is clear that the materials of the past are often — perhaps usually — manipulated and changed to serve the present, accepting Hobsbawm's usages is tantamount to denying the validity of the primary meaning of the word *tradition:* elements of culture that are handed over or handed down through time. Tradition in this sense is far deeper and more extensive, transcending by far the manipulations of the past and present associated with nationalism.

Thus far we have concentrated on Irish-language culture in Ireland, but from the Tudor period Gaelic culture was set against English culture and began its long retreat as the dominant order in Ireland. Because English-language culture became dominant — and is still dominant not just in Ireland but in the world — it is sometimes hard to see English culture as other than a baseline, a sort of norm. Just as Irish culture was constructed and invented repeatedly since the eighteenth century, however, so has English culture been, and to understand the relationship of language and tradition in Ireland, we must understand those manipulations as well. Much of the construction of English culture was ancillary to England's role as an imperial power: as Stuart Hall argues, Englishness was "defined as a strongly centered, highly exclusive and exclusivist form of cultural identity" (1997: 20). Englishness was also equated with being "Anglo-Saxon," and that equation was in turn imbricated in a theory of race used for purposes of subjection of the Irish and the populations of the other colonies of the British Empire.[19]

Englishness marginalized the cultures of its colonies, constituting the colonized Other "within the regimes of representation of [its] metropolitan center," and it enabled the English to command "within their own discourses, the discourses of almost everybody else" (Hall 1997:20). English customs, literature, and art forms were promulgated as the epitome of what was "cultivated" and "civilized" not only in Great Britain but throughout the many lands of the empire. In this process essentialism was also at work, for such a construction of Englishness was possible only "by dint of excluding or absorbing all the differences that constituted Englishness, the multitude of different regions, peoples, classes, genders that composed the people gathered together in the Act of Union" (ibid.)

Perhaps not surprisingly, the English-speaking populations of Ireland — the descendants of the Tudor conquest, the Cromwellian conquest, and the Plantation alike, as well as the "Old English" and the descendants of the Irish-speaking population who had turned to the English language — were some of the earliest voices against this monolithic and essentialist view of Englishness. As early as the eighteenth century, members of the Anglo-Irish Ascendancy began to claim a cultural heritage that was different from that of England. Throughout the nineteenth century the claim accelerated, and a literary tradition was defined that diverged in its models, subject matter, and goals from the dominant literary tradition of England. We can trace such a lineage from Jonathan Swift and Charlotte Brooke to Thomas Davis, James Clarence Mangan, and Samuel Ferguson, among others, a lineage that provided an alternative and supplementary

19. Curtis (1968, 1971) discusses these issues as they relate to Ireland.

heritage from the past—a heritage not to be denied by most English speakers in Ireland.[20] A musical lineage can also be traced in English-language culture in Ireland, focusing on, for example, the adaptations of native harp music by Edward Bunting and the melodies of Thomas Moore. Similarly, alternate patriotic histories were delineated, within both the nationalist and the unionist populations of Ireland.

It was at this juncture that the Irish Revival gathered steam in Ireland, marked by the foundation of the Gaelic Athletic Association in 1884 and the Gaelic League in 1893. An important event in the movement was the 1892 address by Douglas Hyde to the Irish National Literary Society titled "The Necessity for De-Anglicising Ireland," in which Hyde, following D. P. Moran, called on the Irish to differentiate themselves culturally, to be more than "West Britons." For approximately two decades the various competing constructions of Irish tradition and culture that we have traced coexisted relatively smoothly under the aegis of the Revival,[21] as proponents worked together for what was seen as the greater good: the cultural and political liberation of Ireland from English domination. The movement brought together cultural efforts and expressions in both languages, Irish and English. One of the goals of the Irish Revival was the development of a national literature in English. That effort involved such things as the deployment in and transculturation to English of Irish-language literary and historical materials, the transference and adaptation of elements of Irish-language poetics from both the learned poetic tradition and the oral folkloric tradition, the exploitation of otherworld and supernatural elements of Gaelic tradition within the context of nineteenth- and twentieth-century spiritualism, and the uptake of certain linguistic elements from Irish. The primary authors of the Revival writing in English extolled aspects of Irish tradition that made literature more vital in the western island than in England—from its "rich and living" language, a speech "racy of the soil," and audiences trained to listen to rhetoric and oratory, to "a popular imagination" that was "fiery and magnificent, and tender," still possessing a common knowledge of stories that gave the culture a

20. It was the nineteenth century that also witnessed the beginning of a literature in English by Irish writers from a predominantly nationalist, Irish-speaking background, most prominently perhaps William Carleton (1794–1869).

21. Debates in newspapers about Celticism, splits in the dramatic movement, and the like notwithstanding.

surviving stock of primary myth and a sense of the sanctity of legend based on the sanctity of the land itself.[22]

This sense of the possibilities for a literature in English that might issue from drawing on both currents of culture in Ireland led to a tremendous outpouring of creativity that resulted in Ireland's producing what is arguably the strongest group of writers of any English-speaking land in the twentieth century. Strengths of the movement included the development of representations of Hiberno-English, as well as the construction of the so-called Anglo-Irish idiom, a means of representing the Irish language, as well as Gaelicized ways of speaking in English. A literary pedigree was developed, marking the lineage of Irish writers who had undertaken a patriotic endeavor in English, memorialized by W. B. Yeats in "To Ireland in the Coming Times":

> Know, that I would accounted be
> True brother of a company
> That sang, to sweeten Ireland's wrong,
> Ballad and story, rann and song;
> . . . .
> Nor may I less be counted one
> With Davis, Mangan, Ferguson . . .
>
> (Yeats 1983:50)

There were, of course, problematic aspects to this cultural burgeoning, not the least of which was a tendency to sentimentalize and romanticize Irish folk tradition that ignored some of its most violent and pernicious aspects.[23]

Meanwhile, literature in Irish was also benefiting from the Irish Revival. Despite the precipitous decline of Irish speakers during the period 1850–1911, at the very moment when one might have expected the death of tradition in the Irish language, it was taking on new life. Irish-language literature increased its generic range by appropriating and developing dominant genres of English literature, including drama, the novel, and the short story. It was during the Irish Revival that the first plays were written in Irish, ironically in some cases by authors who were native English

---

22. On points such as these, see, for example, J. M. Synge's ([1907] 1982) preface to *Playboy of the Western World*.
23. Angela Bourke takes up these issues in *The Burning of Bridget Cleary* (2000).

speakers, including Douglas Hyde and Augusta Gregory.[24] During the Revival and the decades thereafter, novels in Irish were written, including the works of Séamus Ó Grianna and Seosamh Mac Grianna, and the short story was mastered by Liam O'Flaherty, Pádraic Ó Conaire, and Patrick Pearse. In the first decades of the twentieth century, translations were made in Modern Irish of medieval texts, so that modern Irish speakers did not have to depend on English translations and adaptations of the native literature. New genres were also initiated in Irish, notably the peasant biography pioneered by Tomás Ó Criomhthain, Péig Sayers, and Muiris Ó Súilleabháin. A massive undertaking of collecting Irish folklore was begun before 1922, expanding radically thereafter with the establishment of An Cumann le Béaloideas Éireann (Folklore of Ireland Society) in 1926 and the Coimisiún Béaloideasa Éireann (Irish Folklore Commission) in 1935.

The course of language and tradition in Ireland was not always smooth after 1922. In Northern Ireland there followed the reassertion of colonialist attitudes and norms, whereby the Catholic descendants of the Irish-speaking population became a minority dispossessed of language, culture, and tradition. Because of continuing facets of colonization and a reassertion of Britishness associated with Protestant dominance in Northern Ireland after 1922, therefore, the situation of artists in the North diverged from that of artists in the South. With the formation of the Irish state, Irish became the first official language of the nation and ultimately an essential part of the educational system, required for employment in the civil service, for example. The tenets of nineteenth-century nationalism were in many ways institutionalized as cultural policies of the state, along with a marked sectarianism that colored the interpretation of tradition and the promulgation of the Irish language. The essentialist postulates of the period were also engaged in a polarized opposition to England.

At the same time, during the decades after independence of the Irish state, the first steps toward decolonization were also taken in the Irish Republic. Frantz Fanon has identified three principal stages of cultural engagement under colonialism. In the first, the colonized subjects introject and internalize the standards of the colonizer; in the second stage a definition of national identity begins to emerge, but it is constrained by the categories of the colonizer, often defined in opposition to the colonizer as

24. Tymoczko 1993:n.6 and O'Leary 1994:ch.5 provide accounts of the earliest plays written in Irish.

Other. Only in the third stage do true autonomy and a decolonized identity begin to be established, when the dyadic relationship of colonized and colonizer is superseded, and the emerging cultural terms become freed of the constraints of both the colonizers and nationalism.[25] If the first stage is most apparent in the nineteenth century in Ireland and the second during the Irish Revival, we can say that it was principally after 1922 that cultural figures in the Irish state began to move toward decolonization. Writers as different as James Joyce, Flann O'Brien, Patrick Kavanagh, and Austin Clarke took their diverse stands against essentialist definitions of Irish tradition, even as they asserted their own identities as Irish writers. Still another significant achievement of the Republic was integrating pre-colonial literature, history, and language into an English-language cultural framework, thus normalizing an autonomous Irish perspective within the broader framework of culture carried in English. Schooled in the litera-ture, language, and cultural heritage of Gaelic Ireland, Irish artists and thinkers were also masters of the English language, English culture, and the English-language heritage of Ireland. From an amalgam of the two, they began the work of forging a distinct Irish culture in the Republic, a notable feature of the current cultural confidence in Ireland, where a re-commitment to the Gaelic heritage and the Irish language is so notable, epitomized perhaps in the popularity of all-Irish schools for the young.

In the postwar period Thomas Kinsella emerged as one of the most articulate voices on this complex positioning of Irish writers with respect to language and tradition. In an early essay titled "The Irish Writer" (1970), Kinsella discussed the dual-language heritage of Irish writers that distinguished them from English writers. His choice of terminology — his perception of Ireland as a *divided* tradition — bespeaks the continued op-positional and polarized cultural and linguistic context of Ireland as late as the 1970s. Yet his recognition of the necessity of looking for "the past in myself," accepting the reality of both a great inheritance and a great loss, indicates that Kinsella was beginning to articulate a project of decoloniza-tion for Irish writers. In this articulation he anticipated postcolonial the-ory at the end of the twentieth century as it has been constructed by Edward Said, Homi Bhabha, and others. It is suggestive of the growing decolonization of Irish writers that Kinsella relabeled his perception of

25. See Fanon (1966:178–79) and Cave (1991), the latter of whom discusses the Irish situation in particular.

Ireland's linguistic and cultural heritage when he expanded his essay to a monograph in 1995, naming it a *dual* tradition and moving toward a greater consciousness of the power of hybridity that resides in such a multilingual tradition as that of Ireland. The project articulated by Kinsella has in many ways come to fruition in the work of writers who situate themselves within the Irish-language heritage of Ireland, in addition to its English-language heritage, such as the *Innti* poets, of whom Nuala Ní Dhomhnaill is the most well known. Such work presupposes a belief that Irish literature is entitled to have its own complex voicing within the contemporary international artistic community.

Ireland has been one of the first countries to grapple with many of the cultural problems of modernity, from linguistic and cultural shifts to issues having to do with hybridity and diaspora. Of the many cultures with multiple languages and traditions, Ireland has also been a leader both in forging a cultural response to oppression and colonialism and in blending its complex linguistic and cultural heritage into an autonomous whole. The tremendous quality and richness of Ireland's modern literature and cultural presence cannot be divorced from the mixings and crossings in its dual tradition since the Tudor period, as well as its long history of linguistic interface from the earliest times. In exploring the themes of language and tradition in Ireland, therefore, we offer a view on broader questions related to cultural formation, cultural change, and cultural power which are currently facing many nations of the world.

The implications of such a view can perhaps be most easily glimpsed in terms of translation. Translation is a process that confronts and reveals the asymmetries of cultures and traditions, as well as the anisomorphisms of languages: indeed, some would claim that the task of translation is more one of cultural transposition than linguistic transfer. Translation is also a process that involves losses and gains, as such asymmetries and anisomorphisms are negotiated and mediated. Increasingly translation is theorized as a performative process as well, involving creation and construction, on a par in certain ways with other original types of artistic creation. Translation, therefore, is a one-to-many mapping: there is no single right way to translate. Moreover, even as translation changes and mutates cultural materials, it is responsible for the survival of the heritage of the past and its dissemination in the present. Thus in many circumstances translation is responsible for the persistence of tradition, as we have been using the word in this essay, and its communication within Ireland itself and the world at large.[26]

In Ireland, both in the North and in the South, it has become virtually impossible to separate the traditions of English-language and Irish-language cultures. Irish artists and writers, as well as the general populace, must be set in the context of both cultures, for they work across language and cultural boundaries freely, owning all that has been handed over from the past in Ireland, whatever its linguistic origin. In a sense, therefore, Ireland has become a translational culture where asymmetries exist and coexist in language, tradition, and culture—where such asymmetries are acknowledged, exploited, transcended, remembered, assumed, and forgotten. Two cultural traditions once separate have become blended and hybridized, with artists in particular moving freely back and forth across linguistic and cultural boundaries, creating and configuring their own individual patternings and amalgams from the varied and rich cultural fields they inherit. It is this translational condition that has allowed tradition to thrive in Ireland, albeit often in changed, altered, and blended states. As a translational island, Ireland is perhaps a forerunner of the era when globalization will mean that no culture can remain purely local, that all languages and traditions must alter and change if they are to survive. Irish solutions to the issues raised suggest ways forward—not only by example but by counterexample as well.

These varied and complex questions about language and tradition are taken up by the authors of the essays in this collection. Although some scholars lag behind Irish culture itself, working primarily with only one of the linguistic strands of Ireland's cultural tradition, the contributors to this volume all work with Irish-language literature and culture, as well as English. Cóilín Owens addresses the question of the formation of the artist in Ireland in "Stephen Dedalus, Fili, "showing that James Joyce configures Stephen Dedalus — and perhaps himself — as a poet of a dual culture, inheriting the traditions of the early Irish poet, the *fili,* as well as those of the English poet. Owens demonstrates conclusively how thoroughly Joyce had absorbed knowledge about the early Irish poets, applying those paradigms — notwithstanding his naturalistic representations and modern dress — to the character Stephen Dedalus. Anticipating the critical dis-

---

26. Tymoczko 1999 takes up these various points. Translation of poetry in Modern Irish, for example, has made possible bridges between Irish writers and audiences, and those of other parts of the world, from Japan to the principal and lesser-used languages of Europe.

courses of postcolonial theory, Joyce was grappling with the problematic
of an artist in a colonized culture—a culture with a dual-language tradition — differentiating the experience of artists formed within a dominant
cultural tradition and those formed in situations where cultural traditions
meet in unequal conditions of power.

In "Gender and Power in *Serglige Con Culainn* and *The Only Jealousy
of Emer*," Joanne Findon explores how a textual tradition can change to
serve the purposes of a new time. Using the index of gender to compare
and contrast the early Irish tale *Serglige Con Culainn* (*The Wasting Sickness of Cú Chulainn*) with W. B. Yeats's play *The Only Jealousy of Emer*,
Findon shows that even where motifs and elements of plot may be retained in a new cultural context, narrative material can become reshaped
to suit another poetic vision and personal beliefs, as well as the exigencies
of altered social constraints. Focusing on features as wide ranging as linguistic shifts, form, subjectivity, and biographical imperatives, Findon
explores the nature of artistic inspiration, creativity, and the power of
rewriting. She shows that transfer across language boundaries is very
complex, not least because the personal agenda and experience of the
agent of transfer may be as important in shaping the result as are cultural
barriers.

Helen Fulton's approach to questions pertaining to language and tradition in Ireland moves away from aesthetic issues to the realm of politics. In
"Hegemonic Discourses in Brian Friel's *The Freedom of the City*," she
argues that Friel's play demonstrates how discourses are deployed to construct power and to negotiate between dominant and subordinate groups
in society. Friel thematizes languages, representing the relations between
England and Ireland in terms of linguistic difference, uncovering the ways
in which linguistic disempowerment leads to cultural dispossession, the
ways that the discursive practices of social institutions ensure the continuing subordination of individual lives. Moving beyond nationalism and
questions of Irish or English, the play presents a society in crisis, which
must resort to coercion by violence because normal hegemonic methods
fail to maintain consensus. Fulton argues that Friel's play reconfigures the
usual binary oppositions used to structure representations of Irish society—Irish Gaelic and English, Catholic and Protestant, nationalist and
unionist—to show that dominant ideologies dismantle such divisions.
Thus discourses of oppression in a culture reconfigure oppositions surrounding institutional power; she suggests that the revival or survival of a

national language — Irish in the case at hand — is secondary to countering hegemonic discourses in the struggle for political and cultural autonomy.

Turning to early Irish literature, Jeremy Lowe investigates the nature of the heroic tradition in medieval Ireland in his essay "Contagious Violence and the Spectacle of Death in *Táin Bó Cúailnge*." Lowe demonstrates that the early Irish text — generally considered Ireland's central traditional heroic narrative — dramatizes the destabilizing effects of warfare, even as it celebrates feats of heroism. Violence in the *Táin* is, therefore, disruptive, suggesting that even in medieval literature traditional values and narrative structures were constantly being questioned, reconsidered, and displaced. Lowe argues that the contradictions inherent in the warrior figure in this text reflect a medieval culture aware of the ambivalence of the heroic ethos and the fact that warlike action remains difficult for any society to assimilate. This dimension is stressed by the lack of any center to the tale — the absence of a locus — as well as the failure of social systems and social rules to control and structure the violence. Violence becomes spectacle in the tale, the broken bodies a sign of the themes explored. Lowe concludes that the *Táin* is the product of a society that interrogated the traditional ideals that ostensibly defined it, representing an ambivalence toward violence and warfare that continues to be relevant in Ireland today, more than a thousand years after the tale was first written down. Thus, the heroic tradition of medieval Ireland invoked by Irish patriots in the past and in the present was not as essentialist, as simple, or as warlike as has been supposed.

In "Interpretations and Translations of Irish Traditional Music," Sally K. Sommers Smith turns to cultural traditions that transcend the textual. Because Ireland has been famous for its music since the Middle Ages, musical traditions in Ireland offer a case study for many of the issues at the heart of this volume. Using Irish music as a touchstone, Smith undermines common misconceptions about traditional music, shedding light on the nature of *tradition* per se. She demonstrates that in Ireland traditional music often has a known composer, that it is not exclusively aural or illiterate, and that it may be influenced by popular or foreign music; she also dismantles the preconception that traditional music rises like an autochthonous element from a land and a people. Smith argues that the Irish evidence indicates that traditional music cannot be exclusively connected with the notion of nation; rather, traditional music, like literature, is subject to outside influences, cultural evolution, and individual creation. It is all the more ironic, then, that Irish music had to be "civilized" for "cultured" English audiences and stripped of perceived political menace through adaptation to English standards of harmony and performance.

Michael Cronin explores the practical issues of negotiating across multiple languages in "Interpreting Ireland: Literary and Historical Perspectives on the Role of Interpreters in Ireland." Cronin foregrounds the role of individual interpreters, illustrating how interpreters are symbolically implicated in the relations between linguistic communities. He demonstrates that the position of specific languages in interpreting practices is an index of the power structure within a multilinguistic polity or nation; thus, the shift of Irish from an equal partner in linguistic transactions to a language with decidedly secondary status mirrors the shift of power relations between the Irish-speaking community and the English-speaking one. The essay concludes with questions about linguistic interface in Ireland at present, as Ireland becomes an immigrant nation, drawing people from around the world who have opened a new period of multilingualism in the island.

A key period of linguistic interface in Ireland — in which interpretation was a central issue — was the seventeenth century, and this is the period that Catherine McKenna focuses on in "Triangulating Opposition: Irish Expatriates and Hagiography in the Seventeenth Century." Through a careful analysis of the cultural politics of hagiography, McKenna shows that the collection and dissemination of saints' lives in the period became a vehicle for engaging European attention to and support for the position of Gaelic Catholic Ireland. The use of Latin by Irish hagiographers, moreover, became a way to transcend the dominance of England and the English language, a way to circumvent the hegemony of the colonizers, to reach beyond their grasp and access a wider power base. She argues convincingly that Latin was a third term in the equation of cultural politics in Ireland for centuries, serving as a means of promulgating images of the nation and asserting the sovereignty of Ireland in international politics. She concludes that the elements used to define Ireland and Irish culture in Latin hagiography on the Continent in the seventeenth century set the terms of debate that shaped the nationalistic dialectic within Ireland in the following centuries.

The question of language in Ireland has been heavily politicized since the ascendancy of the nineteenth-century tenet that national sovereignty was contingent on the possession of a national language. Almost all the articles in this volume touch on this issue in one way or another, but the essay by Gordon McCoy and Camille O'Reilly titled "Essentializing Ulster? The Ulster-Scots Language Movement" focuses directly on the politicization of language in Ireland. McCoy and O'Reilly chronicle how an Ulster-Scots language movement has developed in response to the Irish-language revival in Northern Ireland, thus illuminating the relationship between politics and language. The proponents of the movement resist the ascription of dialect status to Ulster-Scots, and many have promoted orthographic systems that will maximally differentiate the speech from standard English spelling. The politics of parity in the North, as well as European policies that support lesser-used languages, have funded the Ulster-Scots movement at a critical time in the renegotiation of power in Northern Ireland, adding yet another element to the debate on language, tradition, and cultural identity in Ireland.

Language in Northern Ireland is addressed in another form by Thomas Dillon Redshaw in "Patrimony: On the *Tête Coupée* in John Montague's *The Rough Field.*" Redshaw shows how the loss of the Irish language that was a central concern of Irish cultural nationalism at the end of the nineteenth century is personalized in the poetry of John Montague. Redshaw demonstrates how thoroughly the poet has assimilated the cultural, historical, and linguistic richness of his native County Tyrone. For Montague, language, landscape, history, politics, and family all become intertwined. The ancient Celtic cult of the severed head and early Irish headhunting become symbolic centers for exploring identity and patrimony in both the most immediate and the largest senses, as well as a means of articulating the problem of the artist who must speak with a "grafted tongue." Montague constructs a literary tradition for Northern Ireland, looking back to writings from the north in both English and Irish, opening discourses that in turn have been taken up by Seamus Heaney and others.

Concluding the volume is an essay by Declan Kiberd titled "John McGahern's *Amongst Women*," in which Kiberd argues that the epic quality of McGahern's work owes much to his deep immersion in Tomás Ó Criomhthain's *An tOileánach* (*The Islandman*, 1929), the classic account-from-within of Blasket Island life in the late nineteenth and early twentieth centuries. Kiberd explores McGahern's themes pertaining to violence, to the relations between men and women, and to the natural world in Irish rural life, concluding that McGahern has a genius for translation, for translating elements of an ancient, heroic Irish culture into the form of an English novel, a genre often considered inherently inimical to those old ways of life. Kiberd's argument illustrates that in Ireland contemporary artists draw from all aspects of Ireland's multilingual culture, crossing freely the lines of language and tradition.

The essays taken together, therefore, illuminate the workings of tradition within Ireland and the interplay of tradition and culture, as each serves to define and construct the other. The role of language in this interplay is paramount, and the multilingualism of Ireland sets in relief the continuities and displacements of Irish traditions, their fractures and linkages. In turn, Ireland's history highlights the relation of language and tradition to politics and power. The essays reveal that even within the compass of a small island, the layered nature of tradition across time is patent, and that from the earliest period to our own, evidence shows tradition to be flexible rather than static, a protean legacy from the past ready to serve the needs of the present and future. Thus, the book is a contribution to the dialogue about the nature and value of tradition, issues that increasingly face people everywhere as language, culture, and tradition are being renegotiated throughout the world.

Works Cited

Bieler, Ludwig, ed. and trans. 1979. *The patrician texts in the Book of Armagh.* Dublin: Dublin Institute for Advanced Studies.

Bourke, Angela. 2000. *The burning of Bridget Cleary: A true story.* Pimlico: Viking.

Cave, Richard Allen. 1991. Staging the Irishman. In *Acts of supremacy: The British Empire and the stage, 1790–1930,* by J. S. Bratton, Richard Allen Cave, Brendan Gregory, Heidi J. Holder, and Michael Pichering, 61–128. Manchester: Manchester University Press.

Cronin, Michael, and Cormac Ó Cuilleanáin, eds. 2003. *The languages of Ireland.* Dublin: Four Courts.

Curtis, L. Perry, Jr. 1968. *Anglo-Saxons and Celts: A study of anti-Irish prejudice in Victorian England.* Bridgeport, Conn.: University of Bridgeport.

———. 1971. *Apes and angels: The Irishman in Victorian caricature.* Washington: Smithsonian Institution Press.

Edwards, Ruth Dudley. 1973. *An atlas of Irish history.* London: Methuen.

Evans, E. Estyn. 1957. *Irish folk ways.* London: Routledge.

Fanon, Frantz. 1966. *The wretched of the earth.* 1961. Trans. Constance Farrington. New York: Grove Press.

Hall, Stuart. 1997. The local and the global: Globalization and ethnicity. In *Culture, globalization, and the world-system: Contemporary conditions for the representation of identity,* ed. Anthony D. King, 19–40. Minneapolis: University of Minneapolis Press.

Havelock, Eric A. 1963. *Preface to Plato.* Cambridge: Harvard University Press.

Hobsbawm, Eric. 1983. Inventing traditions. In *The invention of tradition,* ed. Eric Hobsbawm and Terence Ranger, 1–14. Cambridge: Cambridge University Press.

Hughes, Kathleen. 1972. *Early Christian Ireland: Introduction to the sources.* Ithaca: Cornell University Press.

Ireland, Colin A. 1996. Aldfrith of Northumbria and the learning of a *sapiens. A Celtic florilegium: Studies in memory of Brendan O Hehir,* ed. Kathryn A. Klar, Eve E. Sweetser, and Claire Thomas. 63–77. Lawrence, Mass.: Celtic Studies Publications.

———. 1999. *Old Irish wisdom attributed to Aldfrith of Northumbria: An edition of "Bríathra Flainn Fhína maic Ossu."* Tempe: Arizona Center for Medieval and Renaissance Studies.

James, Simon. 1999. *The Atlantic Celts: Ancient people or modern invention?* London: British Museum Press.

Kelleher, John V. 1963. Early Irish history and pseudo-history. *Studia Hibernica* 3:113–27.

———. 2002. Early Irish history and pseudo-history. In *Selected writings of John V. Kelleher on Ireland and Irish America,* ed. Charles Fanning, 219–39. Carbondale: Southern Illinois University Press.

Kiberd, Declan. 1998. Romantic Ireland's dead and gone: The English-speaking Republic as the crucible of modernity. *Times Literary Supplement,* 12 June, 12–14.

Kinsella, Thomas. 1970. The Irish writer. In *Davis, Mangan, Ferguson? Tradition and the Irish writer,* by W. B. Yeats and Thomas Kinsella, 57–70. Dublin: Dolmen.

———. 1995. *The dual tradition: An essay on poetry and politics in Ireland.* Manchester: Carcanet Press.

Larkin, Emmet. 1972. The devotional revolution in Ireland, 1850–1875. *American Historical Review* 77:625–52.

Lee, Joseph J. 1978. Women and the Church since the Famine. In *Women in Irish society: The historical dimension,* ed. Margaret MacCurtain and Donncha Ó Corráin, 37–45. Dublin: Arlen House.

Lord, Albert B. 1960. *The Singer of Tales.* Cambridge: Harvard University Press.

Macalister, R. A. S., ed. and trans. 1938–56. *Lebor gabála Érenn, The book of the taking of Ireland.* 5 vols. London: Irish Texts Society.

Mac Neill, Máire. 1962. *The festival of Lughnasa.* London: Oxford University Press.

O'Brien, M. A., ed. 1962. *Corpus genealogiarum Hiberniae.* Dublin: Dublin Institute for Advanced Studies.

O'Connor, Frank. 1967. *The backward look: A survey of Irish literature*. London: Macmillan.

O'Leary, Philip. 1994. *The prose literature of the Gaelic revival, 1881–1921: Ideology and innovation*. University Park: Pennsylvania State University Press.

Ong, Walter J. 1988. *Orality and literacy: The technologizing of the word*. 1982. London: Routledge.

Ó Súilleabháin, Seán. 1970. *A handbook of Irish folklore*. 1942. Detroit: Singing Tree.

Richter, Michael. 1988. *Medieval Ireland: The enduring tradition*. 1983. New York: St. Martin's.

———. 1999. *Ireland and her neighbours in the seventh century*. New York: St. Martin's.

Scowcroft, R. Mark. 1987. *Leabhar gabhála* — part I: The growth of the text. *Ériu* 38:81–142.

———. 1988. *Leabhar gabhála* — part II: The growth of the tradition." *Ériu* 39:1–66.

Stevenson, Jane. 1989. The beginnings of literacy in Ireland. *Proceedings of the Royal Irish Academy* 89 C:127–65.

———. 1995. Literacy and orality in early medieval Ireland. In *Cultural identity and cultural integration: Ireland and Europe in the early middle ages*, ed. Doris Edel, 11–22. Dublin: Four Courts.

Synge, J. M. [1907], 1982. Preface. *Collected Works*. Vol. 4. Ed. Ann Saddlemyer, 53–54. Gerrards Cross, Bucks: Colin Smythe.

Thurneysen, Rudolf. 1927. Aus dem irischen Recht IV. *Zeitschrift für celtische Philologie* 16:167–230.

Tymoczko, Maria. 1985–86. Animal imagery in *Loinges mac nUislenn*. *Studia Celtica* 20–21:145–66.

———. 1993. Amateur political theatricals, *tableaux vivants*, and Yeats's *Cathleen ni Houlihan*. *Yeats Annual* 10:33–64.

———. 1999. *Translation in a postcolonial context: Early Irish literature in English translation*. Manchester: St. Jerome Publishing.

Williams, J. E. Caerwyn, and Patrick K. Ford. 1992. *The Irish literary tradition*. Belmont, Mass.: Ford and Bailie.

Yeats, W. B. 1983. *The poems: A new edition*. Ed. Richard J. Finneran. New York: Macmillan.

CÓILÍN OWENS

Stephen Dedalus, *Fili*

Contrahit orator, variant in carmine vates

Stephen Dedalus of James Joyce's *A Portrait of the Artist as a Young Man* is a poet in the ordinary senses of the word. His earliest recollections of childhood introduce a distinction between the story his father told and "his song" (PA 7.1–11).[1] He soon comes to observe that poetry has formal qualities ("verses [read] backwards . . . were not poetry," 16.7–8) and that it can be evaluated (*"Balbus was building a wall"* was a mere graffito: "a cod," PA 43.18–19). In such ways we see Stephen become a reader and a judge of poetry, enabling him to value Byron above Tennyson (PA 80.27–81.11) He has a cultivated sense of language, mentally measuring poetic phrases ("a day of dappled seaborne clouds," PA 166.27). Whereas Stephen never claims to be a poet himself, he allows his fellows to call him by that sacred name (e.g., PA 231.8), and of course, he writes in the certified modern poetic form of the villanelle (PA 223–24). Finally, we read his sophisticated allocutions on the nature and divisions of artistic representation (lyric, epic, and dramatic). Thus we are led to consider Stephen a bearer of the epithet "poet" in these several senses: a creator of verse, an aesthete, a critic, and a literary theorist.

None of these contexts implies a specifically Irish, Gaelic, or Celtic reference. Stephen may have some regrets about it, but his nation's colonial history seems to have cast him as a poet of the English language. Rejecting Davin's appeals to patriotism, he savors no Gaelic phrases. He may feel like Dante, think like Nietzsche, but he writes like the Decadents. Nevertheless, it may be worth examining the implications of this portrait of the young poet which, beginning with the maker of *"the geen wothe"* (PA 7) and ending with the would-be forger of the conscience of his race, is

---

1. J. Joyce 1964 hereafter abbreviated PA; all page and line references are to the edition by Chester G. Anderson.

28

bound in green.[2] Joyce's punctilio about such formalities suggests the hypothesis that his depiction of Stephen's gifts, training, and accomplishments may be significantly illuminated by comparison with the native Irish definitions of poet as *fili* (O. Ir., pl. *filid*).[3]

In this essay I consider the textual evidence for but a few of the Irish elements underlying the notion of the poet as *hieros* in *A Portrait of the Artist as a Young Man*.[4] When Stephen thinks of himself as "a priest of the eternal imagination" (PA 221.14), the text implies more than an appropriation from his Jesuit teachers: it is informed by the historical nexus between the *fili* and the *druí*, 'druid'. A corollary of the argument here is that one of Joyce's technical achievements is the cunning camouflage of this insular figure of the fili within the dense tapestry of *A Portrait of the Artist*. As he confided to Henrik Ibsen in a letter of 1 March 1900, "we always keep the dearest things to ourselves" (J. Joyce 1966:1.52).[5]

Before turning to Joyce's text, a survey of some salient features of the Irish fili will be useful. The filid of early medieval Ireland were reputed to have magical or visionary powers akin to those of the druids and were credited with possessing the gift of prophecy. This was especially true after the suppression of the druidic class under Christian hegemony, when this hieratic aspect of the character and capacities of the filid was augmented after inheriting some of the functions of the druids. The filid were respected for the discipline of their craft: up to twelve years of schooling in

2. The reading *geen* follows Gabler's 1993 edition of *Portrait*, where it is taken from Irish National Library MS. 920. See J. Joyce 1993:25.

3. Mod. Ir. *file* (pronounced "fill-eh"), pl. *filí*. A convenient summary of the nature of the Irish fili is found in Welch 1996, s.v. "áes dána," "bardic poetry." For more detailed information, see Knott and Murphy 1966; Bergin 1970; Tymoczko 1994:139–40; Simms 1998; and sources cited. Sources contemporary to Joyce include Hyde 1895, [1899] 1980, 1902; Sigerson 1897; *Encyclopaedia Britannica* 1910, s.v. "bard"; as well as specific materials cited below.

4. A complex issue in making the argument that follows is the difficulty of reconciling three different perspectives: what Joyce thought about the Irish fili (based in part on the scholarship and popular views of *his* contemporaries), what he permits Stephen to think, and what today's scholars think. Then we have Joyce's peculiar uses of language deriving from his extraordinarily retentive memory and elastic sense of reference. It will help to keep these factors in mind in evaluating the argument here.

5. The implications of the argument advanced in this essay are the subject of my forthcoming monograph to be entitled "The Literary Fenianism of *A Portrait of the Artist*." In this larger project I argue that if Joyce's early works express a young man's conflict with popular and received ideas about community, they are also in contention with the amateur Celticism, popular nationalism, and vulgar Catholicism of the time. Joyce has designed *A Portrait of the Artist* so that the contention between the natural imagination and received dogmas is imagined in historical and mythological terms native to Ireland.

the complex formal meters that were one of the defining aspects of poetry in the culture of ancient Ireland. The seven orders of filid enjoyed a high social status, superior even to the legal authorities, the brehons (O. Ir. *brithemain*), and were clearly distinguished from the bards, who belonged to one of the lower orders of verse-makers (MacKillop 1998, s.v. "bard," "fili").

Before the long career of native Irish Gaelic culture was brought to a close, the role and definition of the poets as a class underwent several significant changes. As the etymology of *fili* suggests (from Indo-European **vel-*, 'see'), the poets of pre-Christian Ireland were regarded as seers, possessed of particular kinds of insight or mystical knowledge, the expression of which required a specialized language. During their years of training, the filid were expected to learn a very large repertoire of tales, history, and genealogy and to internalize a complex prosodic system, to engage in riddling contests, and to demonstrate the ability to contend in speech. The poetry of the filid, therefore, cultivated in poetic schools, emerges in highly complex yet spontaneously generated forms. These ornate poetic forms were governed by elaborate patterns of meter, rhyme, assonance, and alliteration, so that the effect of a stanza of their professional poetry is as much aural as intellectual.[6] The notion of poetry associated with the Irish fili is highly prescriptive, founded on rigorous grammatical training, while also requiring competency in up to fifty meters.[7] The classes of filid were distinguished by their relative mastery of the repertoire of tales and expressive forms, and they enjoyed an elite status in part as a result of this training.

During the later Middle Ages, the class of native poets (loosely known as *bards* or *filid*, with the terms often interchanged in modern scholarly and popular discourse) organized themselves into hereditary schools. These schools specialized in rigorous formal training and reinforced the elitist and conservative proclivities of the ancient caste from which the filid were descended, eventually moving the poets into untenable political and aesthetic positions. Students in the bardic schools of late medieval and early modern Ireland lived in a college, removed from their families throughout the winter half of the year, for a sequence of seven years. Under the direction of a hereditary *ollam* (the highest rank of poet), they

6. For a brief account see Deane et al. 1991:1.274–96.
7. See Murphy 1961, which gives a sense of the metrical complexity to be mastered by the early Irish poets.

studied languages (Irish and Latin); grammar; metrics; genealogy; law; *dindshenchas,* 'the lore of places'; mythology; and history. They were required to memorize a substantial canon of works in a number of progressively complex traditional meters. This bardic training followed the ancient tradition of intensive training of memory, inherited from a period when writing was regarded as an admission of a singular weakness in that vital faculty. The classic account of the training of a Gaelic poet is to be found in the *Memoirs of the Marquis of Clanricarde* (1722), which was available in Joyce's time in many summaries, including several by Douglas Hyde (1895, 1899, 1902).[8]

A distinctive feature of the training of the filid was the assignment of a particular form and subject to the students: "The said Subject . . . having being given over Night, they work'd it apart each by himself upon his own Bed, the whole next Day in the Dark, till at certain Hour in the Night Lights being brought in, they committed it to writing" (quoted in Bergin 1970:6). This habit of composing in the dark has been interpreted as a relic of a ritual or ceremony of divination handed down from pagan times, long after its original purpose had been forgotten. In view of the apparent primeval relationship between druid and poet, there has been speculation that this practice is associated with such rituals as *imbas forosnai,* 'great knowledge that illuminates', in which, according to the ninth-century tract *Sanas Cormaic (Cormac's Glossary),* before retiring to sleep, the practitioner partakes of some specially prepared food that disposes him to inspired declamation the following morning. According to this same text, it was one of several pagan practices of which the Christian church disapproved.[9] Dáithí Ó hÓgáin observes that all such expressions can be taken as survivals of the shamanic rituals of archaic cultures generally.[10] The Clanricarde account goes on to explain that "the reason of laying the Study aforesaid in the Dark was doubtless to avoid the Distraction which

8. See also the original in Clanricarde 1722.

9. On these interpretations see Bergin 1970:10 and MacKillop 1998, s.v. "imbas forosnai." There was an alternative translation of the term *imbas forosnai,* based on medieval practices of etymology that are now regarded as inaccurate but that Joyce may have encountered, 'enlightenment between the hands', suggesting grounds to consider a link here with Stephen's masturbation. See Carens 1981 and Benstock 1977:148–54.

10. The ritual has analogues in oral and folk traditions in the many tales of dreamers partaking in the life of the *síd,* the Irish otherworld, and arising to produce spontaneous verse afterward (Ó hÓgáin 1990, s.v. "poets"). Cf. Yeats's poem "The Scholars," in which editors "annotate the lines / That young men, tossing on their beds, / Rhymed out in love's despair" (Yeats 1983:140–41).

Light and the variety of Objects represented thereby commonly occasions. This being prevented, the Faculties of the Soul occupied themselves solely upon the Subject in hand, and the Theme given; so that it was soon brought to some Perfection according to the Notions of Capacities of the Students" (quoted in Bergin 1970:6–7).

In the poetic schools the assigned subjects included odes in praise of the patron chief; elegies; meditations; *dánta grá* (love poems); religious subjects; and, in the seventeenth century, *aislingí* (sexual dream-poems, visionary allegories of political liberation). As George Sigerson, a lecturer at the Royal University in Joyce's time, pointed out, a study of bardic poetry provides a salutary corrective to "those who are wont to associate Irish poetry with effusiveness of thought and luxuriance of language"; on the contrary, such a study discloses that "bardic poetry was characterized by classic reserve in thought, form, and expression" (Sigerson 1897:23). The intensive schooling of the fílid in a specialized language abounding in archaisms, recondite words, riddles, literary metaphors, and references to myth and ritual often rendered their poems unintelligible to the vulgar (MacKillop 1998, s.v. "bérla na filed"; Knott and Murphy 1966:65–68).[11] The rules governing poetry were hidebound, like those of a modern scientific grammarian, and the textbooks were highly prescriptive, emphasizing dignity and complexity over self-expression and spontaneity. The Irish fílid flourished from the dawn of history to the seventeenth century, that is, up to the time of Thomas Nashe (1567–1601) and John Dowland (1562–1626), the latter an Irishman who wrote in the English court tradition. The prevailing view during Joyce's time — a view which he apparently shared — was that the fílid were largely untouched by the Renaissance.[12] Standing by their patrons, the Gaelic chieftains, the fílid fell with them as well. Culturally the fílid represented for Joyce a tradition of wordcraft independent of classical learning in the first instance and of its revival in the second. They might be viewed, therefore, as the tribal antecedents of any modern Irish poet who would seek to restore a native tradition as did, in their own ways, Yeats, Hyde, and A.E.

Even a cursory outline of Stephen's training, character, and aesthetic values in *A Portrait of the Artist as a Young Man* would encourage us to

11. Osborn Bergin observes that practically all bardic poetry is written in one standard literary dialect, which remained almost unchanged for five hundred years and rigorously excluded forms and usages not sanctioned by previous practitioners (1970:13).

12. Recent scholarship has modified this position; see, for example, Mac Craith 1992.

hypothesize that the apparently naturalistic account of his late-Victorian bourgeois education contains elements that indicate a relationship with the apparently lost native tradition that shaped the gifts of the fili. Among these elements are Stephen's removal from his family to a seasonal school for training under a distinct cadre of tutors; the elevated status that training granted to the study of Latin, history, rhetoric, and the development of memory; his resulting predilection for the language underwritten by the literary tradition rather than the marketplace; his hieratic conception of the poet's calling and the images of augury surrounding this avocation, as well as the corollary tension with the Christian priesthood; his conception of the poet as removed from ordinary life, as bearing hereditary gifts, belonging to a superior caste, and having responsibility as a keeper of the tribe's conscience; the peculiar method of his production of the villanelle, as the spontaneous, yet highly formal, production of a well-trained mind in a supine body emerging from sleep; and, finally, the visionary content of the villanelle itself, amenable to interpretation as a political allegory and a version of the aisling.[13] These are some of the discernible cerements of the soul that frets in the shadow of Stephen's secondary patrimonies, Catholic dogma and the genius of English language and literature. Some aspects of Stephen's portrait merit more detailed consideration than this litany provides, and to these questions I now turn.

The mysticism of Yeats and A. E., the patrons of the Irish Literary Revival, was in part shaped by their acquaintance with the visionary role of the Irish filid, and to some extent each modeled his role as poet on that earlier pattern (Tymoczko 1994:305). In contrast with them, Joyce, who regarded claims to mystical infusions with a mixture of respect (in Yeats's case) and disdain (in A. E.'s),[14] was nonetheless partial to the view that a complex engagement with reality required complex means of expression. So he cultivated and formulated his epiphanies, and he indulged in playful demonstrations of intellectual superiority, signing himself "the Nolan" and "Stephen Daedalus" and sending generations of readers to scores of reference works to pursue his fine-spun schemes. He has Stephen remind the dean that, like his forebears among the Irish filid, he distinguishes between the language of the literary tradition and the marketplace (PA

13. The temptress in this poem is the embodiment of Stephen's religious and erotic desires and is amenable to conventional, though less than facile, patriotic interpretation.
14. Joyce's youthful views on these two figures are expressed in "The Holy Office."

188.7–8), the aesthetic implications of which he subsequently impresses on Lynch (PA 213.29–31).

In ancient Irish usage, by contrast with the fili, the bard was a poet of inferior rank. In the Anglo-Irish chronicles, the term was employed in an indiscriminately derogatory manner toward all ranks of native poets, whereas in modern Celtic studies scholars use it to describe without prejudice the late medieval and early modern practices of the Irish schools of poetry. Nonetheless, some of the derogatory connotations that derive from former colonial condescension remain attached in colloquial use. Joyce's various uses of the term *bard* indicate that he was sensitive to these nuances in contemporary usage and to the underlying historical shifts accounting for them. Addressing the Triestines on the subject of Irish history and culture, he did not trouble his audience about distinctions within the Irish poetic orders beyond noting that with the death of James Clarence Mangan "the long tradition of the triple order of the old Celtic bards ended" (J. Joyce 1959:174, cf. 176), evidently citing the broad divisions of the learned classes into druids, bards, and vates, divisions that are attested by Greek and Roman writers (Mac Cana 1970:14). On the other hand, when he addressed the ranks of the Irish Revivalists in "The Holy Office" and "Gas from a Burner," he assumed a more knowing stance. He invoked the historical distinction between the Irish filid, endowed with hieratic power deriving from their historical affiliation with the druids, a power that guaranteed the lethal effect of their satire, and bards who produced merely occasional encomia. In "The Holy Office" (J. Joyce 1959:149–52) the implied author is a pagan priest-poet who purges the mumming company of the Abbey Theatre "bards" of their sentimentality and self-deception. Similarly, such contrasts between the slovenly bard and the lethally satirical fili inform the terms of engagement between Malachi Mulligan and Stephen Dedalus in the opening chapter of *Ulysses*.[15] To Mulligan's harassment about Stephen's lack of hygiene — "the bard's noserag" (U 1.73), "you dreadful bard" (U 1.134), and "the unclean bard" (U 1.475) — Stephen inwardly reflects on the superior edge of his satiric weapon: "He fears the lancet of my art as I fear that of his. The cold steel pen" (U 1.152–53).

The word *druí* (Mod. Ir. *draoi*) is probably derived from an Indo-European compound *dru-wid*, 'knower of trees'. The first element of the

15. J. Joyce 1986 hereafter abbreviated U; all episode and line references are to the edition by Gabler et al.

compound is cognate with the Greek and Irish words for *oak,* the tree with which the druids are constantly connected in the early sources.[16] Joyce was familiar with this association, as we read in his lecture "Ireland, Island of Saints and Sages": "The Druid priests had their temples in the open, and worshipped the sun and moon in groves of oak trees" (J. Joyce 1959:156). The druids were the highest of the learned classes, which included the filid (seemingly equivalent to the Continental *vates* known to Caesar) and the bards. It seems that the druids and vates/filid, as learned philosophers, were closely related in function, but whereas druids presided at sacrifices, the vates/filid were associated with prophecy, inspiration, and poetry. We know from the reports of Caesar and Diodorus Siculus, among others, that the druids were at the center of Continental Celtic society and that they believed in the transmigration of souls, the soul's immortality, and an afterlife without retributive justice. They held that life was at base spiritual and eternal, though in a morally indifferent universe. From their exalted position, they made decisions on matters of custom, law, nature, and cosmology, discerning from the five elements presiding over human affairs — the sky, earth, sea, sun, and moon — the future of mankind. Their mystical powers enabled them to utter sacred rhetoric for the edification and guidance of king and people (Ó hÓgáin 1990, s.v. "druid").

With the supremacy of Christianity and the suppression of the druids in ancient Irish society, it seems that some of the druids' powers and prerogatives passed to the filid. As Eleanor Knott observes, the rivalry between the church and the filid was not that between sacred and secular literature but between Christianity and residual druidism (Knott and Murphy 1966:21–22). Evidence for this overlap of position and power, especially under Christian auspices, is found in the magical rituals, which despite Christian interdiction survived in the practices of the medieval filid.[17] Anne Ross points out that the oral training of the druids — embracing up to twenty years — "dovetails well with the Irish information about the training of the filid which was done entirely orally, and took from seven to twelve years" (Ross 1967:55). Marie-Louise Sjoestedt notes that in consequence of the inheritance of druidic status, the poets of the Celtic social order found themselves the guardians of the religious, literary, and learned traditions

16. For a summary of the druids, see Mac Cana 1970:14 and MacKillop 1998, s.v. "druid."

17. Hyde [1899] 1980:241; Carney 1967.

of Ireland, thus transcending territorial rivalries that dogged the political order (Sjoestedt 1982:5). The Irish filid, then, retained features of scholar-magicians, as the preservers of archaic traditions in mythology and ritual. As one might predict of a pastoral culture, the fertile figure of the bull appears in several divinatory rituals in the early texts. One of these, de-scribed in *Togail Bruidne Da Derga (The Destruction of Da Derga's Hos-tel)*, discerns the future king by having druids preside over the sleep of a man who has feasted on the meat and broth of a slaughtered bull: a vision of the future king appears in the dream induced by this *tarbfeis*, 'bull-sleep/bull-feast'.[18]

It is such relatively recherché elements of the Celtic and Gaelic tradi-tions of the fili that engage Joyce's interest, rather than the aspects of Celticism favored by the Revivalists, including the invocation of rural folkways, the otherworld, popular nationalism, the celebration of mythic heroes, the mystification of twilight, and so forth. Moreover, where Joyce invokes these cultural conventions, he does so in a manner we retrospec-tively recognize as "Joycean." In *Portrait of the Artist*, for example, dur-ing one of the conversations outside the National Library, the exchange moves from heredity to ballocks, and Temple calls Stephen a poet (PA 231.8). Stephen withdraws from the vulgar banter into an illuminating reverie provoked by this taunt: "he remembered an evening when he had dismounted from a borrowed creaking bicycle to pray to God in a wood near Malahide. He had lifted up his arms and spoken in ecstasy to the sombre nave of the trees, knowing that he stood on holy ground and in a holy hour" (PA 232.19–22). Reawaking to the scene with his friends, Stephen beats his ashplant against the base of one of the pillars in the colonnade and, despite the idle chatter around him, finds himself imbued with "A trembling joy, lambent as a faint light, [which] played like a fairy host around him" (PA 232.35–36). This reverie summons him mentally to "the age of Dowland and Byrd and Nash" (PA 233.6–7).

There is an interesting contrast here between Stephen's conscious return to Elizabethan and Stuart England (the apogee of England's cultural his-tory) and the last age of Gaelic civilization, which finally fell victim during that same period to its imperial neighbor. The context makes some impor-tant connections that illuminate the present inquiry: Stephen's being called a poet by Temple causes him to reflect on his invocation of sylvan spirits (in

18. See the account of P. W. Joyce ([1903] 1913:1.245) that Joyce may have known.

the "sombre nave"). These images of woods, poetry, magic, and divination direct our attention, though not that of Stephen (who thinks of exquisite court lutenists), to the presumed druidic origins of the calling of the fili. Stephen's conception of the poetic imagination as priestly is anticipated by an Irish tradition more ancient than those introduced by Saint Ignatius Loyola or, indeed, Saint Patrick. The conflicts of loyalties which Stephen experiences with respect to these apostolic successors are replicated in a more covert manner in the voice of the text, but consistent with Joyce's textual ironies in many other directions, they are partially concealed from Stephen himself.

We can observe this semiconsciousness as well, for example, in Stephen's wondering about the significance of the birds circling over Molesworth Street (PA 224.3–226.7). There is ample evidence from written and iconographic records of the divination practices of the Irish and Continental druids that the flight of certain birds (the wren, the raven, the eagle, and the swan, for instance) yielded information about the future (Ross 1967:257–61). Pertinent to the present argument, we see that Stephen observes the birds after emerging from the colonnade of the pillars of the National Library (an ironic image of the oak grove), and he is looking across Kildare Street (Ir. *Sráid Cill Dara,* 'The Street of the Church of the Oak'), which in turn evokes his earlier spiritual and linguistic training at Clongowes Wood, itself located in County Kildare.

Stephen's dependence on an ashplant at this point is significant. On the naturalistic level the ashplant is merely Stephen's walking stick (his home in Fairview is two miles away), but because it was adapted from a drover's uses, it becomes, in Buck Mulligan's memorable jibe, the instrument of a "bullockbefriending bard" (U 2.431, 14.1115). The ashplant, made of ash, evokes the rowan tree, which along with the oak was a druidic favorite. Joyce's conflation of the ash and rowan trees is justified by the associations with divination and protection against the fairies that they share in both the ancient literature and modern folklore.[19] Here and elsewhere in *A Portrait of the Artist,* Stephen's ashplant functions as a *flesc filed,* 'a poet's rod', and an instrument of augury and is thus an element in the submerged myth of Stephen as fili (cf. PA 224–26, 232, 237).

These links between divination, poetry, and sacred woods contrast with the image of Stephen at the end of the same scene, standing outside

---

19. See MacKillop 1998, s.v. "ash," "rowan,"; Garvin 1976:27–32.

Maple's Hotel and reflecting with slightly displaced anger on its Anglo-
Irish patrons (PA 237.35–238.9).[20] He imagines them in social stereotype,
"the sleek lives of the patricians of Ireland" behind the "colourless po-
lished wood" with their "polite disdain" for native culture. In a spasm of
reverse snobbery toward these dull usurpers of a high station, he reflects a
theme of much seventeenth- and eighteenth-century Gaelic poetry toward
the lowborn Planters. This passage is additionally interesting in the present context because in its diction, images, and false etymological pun
("patricians"), it links an alien social class with the alien wood of the
maple tree and with the archetypal British presence in Ireland of Saint
Patrick.[21] In striking contrast with the oak, the ash, and the rowan, there is
no native Irish word for the maple tree, and it makes no appearance in
Irish toponymy, literature, or folklore.

In view of these large and obscurely ingrained powers, Stephen's mind
is justly troubled about his own future in an Anglocentric and Anglophone world that adulates materialism and rationalism. He is aware that
in taking on the mantle of poet, he is a descendant of an ancient caste who
"for ages had gazed upward as he was gazing at birds in flight" (PA 225.4–
5). He recognizes that his sense of wonder and foreboding is adumbrated
by these mysterious shapes cut in the "airy temple" above him, antecedent
to both Christian and rational orders. But against Stephen's conscious
recollection of phrases from Cornelius Agrippa and Emanuel Sweden-
borg, the narrative places him in a setting closer to home, summoning
through "an Irish oath" (PA 225.17) a druidic presence. This scene, like
that in the Malahide wood, is appropriately interrupted by representatives
of the public order, the Royal Irish Constabulary (PA 226.16, 232.22).
The schoolbook illustration of Latin scansion, "*Contrahit orator, variant
in carmine vates*" (The orator summarizes; the poet-prophets elaborate in
their verses; PA 179.23, my translation), nicely conceals and reveals these
links between the orator (in the present connection, Father Arnall, who
has delivered the hellfire sermon of chapter 3) and the vates/fili. Thus in
contrast with the express rationality of public speech, in the imaginative

20. Maple's Hotel, 25–28 Kildare Street, was "small, quiet, fashionable, and expensive"
(Gifford 1988:275). The argument that there is a contrast in *A Portrait of the Artist* between
the rowan and the oak as Irish, on the one hand, and the maple as associated with Anglo-
Irish, on the other, will be developed in detail in my longer study.
21. For his own reasons Joyce links St. Patrick with the British presence in Ireland; this
linkage will be explored in my monograph.

design of *A Portrait of the Artist* we may discern traces of Stephen's true avatar, the magical hand of the druid-seer-poet.

When Stephen decides to dedicate himself to the priesthood of art, to become "a priest of the eternal imagination" (PA 221.14), he commandeers the presumed sacramental powers of the Catholic priesthood to the service of artistic creation. In this transfer he is unconsciously replaying the historical record that recalls the inheritance by the filid of powers previously the druids' preserve. His decision is thereby underwritten by the submerged native holy order of druids whose belief in the soul's immortality he retains. This theme takes a narrative form in some early texts; as *Lebor Gabála Érenn* (*The Book of Invasions*) has it, Parthalon, the chief of the first settlers in Ireland, like Milesius, the ur-Gael, included in his retinue a druid, whose functions included the sanctification of the land, preparing the way for the spiritual habitation of Ireland. This druidic order remained a central feature of Celtic culture until its displacement or absorption by a later society that, like Stephen's, was expressly Catholic Christian. Thus, as Stephen turns away from the office of the Jesuit priesthood proffered him by the spiritual director of his sodality (PA 153–64) to the priesthood of art (PA 164–73), he does so in terms that reflect the shamanistic nature of the pre-Christian druids.

It is hardly an accumulation of accidents, then, that the images of vision, ritual, fertility, national liberation, bull, and winged deliverance fleck the design of the account of Stephen's mystical election on Dollymount Strand (PA 164–73). The many references to bulls, suggestive of the bull ritual — Bull Wall, Clontarf (Ir. *Cluain Tarbh*, 'The Meadow of the Bulls'), Bous Stephanoumenos, and so forth — as well as Stephen's swooning into "the languor of sleep" (PA 172.26) and his vision of "the great artificer whose name he bore . . . new and soaring and beautiful, impalpable, imperishable" (PA 170.5–7), all appear to invoke the setting for a ritual. These elements frame Stephen's reflections on the arrangement of the clouds and the relationships of the sky and sea, suggesting, therefore, a complex allusion to the druidic capacity for reading the natural elements.[22] The cumulative effect of this cluster of allusions establishes Stephen's creative links with the spiritual-imaginative role of the druid, whose inspired but difficult words make him the avatar of the Irish fili, the embodiment of the creative imagination. This context, finally, allows us to

22. As well as, perhaps, the induced dream by which the future king of the realm is discerned.

appreciate the fuller force of the double insult that Stephen anticipates, namely, being called by Mulligan a "bullockbefriending bard" (U 2.431, 7.528, 14.1115): an impotent and vulgar performing bard-orator, rather than a singing vates.

Stephen's villanelle is, of course, his claim to certification as a fili. The particular circumstances under which he delivers this text resembles the rite of passage in which people became poets: having taken soup, Stephen goes to bed and wakes up to deliver his poem in semidarkness. In this connection, it is significant that Joyce switched the genesis of the villanelle from the street in *Stephen Hero* (J. Joyce 1963:210–11), with its weak citation of the Celtic Twilight (it was a misty evening), to the more historically grounded environment of the poet's bed in *A Portrait of the Artist*. Again, the irrational conditions of the fili's inspiration are echoed in Stephen's swooning at the vision of the bird-girl, his muse on the strand. The image of the poet projected in *A Portrait of the Artist* seems, in sum, to draw on the more exalted aspects in Stephen's conception of the poet — the hieratic, the visionary — but in delivery, ironically, to achieve something closer to the technically complex but conservative expression of the villanelle. Thus, the approach I am developing to the figure of Stephen is consistent with and confirms Joyce's ironic representation of Stephen that has been established since Hugh Kenner's *Dublin's Joyce* as the dominant reading of *A Portrait of the Artist as a Young Man*.

Let us turn for a moment to another feature of native Irish poetic identity and practice. In response to the demands of their patrons, the filid produced a large body of official and formulaic poetry. Two of the most distinctive aspects of this body of poetry are poems in praise of patrons and poems satirizing enemies. The satire of the filid was famed even among the English, and it was reputed to be able to raise welts on the subject of the satire and, in extremis, to cause death. Thus, for example, we read of the death of the Englishman John Stanley who died in 1414 from "the virulence of the lampoon" of one of the filid named Ó hUigínn.[23] Their functions as preservers of tribal memory and as opponents of Anglicization gave the filid political status and made them the particular targets of eventually successful English colonial repression.[24] Nevertheless, it is among the ironies of literary history that during the seventeenth century, when this class was under the greatest threat, it was in some ways

23. Ó hÓgáin 1990:364, 368. See also Robinson 1912 on the poets' power of satire.
24. Deane 1991:1.236.

most productive. Indeed, the filid did not finally die out for another century, but, again, not before producing the final flourish of the Jacobite aisling (Welch 1996, s.v. "bardic poetry," "aisling").[25]

There is evidence that Joyce undertook *Stephen Hero* with this tradition of the native satirist in mind, and thus, the centrality of the figure of the Irish poet in *A Portrait of the Artist* can be traced to the inception of the novel. In a diary entry for 29 February 1904, Stanislaus Joyce testifies regarding the project on which his brother had just embarked: "The Irish are represented as being very much afraid of the satire of the wandering poets. This 'satire' is really a habit of nicknaming very prevalent in this country" (S. Joyce 1971:13). James Joyce was clearly aware of the continuities and discontinuities in the history of the filid, and it was evidently on his mind as he undertook the revision of *Stephen Hero* in September 1907. In the manuscript for the undelivered lecture "James Clarence Mangan," prepared some months before, he outlined the development of Irish literature from its origins to "the age of wandering minstrels, whose symbolic songs carried on the tradition of the triple order of the old Celtic bards" (J. Joyce 1959:176). Moreover, a flurry of correspondence with Oliver St. John Gogarty in late 1907, when Joyce was writing the first chapters of *A Portrait of the Artist*, reveals something of his spirit and intentions, since it provoked Gogarty's jibe, "Is there any reason why your Ashplant shall not be made the center of the Collection in 'National Joyce Museum, Cabra'?" (Ellmann 1982:263). In 1909, when the first three chapters of *A Portrait* were finished (Ellmann 1982:270), Joyce was still brooding on Gogarty's just fear of the lancet of his satirical powers, as an entry (later used in *Ulysses,* as we have seen) in his Trieste notebook indicates (Ellmann 1982:277).

There were many accounts of the status of the filid and of the schooling of Irish poets available in Joyce's time. Among them were Hyde's *Literary History of Ireland* (1899) and *Filidheacht Ghaedhealach: Irish Poetry* (1902); P. W. Joyce's *Social History of Ancient Ireland* (1903), where there is a description of the bardic training ([1903] 1913:1.242–45); and George Sigerson's historical anthology *Bards of the Gael and Gall* (1897). The latter must have been attractive to Joyce if for no other reason than

---

25. In Joyce's time these terms and conventions figured in many scholarly and popular accounts, including the works of Douglas Hyde, the lectures of Eoin Mac Neill at the Royal University, Thomas Moore's *Melodies,* James Clarence Mangan's poems, and the pages of the *United Irishman.* See Welch 1996, s.v. "aisling," and Tymoczko 1994:101–7.

that Sigerson's favorite thesis was that Gaelic literary tradition was hospitable to foreign cultural influences, a strand of his argument not unrelated to Sigerson's own Scandinavian origins.[26]

It is interesting to reflect that some of the features that mark Stephen as a fili are true of Joyce as well. Joyce's own schooling at Clongowes and Belvedere, with its emphases on grammar, history, and languages, fitted him for a life of letters. The Intermediate Education syllabus of his time, the tutelage of his Jesuit masters, and his removal from family broadly resembled the regimen of the bardic school system. Moreover, Hyde's short list of families who produced the *ollamain* (the highest grade of poets and, hence, the teachers) for these schools would have caught Joyce's attention, because it includes the O'Dalys and the Conmees (Hyde [1899] 1980:524), the names of two of Joyce's actual Jesuit masters at Clongowes, Father James Daly and Father John Conmee. The first, Joyce fictionalizes as the "common name" of Dolan. We have seen that in the revision of *Stephen Hero* which resulted in *A Portrait of the Artist,* Joyce adjusted his text so that Stephen delivers his villanelle, a conventional but formally demanding composition, in the manner prescribed in accounts of the bardic schools: in semidarkness, upon a bed, emerging from a doctored sleep, extempore, and so forth; and whatever else one may remark on the virtues of Stephen's poem, it is surely an exhibition of technical skill. Joyce may well have been struck with the analogy between the poets' practice and his own situation, when in July and August 1907 he was hospitalized with rheumatic fever. Among the results of that enforced withdrawal was the final version of "The Dead," which Stanislaus reports his brother dictated to him verbatim from his bed early in September of that year (Ellmann 1982:264 n). Another result was the overall conception of how he was to revise *Stephen Hero* according to a radically new scheme; the result was *A Portrait of the Artist,* which he immediately commenced (264). Furthermore, the latter composition substantially meets the requirements of the aisling: the temptress is the embodiment of Stephen's religious and erotic desires, and the text is available for conven-

26. This "gaelish gall" is referred to several times in *Finnegans Wake* (J. Joyce 1939:63.6; 134.22; 515.7; 515.15; 530.21). See also Tymoczko 1994:304–6. In *Ulysses* Sigerson is credited with the opinion that the national epic had yet to be written (U 9:309). If *Ulysses* is intended as the fulfillment of Sigerson's hope, it is easy to argue that *A Portrait of the Artist as a Young Man,* its lyric prelude by a twentieth-century Irish "bard," though "animated by other ideals" (J. Joyce 1959:174), enters the list of European classics intertextually bonded with works generated from the Irish Gaelic tradition.

tional, though less than facile, patriotic interpretation, the pursuit of which is beyond the scope of the present essay.

Let us conclude by returning to Stephen Dedalus, fili, as he envisions his poetic vocation and commits himself to it. Joyce would have known from many sources, including Hyde and Henri d'Arbois de Jubainville (cf. Tymoczko 1994:233, 293–96), that in Irish mythology the first poet was Amairgen, who, with the sons of Míl, the progenitors of the Goidels, first set foot on Irish soil on Bealtaine, 1 May. According to *The Book of Invasions,* this was the moment that Amairgen — the primordial fili and Stephen's mythic ancestor — delivered the first poem in the Irish tradition:

> I am the wind which blows over the sea
> I am the wave of the Ocean
> I am the ox of the seven combats
> I am the vulture upon the rock
> I am a tear of the sun
> I am the fairest of plants
> I am a wild boar in valour
> I am a salmon in the water
> I am a lake in the plain
> (Trans. R. I. Best in d'Arbois de Jubainville 1903:136)

The creative power of the archetypal poet is here identified with the life force, which vivifies its subjects. As Stephen conceptualizes the vocation of poet, he similarly seeks creative energy in the acceptance of life as he finds it, sordid and exalted, suspending moral prejudgment, "to recreate life out of life" (PA 172.9). As d'Arbois de Jubainville notes, Amairgen's poem gave the Milesians power over the Túatha Dé Danann: "This divine science, indeed, penetrating the secrets of nature, discovering her laws, and mastering her hidden forces, as, according to the tenets of Celtic philosophy, [is] identical with these forces themselves, with the visible and the material world; and to possess this science was to possess nature in her entirety" (d'Arbois de Jubainville 1903:137). It is a vision that informs not just Stephen's projected work as artist but also the work of Joyce himself.

Stephen's parting resolution, "to forge in the smithy of my soul the uncreated conscience of my race" (PA 253.1–2), is framed in a startling metaphor for poetic creation which links the crafts of metalworker and fili, a metaphor that was well established in medieval Ireland. The nexus is clearly seen in the triple goddess, the three Brigits, patrons of poetry, smithcraft, and healing (MacKillop 1998, s.v. "Brigit"; Mac Cana 1970:

34; cf. McCone 1990:162). An instructive example of the metaphor of poetry and the work of the forge in late bardic poetry appeared in the *Irish Review* in 1912, the year that Joyce resumed work on the final drafts of *A Portrait of the Artist as a Young Man*. Translated as "The Empty School," the poem describes the fellowship of the poetic school, the technical training, and the poetic production of the Gaelic *fili*. The three aspects of the poet's training—his memory, his creativity, his self-criticism—are rendered in terms of forgery: the red embers of memory, the anvil of the creative mind within the reclining body, and the hammering of the critical faculty after delivery (Bergin 1970:159–60, 286). This forceful triad corresponds in surprising ways to the triple arms that Stephen allows himself: "silence, exile, and cunning" (PA 247.4–5).

Works Cited

Arbois de Jubainville, Henri d'. 1903. *The Irish mythological cycle and Celtic mythology.* 1884. Trans. R. I. Best. Dublin: O Donoghue.

Benstock, Bernard. 1977. *James Joyce: The undiscover'd country.* New York: Barnes and Noble.

Bergin, Osborn, ed. and trans. 1970. *Irish bardic poetry: Texts and translations, together with an introductory lecture.* Ed. David Greene et al. Dublin: Dublin Institute for Advanced Studies.

Carens, James. 1981. The motif of hands in *A Portrait of the Artist as a Young Man. Irish Renaissance Annual* 2, ed. Zack Bowen, 139–57.

Carney, James. 1967. *The Irish bardic poet.* Dublin: Dolmen.

Clanricarde, Ulick de Burgh, and R. Lindsay. 1722. *Memoirs of the Right-Honourable the Marquis of Clanricarde . . . Containing Several Original Papers and Letters of King Charles II, Queen Mother, the Duke of York . . . &c. Relating to the Treaty between the Duke of Lorrain and the Irish Commissioners, from February 1650 to August 1653.* London: Woodman.

Deane, Seamus, et al., eds. 1991. *The Field Day anthology of Irish writing.* 3 vols. Derry: Field Day Publishing.

Ellmann, Richard. 1982. *James Joyce.* 2d ed. New York: Oxford University Press.

Encyclopaedia Britannica. 1910. 11th ed. New York: Encyclopaedia Britannica.

Garvin, John. 1976. *James Joyce's disunited kingdom and the Irish dimension.* Dublin: Gill and Macmillan.

Gifford, Don, with Robert J. Seidman. 1988. *"Ulysses" annotated: Notes for James Joyce's "Ulysses."* 2d ed. Berkeley: University of California Press.

Hyde, Douglas. 1895. *The story of early Gaelic literature.* London: T. Fisher Unwin.

———. [1899] 1980. *A literary history of Ireland from the earliest times to the present*. Reprint, New York: St. Martin's.

———. 1902. *Filidheacht Ghaedhealach: Irish poetry: An essay in Irish with translation in English and a vocabulary*. Dublin: M. H. Gill and Son.

Joyce, James. 1939. *Finnegans wake*. New York: Viking.

———. 1959. *The critical writings of James Joyce*. Ed. Ellsworth Mason and Richard Ellmann. New York: Viking.

———. 1963. *Stephen hero*. Ed. John J. Slocum and Herbert Cahoon. New York: New Directions.

———. 1964. *A portrait of the artist as a young man: Text, criticism, and notes*. Ed. Chester G. Anderson. New York: Viking.

———. 1966. *Letters of James Joyce*. Vol. 1, ed. Stuart Gilbert. 1957. Reissued with corrections. New York: Viking. Vols. 2 and 3, ed. Richard Ellmann. New York: Viking.

———. 1986. *Ulysses: The corrected text*. Ed. Hans Walter Gabler et al. New York: Random House.

———. 1993. *A portrait of the artist as a young man*. Ed. Hans Walter Gabler with Walter Hettche. New York: Garland.

Joyce, Patrick Weston. [1903] 1913. *A social history of ancient Ireland*. 2 vols. Dublin: Phoenix.

Joyce, Stanislaus. 1971. *The complete Dublin diary of Stanislaus Joyce*. Ed. George Healey. Ithaca: Cornell University Press.

Kenner, Hugh. 1956. *Dublin's Joyce*. Boston: Beacon.

Knott, Eleanor, and Gerard Murphy. 1966. *Early Irish literature*. New York: Barnes and Noble.

Mac Cana, Proinsias. 1970. *Celtic mythology*. London: Hamlyn.

Mac Craith, Michael. 1992. Gaelic courtly love poetry: A window on the Renaissance. In *Celtic languages and Celtic peoples: Proceedings of the Second North American Congress of Celtic Studies held in Halifax, August 16–19, 1989*, ed. Cyril J. Bryne, Margaret Harry, and Pádraig Ó Siadhail, 347–68. Halifax: St. Mary's Univeristy Press.

MacKillop, James. 1998. *Dictionary of Celtic mythology*. New York: Oxford University Press.

McCone, Kim. 1990. *Pagan past and Christian present in early Irish literature*. Maynooth: An Sagart.

Murphy, Gerard. 1961. *Early Irish metrics*. Dublin: Royal Irish Academy and Hodges, Figgis.

Ó hÓgáin, Dáithí. 1990. *Myth, legend, and romance: An encyclopedia of the Irish folk tradition*. London: Ryan.

Robinson, Fred Norris. 1912. Satirists and enchanters in early Irish literature. In *Studies in the history of religions presented to Crawford Howell*, ed. David Gordon Lyon and George Foot Moore, 95–130. New York: Macmillan.

Ross, Anne. 1967. *Pagan Celtic Britain: Studies in iconography and tradition*. London: Routledge and Kegan Paul.

Sigerson, George. 1897. *Bards of the Gael and Gall.* London: T. Fisher Unwin.

Simms, Katharine. 1998. Literacy and the Irish bards. In *Literacy in medieval Celtic societies,* ed. Huw Pryce, 238–58. Cambridge: Cambridge University Press.

Sjoestedt, Marie-Louise. 1982. *Gods and heroes of the Celts.* 1940. Trans. Myles Dillon, 1949. Berkeley: Turtle Island Foundation.

Tymoczko, Maria. 1994. *The Irish "Ulysses."* Berkeley: University of California Press.

Welch, Robert, ed. 1996. *The Oxford companion to Irish literature.* New York: Oxford University Press.

Yeats, W. B. 1983. *The poems: A new edition.* Ed. Richard J. Finneran. New York, Macmillan.

JOANNE FINDON

Gender and Power in *Serglige Con Culainn* and *The Only Jealousy of Emer*

The principal source of Yeats's play *The Only Jealousy of Emer* is the medieval Irish tale *Serglige Con Culainn* (*The Wasting Sickness of Cú Chulainn*), a narrative remarkable for its delineation of female concerns and women's power.[1] Unlike many modern critics, Yeats was perceptive enough to recognize the centrality of women and their desires in the medieval story, and he accordingly made the female characters his focus. Yet *The Only Jealousy of Emer* dilutes the female power present in the original through a series of crucial modifications, most critical of which is the introduction of a male god who does not occur in the original. Although I am not the first to note the differences between the early tale and Yeats's play (Clark 1990), my purpose here is to focus specifically on the connections between gender and power and the ways in which these connections have shifted in Yeats's treatment of the tale.

Yeats probably knew the story of Cú Chulainn's lovesickness principally through Lady Augusta Gregory's translation in *Cuchulain of Muirthemne*.[2] Her translation omits several passages present in the original and as a result obscures somewhat the medieval tale's ambiguous treatment of Cú Chulainn as hero (Gregory [1902] 1970:210–22).[3] Yet Greg-

---

1. I have argued this point at length in *A Woman's Words: Emer and Female Speech in the Ulster Cycle* (1997). The early Irish tale *Serglige Con Culainn* is found in two manuscripts, the twelfth-century Lebor na hUidre and the seventeenth-century manuscript Trinity College H.4.22, which seems to derive from the former. The standard edition is that of Dillon (1953a). The early version of the tale is a mixture of two recensions, one Old Irish (ninth century) and the other Middle Irish (eleventh century). The translation in Dillon 1953b is more complete and more accurate but less accessible to nonspecialists than the translation in Gantz 1981. For further discussion of the literary aspects of the tale, see Carey 1994, 1999; Ó Cathasaigh 1994; and Findon 1997:ch.4. For general background on Yeats's *The Only Jealousy of Emer*, see especially Skene 1974; Vendler 1963; and Koritz 1989.

2. Although O Hehir (1988, 1991) and Marcus (1970) have pointed out that Yeats had access to other translations of early Irish material, none of the other collections of translated texts they discuss contains *Serglige Con Culainn*.

3. The two different spellings of the hero's name in this paper reflect the difference between the Middle Irish spelling and the later spellings that were used by nineteenth-century and twentieth-century translators, including Gregory, and adopted by Yeats. Thus,

ory's version is, on the whole, representative of the original medieval tale. It is at Yeats's hands that the tale undergoes a complete metamorphosis. He incorporates into the plot an episode from another tale in Gregory's collection, *The Only Son of Aoife,* in which Cú Chulainn kills his own son and fights the waves of the sea (Gregory [1902] 1970:237–41).[4] Neither the slaying of his son nor the battle with the waves is connected with Cú Chulainn's wasting sickness in either Gregory's translation or in the original early Irish text.

Yeats reshaped the material according to his own poetic agenda and personal beliefs, adapting the medieval story to the social context of early-twentieth-century Ireland. As a poet he felt free to reshape and recombine elements according to his own creative vision, and the process of writing *The Only Jealousy of Emer* was particularly linked to events in his personal life. However, in reshaping the play so radically, he has (consciously or not) shifted power away from the women in the tale and into the hands of the males.

Before I proceed with the analysis, a summary of the medieval *Serglige Con Culainn* is in order. At the beginning of the tale, Cú Chulainn has a dream encounter with two women from the otherworld who beat him senseless with a horsewhip. After this beating he lies speechless in an enchanted trance for a year. When he finally recovers enough to return to the scene of the fateful visitation, he encounters a woman named Lí Ban, who tells him that her sister Fand, whose husband Manannán has abandoned her, has fallen in love with Cú Chulainn. Fand will sleep with him if he travels to the otherworld to help Lí Ban's husband fight against his enemies. Eventually Cú Chulainn does travel to the otherworld, where he apparently defeats the enemy and then spends a month with Fand. He returns to the mortal world after making a tryst with Fand in the human world. Learning of the tryst, his wife Emer arrives at the trysting place with fifty well-armed female companions to challenge Fand. In an extraordinary scene, Emer confronts first her husband and then her rival. She and Fand debate which of them should be abandoned by the man they both love. Fand finally decides to leave the hero to her worthy opponent and

---

Cú Chulainn refers to the early Irish hero and *Cuchulain* to Yeats's version of the character. It is worth noting that although Emer's name is spelled the same in both medieval and modern versions, in Middle Irish it would have been pronounced "*eh*-ver."

4. The waves episode is present only in the more modern versions of the tale incorporated by Gregory into her collection; it is absent from the earliest medieval version of the tale.

departs sorrowfully to rejoin her own husband, Manannán, who has decided to return to her. Cú Chulainn goes mad with grief at Fand's departure, but at Emer's instigation he is finally restored to health through a druidic potion of forgetfulness, given to the hero and Emer alike.

The original tale emphasizes the struggle of two women for the love of the hero. The conflict is a simple one between Emer and Fand, who, despite her otherworld origin and powers of enchantment, is ultimately vulnerable to Emer's challenge. Much of the story's power lies in Fand's sympathetic portrayal. She is never overtly condemned within the tale itself; indeed, through her long and heartfelt laments at the end, Fand transcends the stereotype of the wicked adulteress. She is certainly the beautiful denizen of the otherworld so common in early Irish tales, seductive and powerful. Yet in this text, her powers are limited in ways only too familiar to human beings living in the "real" world.[5]

Serglige Con Culainn should be read within the historical context of eleventh- and twelfth-century church reform, as well as preoccupations with Ireland's noncanonical marriage laws.[6] The text's construction of the final confrontation between Cú Chulainn and the two women could be seen as a warning against the potentially disruptive nature of the native marriage laws, which allowed men to have several wives at a time in different categories of marriage. Emer can thus be read as a voice of protest against polygyny, the spokeswoman for all wives rejected under native law. Her husband represents the type of man who, in the words of Archbishop Lanfranc to king Toirdelbach ua Briain in 1074, "abandons his lawfully wedded wife at his own will . . . and takes to himself some other wife . . . whom another has abandoned in like wickedness, according to a law of marriage that is rather a law of fornication" (Gwynn 1968:4). Fand, who has been abandoned in turn by her own husband, Manannán, is just such a "wife." One spousal abandonment, this text may be arguing, inevitably leads to another and thus potentially to a whole chain of shattered families, not to mention disabled, love-maddened men and women.

This central conflict between two worthy women is significantly altered in Yeats's play. Yeats's version shifts the focus through a number of additions, omissions, and changes. First, Yeats makes Cuchulain's madness and ensuing coma the result of his inadvertent murder of his son and his

5. In early Irish literature most otherworld figures are so similar to mortals that they can pass easily from one world to the next. They are rarely identifiably "alien."
6. The earliest manuscript version in Lebor na hUidre was revised during this period.

battle with the waves, rather than his thwarted love for Fand. Yeats also develops the role of a third woman, Cuchulain's mistress Eithne Inguba. Furthermore, through staging, masks, and costumes, Yeats distances Fand from both the action and the audience. He also removes or weakens the power of choice that Emer, Fand, and Cú Chulainn all possess in the original tale. Most important, Yeats introduces the male god Bricriu as intermediary and power broker in the struggle between Emer and Fand. The result is a radically different story with completely altered meanings.

First, let us examine the cause of the wasting sickness itself. In *Serglige Con Culainn,* the hero falls asleep after shooting unsuccessfully at a pair of manifestly supernatural birds, at which point he sees two women.

> Co n-accai in dá mnaí cucai. Indala n-aí brat úaine impe. Alaili brat corcra cóicdíabail im ṡude. Dolluid in ben cosin brot úane chucai, ⁊ tibid gen fris, ⁊ dobert béim dind echḟleisc dó. Dotháet alaili cucai dano, ⁊ tibid fris, ⁊ nod slaid fón alt chétna. Ocus bátar fri cíana móir oca sin .i. cechtar dé imma sech cucai béus dia búalad combo marb acht bec. Lotir úad íarom.
>
> Arigsitar Ulaid uli aní sin, ⁊ asbertatár ara ndúscide. "Acc!" ol Fergus. "Náchi nglúasid res atchí." Atracht íarom trena chotlud. "Cid dotrónad?" ol Ulaid fris. Níro fét íarom a n-acallaim. ("Nom berar," for sé "dom ṡergligu .i. don Téti Bricc. Nábad do Dún Imrith, nó do Dún Delca." "Not berthar do ṡaigid Emiri do Dún Delca," for Láeg. "Aicc!" ol sé. "Mo breith don Téti Bric.") Berair ass íarom co mboí co cend mblíadna isin magin sin cen labrad fri nech etir.   (Dillon 1953a:ll. 72–86)

> [H]e saw two women approach: one wore a green cloak and the other a crimson cloak folded five times, and the one in green smiled at him and began to beat him with a horsewhip. The other woman then came and smiled also and struck him in the same fashion, and they beat him for such a long time that there was scarcely any life left in him. Then they left.
>
> The [Ulstermen] perceived the state he was in, and they attempted to rouse him. But Fergus said "No! Do not disturb him—it is a vision." Then Cú Chulainn awoke. "Who did this to you?" asked the [Ulstermen], but he was unable to speak. He was taken to his sickbed in An Téte Brecc, and he remained there a year without speaking to anyone.   (Gantz 1981:157)[7]

Here the sickness is connected directly to the actions of the otherworld women. It also repeatedly linked throughout the early Irish story with the idea of the overwhelming power of erotic love. The actions of the other-world women seem emblematic of the kind of all-consuming passion that

---

7. I am citing Gantz's translation because of its accessibility to nonspecialists. Here Gantz omits some details that are not crucial for my argument.

reduces the lover to helplessness. Cú Chulainn is completely enslaved by love for Fand.

The account in Yeats's *The Only Jealousy of Emer* is very different. In explaining the cause of the hero's deathlike sleep to Eithne Inguba, Emer tells her how Cuchulain inadvertently slew his own son and went mad:

> And thereupon, knowing what man he had killed,
> And being mad with sorrow, he ran out;
> And after, to his middle in the foam,
> With shield before him and with sword in hand,
> He fought the deathless sea.
>
> . . . .
>
> Until at last, as though he had fixed his eyes
> On a new enemy, he waded out
> until the water had swept over him;
> But the waves washed his senseless image up
> And laid it at this door.
>
> (Ll. 71–75, 79–83)[8]

In this passage Yeats connects Cuchulain's coma with his grief over his son's death and the malevolent power of the sea. Later, the character Bricriu says that he himself has come from the court of Manannan the sea god. Clearly, in Yeats's play it is the powers of the otherworld, the *sidhe,* under the authority of the male god Manannan, which have taken Cuchulain hostage at a moment of emotional crisis (over the death of a male child). While Fand is clearly implicated in this process (she is, after all, the same immortal figure who lures the hero in an earlier play by Yeats, *At the Hawk's Well* [1917]), she is not depicted as the direct agent of his death-like sickness here.

Second, the development of Eithne Inguba as Cuchulain's mistress is an important alteration made by Yeats. In the medieval story, the hero's wife is named Eithne Inguba at the beginning of the tale and Emer later on. The name change in the medieval story may be simply the result of the splicing together of two separate manuscript versions of the story; alternatively, the two names may represent two different wives.[9] Because secular marriage laws in early Ireland permitted several forms of marriage, allowing a man to have more than one wife at a time, the latter option is certainly possible (Kelly 1988:68–79). In *Serglige Con Culainn,* however, the two

---

8. All quotes from *The Only Jealousy of Emer* are taken from Yeats 1966, the variorum text edited by Russell K. Alspach.

9. For remarks on the problem of the two wives, see Dillon 1953a:ix, xiii.

women never appear together in any scene, and there is no apparent opposition between them; in fact, they appear to be doublets. Their functions in the narrative are identical: each woman serves to warn Cú Chulainn of the dangers of the otherworld and to anchor him in the mortal world.

In Gregory's translation of *The Only Jealousy of Emer,* Eithne Inguba is not identified as a wife but as a woman "who loved Cuchulain" (Gregory [1902] 1970:210). Yeats has chosen to interpret her as a mistress and has drawn her according to early-twentieth-century attitudes toward mistresses. Eithne herself says: "Women like me, the violent hour passed over / Are flung into some corner like old nut-shells" (ll. 105–6). The development of Eithne Inguba as a mistress who perceives herself to be a secondary figure in the hero's life complicates the plot significantly. Instead of two women vying for the hero's love, there are now three. Eithne Inguba becomes part of the tragedy of the tale, as the self-deluded "winner" in the battle over Cuchulain's love, displacing both Emer and Fand at the end.

Third, the dramatic presentation of the story in Yeats's *The Only Jealousy of Emer,* with its use of music, masks, and dance, serves to distance Fand and her world from both the other characters and the audience. Fand is invisible to Emer until Bricriu grants Emer the necessary powers of sight, and there is no direct communication between the two women. Whereas in *Serglige Con Culainn* the otherworld is a place accessible to mortals, here it has become a "land of no return" from which Cuchulain must be saved at all costs. And while Fand is a sympathetic character in the early tale, in Yeats's play she is represented as a dangerous alien creature. The stage directions for her dance specify that "[h]er mask and clothes must suggest gold or bronze or brass or silver, so that she seems more an idol than a human being. This suggestion may be repeated in her movements. Her hair, too, must keep the metallic suggestion" (l. 219). Compounding the impression of strangeness is Fand's identification with the moon in its fifteenth phase. Yeats has deliberately incorporated Fand into the system articulated in *A Vision,* where characters are placed in different phases on a great wheel. The fifteenth phase is the point of greatest subjectivity — thus Fand is past the phases in which being human is possible (Clark 1990:45). The fifteenth phase is also the position of perfect beauty and perfect, untainted love (Billigheimer 1999:250). But as the goddess of the full moon, Fand is beyond Emer's reach. As Bricriu tells Emer, "No knife / can wound that body of air" (ll. 217–18). This treatment contrasts with the presentation in the early Irish *Serglige Con Culainn,* where Fand is represented as a physical being who can be intimidated by Emer's threats of bodily harm.[10]

The medieval tale is remarkable for the space it affords Fand's speech. Fand's lengthy discussion of the perils of love reveals a type of female subjectivity rare in early medieval literature. The final section of the tale is completely dominated by her voice; even Emer falls silent while Fand speaks. Fand utters two long poems, the first of which is directed toward Emer. In these verses she mourns her own imminent departure from the hero. She gently rebukes Emer for her threat of violence but nevertheless acknowledges her as a worthy opponent when she says, "Emer, the man is yours" (Gantz 1981:175). In fact, Emer and Fand have much in common. Both are aristocratic women of high status, and both are trying to cope with abandonment by a husband. Emer's husband has abandoned her in spirit if not in body, while Fand's husband Mannanán mac Lir has left her altogether. Indeed, it is implied that Fand has sought Cú Chulainn as a *result* of her abandonment, suggesting that the real culprit is Manannán. Fand seeks a man to replace her husband, whereas Emer fights to win Cú Chulainn back.

The frank female subjectivity seen in the medieval tale is removed from Fand in Yeats's version. Fand's powers of communication are focused on the hero alone, and the purpose of her seductive dance and words is entrapment. Fand and Emer have nothing in common except their desire for Cuchulain. They never communicate at all in the play: Emer is granted the power to hear and see the conversation between her husband and the Woman of the Sidhe, but she cannot intervene in it. Fand remains the dangerous seductress, the "evil woman" who cannot be viewed sympathetically.

Yeats's version also largely removes the power of choice from the characters. In the medieval tale even Cú Chulainn, bemused though he is as the women fight over him, unwittingly articulates his own choice, while it is the two rival women, Emer and Fand, who most vigorously voice their needs and desires. When Emer reproaches Cú Chulainn for abandoning her, he argues that Fand is a worthy consort because she is a wealthy woman of his status. Emer replies:

10. Otherworld beings in medieval Irish literature are typically capable of being killed; they are immortal but not eternal. Fand is not atypical in her vulnerability.

"Cáid cech n-écmais, is faill cech n-aichnid, co festar cach n-éolas. A gillai," ar sí, "ro bámarni fecht co cátaid acut, ⁊ no bemmís dorísi diambad áil duitsiu."   (Dillon 1953a:ll. 721–23)

The known is honored, the unknown is neglected — until all is known. Lad, we lived together in harmony once, and we could do so again if only I still pleased you.   (Gantz 1981:175)[11]

Then Cú Chulainn makes a critical remark, one whose import he seems not to grasp.

"Dar ar mbréthir trá," ar sé, "isatt áilsiu damsa ⁊ bidat áil hi céin bat béo." "Mo lécudsa didiu," ol Fand. "Is córu mo lécudsa," ar Emer. "Náthó," or Fand. "Messi léicfidir and, ⁊ is mé ro báeglaiged ó chéin."
(Dillon 1953a:ll. 724–27)

He said, "By my word, you do please me, and you will as long as you live." "Leave me then," said Fand. "Better to leave me," said Emer. "No, I should be left," said Fand, "for it is I who was threatened just now."
(Gantz 1981: 175)

The tensions of the medieval tale all intertwine at this moment. A determined Emer reminds her husband of their former happiness. He acknowledges his continuing desire for her, and Fand realizes that her own power over him is seriously threatened. Despite being a mortal women, Emer is more powerful than Fand here because she knows how to use words as weapons and to calculate their effects. It is Emer's carefully crafted words to Cú Chulainn that prompt his spontaneous admission of desire and in turn Fand's capitulation. Fand cedes the hero to Emer, interpreting Cú Chulainn's admission of desire for his wife as a lack of desire for her. Unlike the hero, Fand assumes that wholehearted love can be given to only one person at a time. Her words later on confirm this belief, when she says:

> Wretched is she who gives her love
> if he takes no notice of her;
> better to put such thoughts aside
> unless she is loved as she loves.
> (Gantz 1981:176)

Yeats reconfigures the issue of choice in his version. The Woman of the Sidhe must relinquish Cuchulain only because Bricriu persuades Emer to

11. Gantz's mild translation underplays the sexuality; literally, the phrase means "if only you still desired me."

renounce the hero's love, and not through any choice of her own. She does not speak to Emer, and Emer is unable to speak to her. Cuchulain seems to have the ability to choose for a few moments; we watch breathlessly with Emer as he is seduced by Fand's promise of complete and perfect love with no remorse or guilt:

> *Ghost of Cuchulain.* And shall I never know again
> Intricacies of blind remorse?
> *Woman of the Sidhe.* Time shall seem to stay his course;
> When your mouth and my mouth meet
> All my round shall be complete
> Imagining all its circles run;
> And there shall be oblivion
> Even to quench Cuchulain's drouth,
> Even to still that heart.
> *Ghost of Cuchulain.* Your mouth!
> [They are about to kiss, he turns away.
> O Emer, Emer!
>
> (Ll. 259–68)

At this pivotal moment the memory of his wife returns to him, and Cuchulain wavers as he mourns the loss of their youthful love and the happiness of their early marriage. But Fand scornfully reminds him of his repeated unfatihfulness to Emer and holds out once again the lure of love without remorse:

> But what could make you fit to wive
> With flesh and blood, being born to live
> Where no one speaks of broken troth,
> For all have washed out of their eyes
> Wind-blown dirt of their memories
> To improve their sight?
> *Ghost of Cuchulain.* Your mouth, your mouth!
> [She goes out followed by Ghost of Cuchulain.
>
> (Ll. 278–85)

In his representation of ideal love as untainted by guilt, Yeats subtly al-ludes to the medieval tale's intriguing "theology" of the otherworld as a sort of alternate Eden where the descendants of a "sinless Adam" (Gantz 1981:170) enjoy love without moral guilt. Yeats's version of this ideal is more sinister, however: there is no remorse in love because of the absence of memory, not because of the absence of sin. Wrongs committed against a lover are simply not recalled. Yeats's "Sidhe" is a place of amnesia, and its joys depend on happy oblivion, an enchantment of both mind and body.[12] Although Cuchulain appears to choose this type of love over the more complicated and painful love of mortals, he is portrayed as already enchanted by Fand as he follows her offstage.

Emer's ability to sway her husband directly through her words has been removed, and she remains frustratingly distanced from the action. One of Yeats's friends, T. Sturge Moore, sensed the inherent difficulty in the play's climax when he wrote, in an otherwise positive comment on the play, "Surely some action of Emer's, not the mere thought of her but a visible intervention, ought to have defeated the Woman of the Sidhe" (quoted in Bridge 1953:39–40). But Yeats chooses to maintain the distance between the combatants. Bricriu tells Emer: "He cannot hear — being shut off, a phantom / That can neither touch, nor hear, nor see" (ll. 192–93). The only choice left to Emer is the one offered by Bricriu: "There is still a moment left; cry out, cry out! / Renounce him, and her power is at an end" (ll. 294–95).

The addition of Bricriu as the intermediary in the struggle is the most drastic change Yeats made to the story. A figure named Bricriu appears as a troublemaker in some medieval Irish tales, but he has no part in *Serglige Con Culainn*.[13] In making Bricriu a god and the power broker in *The Only Jealousy of Emer*, Yeats has transformed the relatively simple and vivid struggle between two women — mortal and immortal — into a conflict between two apparently warring factions of Yeats's Sidhe. The nature of the enmity between Bricriu and Fand is never made clear, even in a draft version of the play, where Yeats included more dialogue between them (ll. 288ee–288yy). Already in this earlier version of the play, the power belongs to Bricriu, and he says to the Woman of the Sidhe:

> I must forego your thanks, I that took pity
> Upon your love and carried out your plan
> To tangle all his life and make it nothing
> That he might turn to you.   (Ll. 288hh–kk)

In the final version of *The Only Jealousy of Emer*, Bricriu says only, "I am Fand's enemy come to thwart her will" (l. 289). Giving Emer no choice but

12. Love without guilt was a common concern of the Aesthetes and others in the 1890s, and Yeats may reflect this notion here.

13. Bricriu appears in several early Irish tales, usually as a mischief-maker. For example, in *Fled Bricrenn* (*Bricriu's Feast*) he constructs an elaborate house and prepares a fabulous feast for the Ulstermen and their wives with the intention of inciting them all against one another once they arrive. The resulting conflicts provide abundant humor as well as heroic exploits. For a translation see Gantz 1981:221–55.

to renounce Cuchulain's love forever adds a depth of tragedy to the story unparalleled in the medieval version, and it lends Emer a tragic nobility. At the same time, however, the mechanism seems forced. Although Emer's choice in Yeats's play is heart-wrenching, no human will ever be called on to make it — at least not in the form presented here. No matter how painful a wayward husband's emotional withdrawal, no mortal wife has to bargain with an otherworld god for his soul or renounce any hope of rekindling his love to save it.

Clearly, Yeats's intentions in adapting the story to dramatic form were vastly different from those of the medieval redactors who shaped the original tale. In his "Note on *The Only Jealousy of Emer*," Yeats explicitly states that he has informed his play with "convictions about the nature and history of a woman's beauty," including the idea of the fifteenth phase of the moon symbolizing the "greatest possible bodily beauty" (Yeats 1923:433). The play was part of an evolving esoteric and poetic system in which a number of personalities (including his own) were plotted on a great wheel representing the phases of the moon. In fact, the play took shape in a period of Yeats's life characterized by both emotional upheaval and intense intellectual excitement — the months immediately following his marriage to George Hyde-Lees after his rejection first by Maud Gonne and then by Maud's daughter Iseult. In an exhaustive discussion of George's automatic script sessions (in which she claimed to be a medium for mystical knowledge), George Mills Harper makes the case that the meaning of *The Only Jealousy of Emer* is closely linked to Yeats's personal struggles (Harper 1987:6–153). Cuchulain is Yeats's surrogate self, and the female characters are abstractions representing his conflicted feelings for the four most important women in his life: Maud Gonne (Fand), Iseult Gonne (Eithne), and a fusion of Lady Gregory and George (Emer) (Pethica 1997:178, 200). Maud Gonne's association with the lure of the otherworld and the seductiveness of ideal love are clear in the play. Harper's study implies that *The Only Jealousy of Emer* is above all an elaborate vehicle for Yeats's personal exploration of his own warring impulses and an affirmation of his final choice of George as his wife. Exactly why the figure associated with George must renounce the hero's love forever while Eithne (Iseult) is the naïve winner is never made clear. It is thus wise to bear in mind Helen Vendler's caveat that "nobody transformed experience more than Yeats (not only in his art, but in his entire personal 'mask') and to find the historical 'real' beneath the fiction is a task almost hopeless, it seems to me, in the plays" (Vendler 1963:207).

At any rate, such a highly personalized schema fails to account for the role of Bricriu, whose presence undermines the personal power of *all* the other characters, especially the women. The heightened tragedy of Emer's self-sacrifice is achieved at the cost of female personal power: Fand as otherworld woman is reduced to an abstract idea, and Emer, having lost her ability to communicate directly with both her husband and her rival, must accept the hard choices offered by a male god. At the same time, Cuchulain, who can see only Fand and none of the other characters, remains oblivious to the mighty forces working on him. If the conflict is truly between the perfect love that Fand symbolizes and the imperfect, mortal love embodied by Emer, the action should more directly reflect the two women's engagement as opposites. But in employing the male figure Bricriu as the screen between them, Yeats dilutes the potential impact of this rivalry.

An explanation derived from the psychology of the play itself rather than from Yeats's personal life might prove more satisfying. Some critics have suggested that Fand is an anima figure for Yeats, and the otherworld a symbol of the poet's unconscious (Knapp 1991:77–79); Fand is thus "an image of his own soul in its pure subjective, feminine form" (Skene 1974: 201). Others have seen Fand as a symbol of the poet's muse and have argued that for this reason Yeats cannot possibly allow Cuchulain willfully to reject her outright but must make another character (Emer) responsible for Fand's defeat (Vendler 1963:228–29). Richard Allen Cave's comments about difficulties in staging the play are potentially more illuminating (Cave 1979:140–43). Cave and his performers concluded that Bricriu embodies the emotional stresses in Emer's love for her heroic husband and particularly the "possessive jealousy over Cuchulain" which allows her to indulge in "those petty sentimental hopes" that he will come to love her again in their old age (141). Cave says: "What right has she to exact such an obligation from him? Insight brings an instantaneous change of perception which is theatrically rendered with brilliant economy. It is, as we now see, Emer's own jealousy that has created the figure of discord (Bricriu) which rises terrifyingly from her marriage-bed; now her sight is cleansed" (141).

This is an intriguing idea, but why should Emer not hope for faithfulness from her husband? And to return to the issue of gender and power, why should a character representing her female jealousy be *male*? As a god and intermediary between mortal and immortal realms, the male Bricriu powerfully reinforces the patriarchal framework in which the play operates. Could Yeats not envision such a role as gendered female, despite his familiarity with powerful women in real life? Must it be the males who make and enforce the rules? Amy Koritz notes that "without Bricriu . . . Emer would be defenceless against Fand. Thus the male god effects the reestablishment of the status quo ante: a faithful wife silently sacrificing herself for an adulterous husband, a loving mistress properly conscious of her second-class and unstable position, and a male hero around whose fate revolves all the action — and all the women" (Koritz 1989:393). One might well argue that in *Serglige Con Culainn* "all the action . . . and all the women" similarly revolve around the hero. But in the medieval tale, the women have the power to act on their own behalf, without the interference of a male intermediary. In Yeats's *The Only Jealousy of Emer,* that ability is denied them — and in consequence, all the characters lose. We may see the action through Emer's eyes, but it still takes place in a man's world.

Clearly, the early Irish materials were a source of great inspiration for Yeats. His rewriting of this medieval tale points to the creativity that can be unleashed in an artist living in a bilingual context. Would Yeats have written a different play if he had been able to read *Serglige Con Culainn* in the original Middle Irish? Perhaps. Yet a comparison of these versions across two languages and two literary traditions throws into high relief the issues that preoccupied Yeats as he reshaped the Irish material. From the outset Yeats seems to have seen in the ancient tale a shadow of *his own story,* something that spoke powerfully to his own conflicted attitudes toward strong women. Like other men of his era, he could look at powerful women before his very eyes (women such as Maud Gonne and Lady Gregory) and still not understand them, blinded as he was by the gender stereotypes of late-Victorian culture. He could borrow characters and plot elements from the medieval tradition while remaining as oblivious to their significance as Cú Chulainn himself. Yeats's creative engagement with the figure of Cú Chulainn was ultimately centered in a profoundly personal language, a language beyond English, beyond Irish, and even beyond any rhetoric of heroism or nationalism — a language grounded in deep anxiety over gender roles and women's power. In this respect Yeats gave voice to the tensions and stresses on both sides of the linguistic divide in Ireland. It is what makes *The Only Jealousy of Emer* so infuriating, so mysterious, and so compelling.

Works Cited

Billigheimer, Rachel V. 1999. Tragedy and transcendence in the dance plays of W. B. Yeats. *Canadian Journal of Irish Studies* 25, nos. 1–2: 247–63.

Bridge, Ursula, ed. 1953. *W. B. Yeats and T. Sturge Moore: Their correspondance, 1901–1937*. London: Routledge and Kegan Paul.

Carey, John. 1994. The uses of tradition in *Serglige Con Culainn*. *Ulidia: Proceedings of the First International Conference on the Ulster Cycle of Tales*, ed. J. P. Mallory and Gerard Stockman, 77–84. Belfast: December Publications.

———. 1999. Cú Chulainn as ailing hero. In *Celtic connections: Proceedings of the Tenth International Congress of Celtic Studies*, ed. Ronald Black, William Gillies, and Roibeard Ó Maolalaigh, 190–98. East Linton, Scotland: Tuckwell Press.

Cave, Richard Allen. 1979. A style for Yeats's dance-plays: "The more passionate is the art the more marked is the selection." *Yearbook of English Studies* 9:135–53.

Clark, Rosalind E. 1990. Yeats's *The only jealousy of Emer* and the Old Irish *Serglige Con Culainn*. *Yeats: An Annual of Critical and Textual Studies* 8:39–48.

Dillon, Myles, ed. 1953a. *Serglige Con Culainn*. Dublin: Dublin Institute for Advanced Studies.

———, trans. 1953b. The wasting sickness of Cú Chulainn. *Scottish Gaelic Studies* 7:47–88.

Findon, Joanne. 1997. *A woman's words: Emer and female speech in the Ulster Cycle*. Toronto: University of Toronto Press.

Gantz, Jeffrey, trans. 1981. *Early Irish myths and sagas*. Harmondsworth: Penguin.

Gregory, Augusta, trans. [1902] 1970. *Cuchulain of Muirthemne*. Reprint, New York: Oxford University Press.

Gwynn, Aubrey. 1968. *The twelfth-century reform*. Dublin: Gill.

Harper, George Mills. 1987. *The making of Yeats's "A vision": A study of the automatic script*. Vol. 1. Basingstoke: Macmillan.

Kelley, Fergus. 1988. *A guide to early Irish law*. Dublin: Dublin Institute for Advanced Studies.

Knapp, Bettina. 1991. *The only jealousy of Emer*: Recycling the elements. In *More real than reality: The fantastic in Irish literature and the arts*, ed. Donald E. Morse and Csilla Bertha, 67–81. New York: Greenwood Press.

Koritz, Amy. 1989. Women dancing: The structure of gender in Yeats's early plays for dancers. *Modern Drama* 32:387–400.

Marcus, Phillip L. 1970. *Yeats and the beginning of the Irish Renaissance*. Ithaca: Cornell University Press.

Ó Cathasaigh, Tomás. 1994. Reflections on *Compert Con Culainn* and *Serglige Con Culainn*. *Ulidia: Proceedings of the First International Conference on the Ulster Cycle of Tales*, ed. J. P. Mallory and Gerard Stockman, 85–89. Belfast: December Publications.

O Hehir, Brendan. 1988. Yeats's sources for the matter of Ireland: I. Edain and Aengus. *Yeats: An Annual of Critical and Textual Studies* 6:76–89.

———. 1991. Yeats's sources for the matter of Ireland: II. Edain and Midhir. *Yeats: An Annual of Critical and Textual Studies* 9:95–106.

Pethica, James. 1997. Patronage and creative exchange: Yeats, Lady Gregory, and the economy of indebtedness. In *Yeats and Women,* ed. Deirdre Toomey, 168–204. 2d ed. Basingstoke: Macmillan.

Skene, Reg. 1974. *The Cuchulain plays of W. B. Yeats: A study.* New York: Columbia University Press.

Vendler, Helen Hennessy. 1963. *Yeats's "Vision" and the later plays.* Cambridge: Harvard University Press.

Yeats, W. B. 1923. *Plays and controversies.* London: Macmillan.

———. 1966. *The only jealousy of Emer.* In *The variorum edition of the plays of W. B. Yeats,* ed. Russell K. Alspach, 529–65. London: Macmillan.

Hegemonic Discourses in Brian Friel's
The Freedom of the City

Brian Friel's play *The Freedom of the City* (1973) cannot be read as anything other than a political play. Inspired by a political event — "Bloody Sunday" — in Northern Ireland, the play dramatizes a similar but fictional event in the Northern Irish city of Derry, whose two names, Derry to the nationalists and Londonderry to the unionists, symbolize the political and ideological divisions that have threatened the stability of Northern Ireland in the modern period. But the play is more than simply a dramatized account of a single historical incident, or what Nesta Jones calls a "drama documentary" (Jones 2000:8). In commenting explicitly on the politics of the "Troubles" in Northern Ireland, the play is also activating the broader issues of the hegemonic power of the state and the negotiation between political authority and individuals in society.

The play has always been read as a political text, in some form or another. As a reaction to a political event in Northern Ireland, *The Freedom of the City* has evoked a series of uneasy critical responses since it was first staged at the Abbey Theatre in Dublin on 20 February 1973. The play describes a fictitious event, the deaths of three civilians at the hands of British soldiers during a civil rights march in Derry in 1970, and the subsequent inquiry into the deaths that exonerates the British army. As Elmer Andrews has said, "Clearly, the play is, in some measure, a response to the events of Bloody Sunday (30 January 1972), when thirteen civil rights marchers in Derry were shot dead by British troops, and to the ensuing Widgery tribunal which, in exonerating the British army, served to exacerbate the shock and outrage felt by many Irish civil rights supporters" (Andrews 1995:129). In an interview with Fintan O'Toole in 1982, Friel said, "I wrote it out of some kind of heat and some kind of immediate passion that I would want to have quieted a bit before I did it," indicating the powerful connection between the play and the historical event that preceded it (quoted in Richtarik 1994:81).

It would be hard to deny that the play has an explicitly political message, though critics have been unable to agree on precisely what this message is.[1] Where they seem to agree is that the play transcends the immediate historicity of Bloody Sunday to make some important statements about Irish society and the problematic relationship between Britain as a state power and Northern Ireland as its possession. In its use of discourse, however, the play signifies a much wider concern, that of the construction of power and the negotiation between dominant and subordinate groups in society. The context of Northern Ireland and the Troubles is, of course, significant in itself, providing a stylized and dramatized view of the impact of state intervention on individual lives, but it is also an arena within which we are shown the power of language to impose control and contain opposition.

The centrality of language to Friel's work as metaphor and theme as well as vehicle has been described by Alan Peacock as "a preoccupation with the dubieties, the duplicities, limitations and simultaneous analytical, expressive and transcendent qualities of language which is ubiquitous in Friel's drama" (Peacock 1993:xv). This centrality has been noted most frequently in relation to his later play *Translations* (1980), in which the Ireland/England divide is represented in terms of linguistic difference and the colonial imperative to translate the dominated into the language of the dominant, both literally and figuratively (Lynch 1997). Writing of this play, Declan Kiberd says its underlying theme is "that once Anglicization is achieved the Irish and English, instead of speaking a truly identical tongue, will be divided most treacherously by a common language" (Kiberd 1995:622). In fact, this theme had already been introduced, though more obliquely, in *The Freedom of the City*. Limited by the discourses available to them, the characters in this play are "divided most treacherously" not simply along national and sectarian lines but from each other as well.

The discursive construction of social positioning in the play can be read against a context in which the English language is itself hegemonic relative to Irish. Stranded without state support following partition in 1921, the Irish language in Northern Ireland, long the minority and low-prestige language, slowly suffocated. Voluntary commitment to its survival and revival, as Reg Hindley (1990:160) has pointed out, proved even less effective than the language policies imposed by the Republic. Following a line of earlier scholars, Kiberd (1998:12) has argued, with some justification, that the Irish themselves, virtually within one generation, chose to

---

1. For some of the varied interpretations, see Andrews 1993; Dantanus 1988; Deane 1985; Peacock 1993; Pine 1990; and Richards 1997.

speak English after the famines of the 1840s, a cultural choice often elided from nationalist textbooks: "It was easier in a Brit-bashing mythology to blame the old enemy for the near-erasure of the Irish language than to recognize that Irish people themselves had made the decision not to speak it."[2]

This view of the decline of Irish begs two questions. First, who were "the Irish" in the middle of the nineteenth century? Clearly, they are made up of at least two cultural and linguistic groups, much as "the Welsh" are today. John Edwards (1984:481) estimates that "between 1600 and 1800, [English] grew to become the language of regular use for about half the population—the more powerful half. Irish speakers were more and more the poor, the disadvantaged, and their language received no official recognition." Thus, it was only some of "the Irish"—generally the more economically deprived—who "chose" to stop speaking the language, because the others could not speak it anyway. Second, we must ask how freely chosen was any decision to stop speaking Irish in an economic context that privileged the English language. As Máirtín Ó Murchú puts it, "these Irish-speaking masses were without economic power, and had no means of determining their own destiny" (Ó Murchú 1992:41). Kiberd (1998: 12) points to a "lack of sentiment" in the sudden switch to English, but a decision based on economic pragmatism, the realities of mass emigration, and, indeed, survival is not necessarily commensurate with an active and preferred choice. While Irish people today do have a choice "to speak or not to speak their native language," as Kiberd (1998:12) says, the economic and social context of that choice—in a relatively buoyant economy with the declining influence of the Catholic church and the increasing significance of a multilingual Europe—ensures that the two alternatives are more evenly weighted now than they were a century ago.

This lack of real choices for the culturally disempowered is a theme that underlies *The Freedom of the City*. By drawing attention to discursive varieties within the hegemonic language, the play illustrates one inevitable consequence of the link between language and culture: the linguistically disempowered become the culturally dispossessed.

In describing the use of language in *The Freedom of the City*, most critics take the position that the voices of "authority" are guilty of misrepresentation in one form or another and that "the truth" fails to emerge

2. See also Kiberd 1995:616. For a brief description of the debate about the contribution of the Irish to the decline of their own language, see Edwards 1984:494.

during the aftermath of the killings.[3] Leaving aside the problem of language as a means of representing "truth" — and Fintan O'Toole (1993: 205–6) argues that Friel himself is well aware of the inadequacy of language in this regard and therefore of the impossibility of writing historical "truth" — such views of the play reduce its meaning to a simple condemnation of authority in its failure to produce and recognize "the truth" and its consequent oppression of subordinated individuals. Such a reading certainly defines the play as a strong critique of British rule in Northern Ireland, as Friel evidently intended it to be. But if we are to recover something of wider relevance from the play, we need to be aware that it is language, rather than politics, that is foregrounded. The emphasis on language and discourse inevitably draws attention to their ideological function as a means of constructing different views of "reality."

The discursive distinctions between the "institutional" and "individual" characters — the first speaking in formal conventional registers, the others in a personal conversational style — suggest a face-value opposition between the "bad" authority figures who deliberately distort "the truth" and the "good" individuals who speak "the truth" as they see it. But the very different interpretations of their situation offered by the three Guildhall characters — Michael's faith in the system compared with Skinner's cynicism, for example — constantly undercut their "everyman" role as guardians of an absolute "truth": they see the world differently from each other as well from the institutional characters. This means we have to look at the discursive mechanisms by which the dominant "authority" views come to be inscribed as "the truth," so effectively that any potential opposition to the findings of the inquiry is deactivated and contained. This process of containment and consensus established in the play, from the deaths to the public funeral, provides a dramatic exemplar of the Gramscian model of hegemony in action, revealing some of the strategies, both discursive and coercive, by which social consensus is maintained.

"The turn to Gramsci," to borrow a phrase from Tony Bennett (1986: xi–xix) and Graeme Turner (1992:210), refers to a movement by cultural theorists away from the perceived limitations of classical Marxist theory and toward a more complex formulation known as "hegemony theory" developed by the Italian journalist and political activist Antonio Gramsci.[4] Two ideas rejected by recent theorists in favor of hegemony theory

3. See, for example, Andrews 1995 and Glass 1996.
4. Antonio Gramsci (1891–1937) was a founding member of the Italian Communist

are the economic determinism of classical Marxism, which simply maintains that the economic base of a society inevitably determines its social
and cultural superstructure, and the concept of "dominant ideology" as
used by the Frankfurt school, with its implications of a passive manipulated majority (Storey 1993:100–110). Gramsci himself was dissatisfied
with Marxist economic determinism, noting that historically economic
crises never seemed to favor the working classes or to result in a fundamental change to the capitalist mode of production. His explanation for
this was hegemony, that is, the processes by which dominant groups constantly negotiate with subordinate groups to win their consent to a status
quo that favors the dominant group.

     Stuart Hall has traced the demise within Marxist theory of an overly
simplistic view of "dominant ideology": "That notion of dominance which
meant the direct imposition of one framework, by overt force or ideological compulsion, on a subordinate class, was not sophisticated enough to
match the real complexities of the case"; instead, "hegemony implied that
the dominance of certain formations was secured, not by ideological compulsion, but by cultural leadership. . . . The critical point about this conception of 'leadership' — which was Gramsci's most distinguished contribution — is that hegemony is understood as accomplished, not without the
due measure of legal and legitimate compulsion, but principally by means
of winning the active consent of those classes and groups who were subordinated within it" (Hall 1982:85). Norman Fairclough has also reformu-
lated the Marxist model in a more Gramscian style when he argues that
"the way in which a society organizes its economic production, and the
nature of the relationships established in production between social classes, are fundamental structural features which determine others" (Fairclough 1989:32). He defines what he calls the "dominant bloc" as those
who produce and control the power of the state: "This political power is
typically exercised not just by capitalists, but by an alliance of capitalists
and others who see their interests as tied to capital — many professional
workers, for instance" (33). Both Fairclough and Hall emphasize the importance of ideology conveyed through the discursive practices of social

---

Party and spent the last eleven years of his life in prison, where he wrote most of the work for
which he is now famous. On the life and work of Gramsci, see, for example, Joll 1977; Femia
1981; Simon 1982; Ransome 1992; and Bellamy and Schecter 1993. Gramsci's own writings
are available in a number of English translations, including *Selections from the Prison
Notebooks,* ed. and trans. Hoare and Nowell-Smith (1971) and *Further Selections from the
Prison Notebooks,* ed. and trans. Boothman (1994).

institutions, "no longer as the institutions which merely reflected and sustained the consensus, but as the institutions which helped to produce consensus and which manufactured consent" (Hall 1982:86). These institutions, representing what Fairclough refers to as "state power," reside not only in the obvious forms of social control such as the police and armed forces but also in "a whole range of social institutions such as education, the law, religions, the media, and indeed the family," institutions that "collectively and cumulatively ensure the continuing dominance of the capitalist class" (Fairclough 1989:33).

These are the very institutions — the police, armed forces, law, education, religion, media, and family — whose discourses are represented in *The Freedom of the City*. In the play they have an explicitly hegemonic function — to negotiate and maintain consent to the rule by the dominant bloc. The composition of the dominant bloc, or the power of the state, as it is represented in the play, conforms more to the Gramscian notion of "cultural leadership" than to the earlier Marxist idea of the capitalist ruling class: in Friel's Derry there is no simplistic opposition between ruling class and working class or between colonized Irish and ruling English. Instead, the dominant bloc comprises a cultural leadership of vested interests — political, religious, media — that cut across all social classes and both nations, from the Irish priest to the English judge.

In its stress on consensus and the manufacture of consent, hegemony theory also recognizes the use of coercion as another, more overt, form of state power.[5] Gramsci identified two aspects of society, the civil and the political, where the former includes social institutions such as the legal system, education, religion, and so on, and the latter comprises state organizations such as political parties, the police, and the armed forces. He associates hegemonic consent mainly with civil society and coercive control primarily with the political level of society, though he acknowledges that hegemony and coercion can exist at both levels of society (Bellamy and Schecter 1993:118–19). Ransome (1992:150) paraphrases Gramsci's position by saying he "distinguishes between coercive control which is manifest through direct force or the threat of force, and consensual control which arises when individuals 'willingly' or 'voluntarily' assimilate

5. Gramsci's distinction (not always clearly maintained) between consent and coercion was developed by Louis Althusser into his dual model of ideological state apparatuses and repressive state apparatuses. For a summary of Althusser's position, see Strinati 1995:146–55.

the world-view or hegemony of the dominant group." If ideological processes and institutional discourses do their work, subordinate groups need
not be forced to consent but will do so in the belief (not necessarily
"false") that their interests are to some extent included in the dominant
culture (Strinati 1995:166).

In *The Freedom of the City* we are shown both the discourses of consensus, represented by the contrapuntal voices of institutional and individual characters, and the forces of coercion, represented by the British
army. The presence of both in the play dramatically illustrates the social
consequences of the failure of cultural and political leadership, which
results in a precariously unstable society in which competing interests are
inadequately reconciled. Through its depiction of both discursive hegemony and coercion, the play dramatizes Gramsci's answer to his own
question about why working-class revolt and economic crisis never succeed in overthrowing bourgeois capitalism, why unequal and oppressive
social systems are able to remain in place largely unchallenged. The play
sets up that situation and shows us the answer: the workings of hegemony
and coercion guarantee the continuation of a dominant view of "reality"
that endorses British rule in Northern Ireland.

Ideology conveyed through discursive practices is, as Fairclough (1989:
34) says, "the key mechanism of rule by consent." Through the different
institutional discourses constructed by the play, we come to realize that
the issue dramatized here is not a simple one of lies and cover-ups by a
corrupt state but an inexorable working out of hegemonic power, both
consensual and coercive. The concept of discourse refers to language as a
social practice, which in turn implies that any individual use of language is
determined and constrained by convention. This is not to imply that individuals are merely "passive victims of systems of thought," a point con-
tested by Sara Mills, but to focus on discourse as a way of theorizing
hegemony as "people's compliance in their own oppression" through their
participation in, and access to, a variety of discourses.[6] Such an understanding of discourse challenges the extent to which we are able to speak
as individuals, separate from our social context and experience (Fairclough 1989:9–10, 28–32). Thus, in the play, the more the characters

---

6. Mills (1997:29–30) offers an interesting discussion about what she sees as the differences between ideology — which she interprets fairly narrowly according to a classic Marxist
model — and discourse as tools for cultural theory. In my analysis I follow Foucault in seeing
little distinction between discourse and ideology.

conform to conventional and recognizable discourses, the less individualized they appear to be.

And yet it is a kind of sleight of hand to suggest that characters such as the judge and the policeman who use an institutional discourse are less individualized (and therefore less sympathetic) than the three characters who appear to converse "naturally" in "their own" voices. This is the opposition that appears to be offered to us, the innocent victims whose essence as individuals stands triumphantly outside the corrupt social discourses of authority, but the nature of language itself refuses to validate this opposition. Individuals in the private sphere also participate in and are constrained by socially determined discourses, and they are inevitably compromised and defined by the various kinds of discourses to which they have access. What the play demonstrates is a hierarchy of discourses that determines the social formation, as well as the process through which this hierarchy is maintained and reproduced, even by the very individuals who are disempowered by it: in other words, the operation of hegemony.

The institutional discourses represented in the play—the law, education, religion, the media—all perform a hegemonic function, to win general consent to a view of reality that favors the dominant bloc. To interpret this strategy as lies or a distortion of "the truth" is to miss the point about hegemony: authority would not be hegemonic if it did not construct the world in a way that supported its own interests. The discourse of the law, represented by the speeches of the judge, establishes its legitimacy by its claims to objectivity and fairness. "Our only function is to form an objective view of the events which occurred in the City of Londonderry," says the judge early in the play (109), and he reinforces this "commonsense" position with such phrases as "fact-finding exercise," "the facts we garner," and "the facts may indicate," as well as deictic references to specific times and places.[7] Yet from the beginning, the content of his first speech undermines this discursive construction of objectivity; in his summing up of what may emerge from the inquiry, the only two alternatives he suggests are equally damning: "The facts we garner over the coming days may indicate that the deceased were callous terrorists who had planned to seize the Guildhall weeks before the events of February 10th; or the facts may indicate that the misguided scheme occurred to them on that very day"

7. All page references citing quotations from *The Freedom of the City* refer to the edition in Friel 1984.

(109–10). The possibility of their innocence is occluded, even while the discourse makes claims to being factual and objective.

In all his speeches the judge's language constructs a context of civil disorder that is then used to justify the need for state intervention in the form of "her Majesty's government" and "British troops" (109). He refers to the "danger of reprisal," "callous terrorists" (109), "revolutionary speeches" (110), "platform of defiance" (149), "illegally demonstrating" (149), and "the mob which had gathered" (151), constructing a view of society as out of control and dangerous, a situation that necessitates the urgent restoration of law and order by the state. Through these discursive strategies, the judge's language works to reaffirm the people's consent to British rule in Northern Ireland and to the continued presence there of the British army. His linguistic construction of events makes this seem a "commonsense" conclusion, where "common sense" has the Gramscian meaning of an ideological position "in the service of sustaining unequal relations of power" (Fairclough 1989:84). It is surely "common sense" to agree that if society is out of control, then the state must act to restore order, but such a version of "common sense" works hegemonically to empower the state and to silence opposing voices, such as Skinner's.

The voice of Dodds represents the discourse of academe and education, focused specifically on the jargon of sociology. In the context of the play, this discourse normalizes a view of the world in which the inequalities of wealth and social class that are the product of industrial capitalism are made to seem "natural" and therefore inevitable and unchangeable. Dodds's main thesis is that there is a "culture of poverty" handed down from one generation to the next in a ceaseless spiral of disempowerment: "by the time children are six or seven they have usually taken on the basic values and attitudes of their subculture and aren't psychologically geared to take advantage of changing conditions or increased opportunities that may occur in their lifetime" (110–11).[8] Encoded in the sociological jargon is the "commonsense" view that welfare or any other kind of assistance is therefore useless. Dodds constructs an ethnographic description of the working class as if they were a tribe in a remote wilderness (an impression reinforced by Dodds's position as an American academic commenting on

8. Pine (1990:42, 111–13) has pointed out that Friel based much of Dodds's discussion of "the culture of poverty" on the work of the anthropologist Oscar Lewis, in particular his book *La Vida: A Puerto Rican Family in the Culture of Poverty, San Juan and New York* (1966). Pine suggests that "the subversion of Lewis amounts to an unsuccessful attempt to universalise the condition of poverty" (111).

this strange nation of Irish people): "Another inheritance is his inability to control impulse: he is present-time oriented and seldom defers gratification, never plans for the future, and endures his here and now with resignation and frustration" (133).

This "us and them" division in the language cements the dominant view of the working class as unified, homogeneous, and "other." At the same time, the working class is almost to be envied for its sense of community and fun-loving togetherness, sharing a spirit of simple enjoyment that "we," the cynical and oversophisticated middle classes, have lost from our lives. Dodds says, "The result is that people with a culture of poverty suffer much less from repression than we of the middle-class suffer and indeed, if I may make the suggestion with due qualification, they often have a hell of a lot more fun than we have" (135).

I am not trying to suggest here that Dodds is in any way a "bad" or unsympathetic character, any more than I think the judge is a "bad" example of his profession. As a character, Dodds himself is clearly not unsympathetic to the plight of the impoverished: he notes the tendency of the dominant class to explain "the low economic status of the poor as a result of their personal shiftlessness and inadequacy" (133), implying that although this may be the dominant view, other explanations are possible. He also alludes to the value of communal movements: "trade union, religious, civil rights, pacifist, revolutionary — any movement which gives them this objectivity, organizes them, gives them real hope, promotes solidarity, such a movement inevitably smashes the rigid caste that encases their minds and bodies" (111).

Yet it is precisely this kind of movement — a civil rights march — that the dominant bloc most fears, for the very reasons that Dodds put forward: because of the possibility that such movements will lead to revolution and civil disorder among an oppressed majority. In the context of the play, the concession to the civil rights march is a means by which the ruling group negotiates with the people to maintain their consent to the status quo: a show of solidarity is allowed, but only within the terms prescribed by the governing authorities.

On the one hand, then, Dodds attempts to be scholarly, detached, and impartial, but on the other, the very nature of his discourse aligns him with hegemonic interests. By and large, Dodds is participating in an institutional discourse that serves to reassert the hegemonic position that class distinction are "natural" and inevitable, preexisting the social formation;

that the working classes are, by reason of their birth, temperamentally suited to being working-class (because they are spontaneous, present-time oriented, fun-loving, and so on) and are therefore content to remain so; that any attempts by the state to improve their lot, through welfare or other means, will have little or no effect; and that any form of communal mobilization poses a threat to the established order unless closely monitored by those in power.

Although the judge is English and Dodds is American, the priest, broadcaster, and balladeer are all Irish. Yet they too contribute to hegemonic consensus — Friel never attempts to simplify the issue into a purely nationalist one. The priest is the most overtly hypocritical character in the play, which perhaps implies a certain authorial dissatisfaction on Friel's part with the church as an agent of "cultural leadership." In his first speech the priest assumes the authority to speak for the people and to interpret events for them, using conventional sermonizing rhetoric such as "solemn requiem Mass," "deep and numbing grief," "administering the last rites," "a consolation to all of us," and "blessed are they that mourn, says our Divine Lord" (124–25). Having thus appropriated a position of authority, the priest interprets the event in line with orthodox Christianity, that is, as an act of sacrifice, not far removed from that of Christ himself. He also sees the deaths as an act of rebellion: "They sacrificed their lives so that you and I and thousands like us might be rid of that iniquitous yoke and might inherit a decent way of life" (125). Here is an example of the kind of civil protest movement referred to by Dodds the sociologist, the uniting of the people against economic oppression under the banner of religion, itself a hegemonic force ready to challenge the existing political hegemony.

By the end of the play, however, the political hegemony has easily defeated this challenge. In his second speech the priest has joined forces with the dominant bloc, consenting to its version of reality in order to maintain his own authority. This speech begins in exactly the same words as the first, undermining their value as sincere expressions of comfort and identifying them instead as empty rhetoric. This time, when the priest repeats his question, "why did they die?" (156), he gives a completely different answer. Instead of being heroes who sacrificed their lives for their friends, the three dead people are now defined as the victims (possibly but not certainly innocent) of an evil conspiracy "to deliver this Christian country into the dark dungeons of Godless communism" (156). And far from urging his flock to maintain the rage, the priest now exhorts: "And to those of you who are flirting with the doctrines of revolution, let me quote to you from that most revolutionary of doctrines—the sermon on the mount: 'Blessed are the meek for *they* shall possess the land' " (156). In the face of the inevitable findings of the inquiry, the priest has decided that discretion should be the better part of valor and that he would be unwise to continue supporting the sacrificial heroism of the dead. As a hegemonic power in its own right, the Catholic church sees no value in openly confronting the political and economic hegemony of the day; the only role remaining for it, then, is to use its teachings to promote class unity (and class difference) and to reconcile its congregation to the inevitability of social inequality and oppression. Like the other institutional characters, the priest consents—and wins the consent of others—to the hegemonic status quo.

The television reporter, Liam O'Kelly, also appears twice, at the beginning and end of the play, using a media discourse appropriate to each occasion. The hegemonic function of media discourses as "reality defining" has long been recognized, with media claims to "impartiality" inevitably compromised by their participation in the production of consent— "shaping the consensus while reflecting it—which orientates them within the field of force of the dominant social interests represented within the state" (Hall 1982:87). It is a matter of "consent" that news services must provide live or on-the-spot coverage of violent events, partly to authenticate the "truth" or actuality of what is happening and partly as a reminder that violence can break out anywhere at any time unless the state is eternally vigilant and empowered to deal with such crises. O'Kelly employs all the usual rhetoric of the live broadcast from the scene of battle, including the affirmation of eyewitness status ("I am standing on the walls overlooking Guildhall Square," 117); the nameless and uncorroborated sources of information ("estimated at about three thousand strong," "unconfirmed reports are coming in," "if the reports are accurate," 117); and the emphasis on the scale of the violence and disorder, which creates a public demand for swift retaliatory action to end the crisis.

In O'Kelly's references to the two sides involved in the struggle, his position is clearly hegemonic. The representatives of command and status are "the Guildhall . . . symbol of Unionist domination," "security forces and the Stormont government," "Brigadier Johnson-Hansbury," and "Chief Superintendent of Derry's Royal Ulster Constabulary," while the references to those who are apparently challenging them include "about fifty armed gunmen," "the terrorists," "usually reliable spokesmen from the Bogside," and "small groups . . . gathering at street corners within the ghetto area" (117–18). The language specifically directs us to understand the power relations involved here and to accept as "common sense" the actions of those who represent legitimate order and justice in the face of an apparent rebellion from "the ghetto area."

O'Kelly's last speech, a commentary on the funeral, again establishes his eyewitness status: "I am standing just outside the Long Tower church" (167). The nature of the funeral as a public event becomes clear as O'Kelly names the officials involved in it and affirms for us their dominant status: "This is surely the most impressive gathering of church and state dignitaries that this humble parish of the Long Tower has ever seen. There is the Cardinal Primate . . . and beside him I see Colonel Foley who is representing the President" (167). The list goes on, meticulously recording everyone's precise title and status, including even the Taoiseach, the Irish prime minister, and it is only when the victims are listed that O'Kelly gets Skinner's name wrong, hinting at the relative unimportance of the dead people, the "ordinary people," compared with the officials. The formal discourse indicates that what we have here is the equivalent of a state funeral, a public recognition of honorable death that, without in any way undermining the findings of the inquiry, enables the mourners, in a safe and contained environment, to perceive the victims as heroes. In such ways is hegemonic consent secured, by making concessions to subordinate groups who then feel their interests are at least acknowledged by, and even included within, the dominant culture.

While the priest and the broadcaster represent a middle-class Northern Ireland with an interest in reproducing the dominant social order, even an unequal and oppressive one, the balladeer represents popular culture and the way in which the majority assimilate events into their own experience. Popular culture is a key site of hegemonic struggle, a place where oppositional challenges to dominant ideas are tried out and ultimately contained and deactivated, "a shifting balance of forces between resistance and incorporation" (Storey 1993:122). The balladeer's two songs are both located in a long tradition of Irish nationalist folk song, celebrating heroic martyrs who fought for "Mother Ireland" against "the British army," only to be felled by "a Saxon bullet" (118, 148). Such a mythologizing discourse, recalling Ireland's prerepublican and prepartition history in terms of war, violence, and rebellion, constructs the Irish as the defeated, the disempowered, the ungovernable, and the recklessly heroic, constantly reproducing a view of the Irish which is only partial and temporary but which has been legitimized in dominant cultural forms (music, film, novels) both within and outside Ireland as universal and unchanging. What might have been, and perhaps once was, a genuine vehicle of popular resistance, has become incorporated into the hegemonic view of Northern Ireland as a society inevitably based on division and war, a view that may then be used to legitimate coercive state control.

The three in the Guildhall—Skinner, Michael, and Lily—are at the receiving end of institutional discourse, and from that position they are participating in the hegemonic negotiation. They are the ones whose consent must be won by the state, and ultimately, in the informal language of the private sphere, they do consent. In the language they use, they take up the subject positions constructed for them by the hegemonic discourses of the institutional powers. The individualized lives of Michael and Lily may not be exactly as Dodds described in his theorized model, but they both accept his view, the dominant view, that their positions in society are natural, inevitable, and perhaps even their own fault, or at least their own responsibility. Michael sees self-improvement as the way out of the "culture of poverty"; Lily blames herself for what she sees as her stupidity and for her disabled son. Theirs are not the triumphantly counterhegemonic voices of individuals proving the authorities to be corrupt and dehumanized; rather, they demonstrate the triumph of the ideology of bourgeois individualism, where the disempowered are encouraged to "take responsibility" for their own disempowerment.

The "public" speeches of the three Guildhall characters at the beginning of act 2, when they comment on their own deaths, are a reminder of the social nature of language and the differences between formal and informal discourse. The speeches suggest the lack of power residing in the language of the individual sphere: because the personal conversations of individuals are constructed as "subjective," they can be dismissed as less truthful than the discourse of institutions. When Lilly tells us "publicly" that she had a flash of insight before she died, we somehow feel she is telling us a "truth" that was never articulated in her own words as an individual in the Guildhall. It is only when Friel artificially instates her as a public person, using a standardized hegemonic discourse, that we really believe that she has spoken an important and meaningful truth. The device of the "public" speeches is a dramatic way of illustrating the difference in power between the language of the private sphere and that of the institutional level of society, showing how this difference is inscribed as a "commonsense" or naturalized distinction. The device indicates to us that there is, after all, nothing triumphantly antihegemonic about the discourse of individuals compared with that of the state: the three Guildhall characters are disempowered not only by their economic situation but also by their exclusion — involuntary in the case of Michael and Lily — from hegemonic discourse.

Michael and Lily symbolize the success of hegemony in winning and maintaining consensus. Throughout the play Michael steadfastly supports the rule of law, the rightness of the system, the integrity of those in authority. He is in awe of the Guildhall ("God, it's very impressive," 119) and what it represents: "I read about the Hon. The Irish Society. They're big London businessmen and big bankers and they own most of the ground in the city" (120). He sees no irony, as Skinner immediately does, in the contrast between the rich fittings of the Guildhall and the slum conditions in which Lily lives. Michael also subscribes to the state's own paternalistic view of itself: if subordinate groups ask for what they want nicely and politely, like good children, the parental state will give it to them. He asserts, "It was a good, disciplined, responsible march. And that's what we must show them — that we're responsible and respectable; and they'll come to respect what we're campaigning for" (128–29).

Michael is the perfectly socialized corporate citizen, using a discourse that supports the importance of the family, homeownership, the need for education, and the superiority of those in power — despite the reality of his own circumstances as an unemployed youth whose participation in every civil rights march has not so far yielded any glimpse of the "better life" to which he aspires. Perhaps the play is hinting here at the Marxist idea of "false consciousness"; certainly he lacks what Dodds has called an "objective view" of his condition (111). In his "public" speech at the beginning of act 2, the "truth" that Michael reveals to us is that a vast difference exists between hegemonic consent, acquired through discourse and negotiation, and actual coercion, the use of violence as a means of subjugation. "Shooting belonged to a totally different order of things," he says, and then, "And that is how I died — in disbelief, in astonishment, in shock" (149–50).

Lily is a subject of hegemony in a slightly different way, socialized by church and state into her role as wife and mother, neither expecting nor apparently needing any personal autonomy but identifying herself entirely through her husband and children, particularly the latter. Even her reasons for joining the march are personal and apolitical, connected with one of her children, not with any sense of anger or injustice at her own position, described so graphically by Skinner: "Because you live with eleven kids and a sick husband in two rooms that aren't fit for animals" (154). Her language is entirely domestic and anecdotal — not so much a heartwarming challenge to the impersonal discourses of authority as a discourse of the disempowered who literally have no access to any institutional discourses and therefore no access to knowledge about how society works beyond their own immediate experience.

Moreover, Lily willingly mimics the patriarchal hegemonic view of women as innately less intelligent and less able than men: "And it's for him I go on all the civil rights marches. Isn't that stupid? . . . Isn't that the stupidest thing you ever heard?" (155). When she is insulted by her husband, whose nickname "the chairman" is a humorous acceptance of her own subordination and that of their class, his reported comment, "You're a bone stupid bitch" (155), is merely a stronger version of the epithets she uses about herself. The character of Lily is disempowered not only by her lack of money and education but also by her acceptance of the limited role allowed her by the church and by secular society, endorsed by the institutional discourses of religion, patriarchy, and the family. There is no risk that Lily will start a revolution. In her "public" speech about her death, Lily acknowledges her limited view of life, as well as her inability to conceptualize experience and, for the first and only time in the play, expresses sorrow and regret for herself: "In a way I died of grief" (150). This brief moment of self-assertion, which we accept as the "truth" about Lily because of the public nature of its discourse, compels us to recognize the extent of Lily's subordination under hegemony, her consent to it in the name of maternal love, and the price she paid for willingly reproducing that consensus.

Finally, Skinner represents a crucial element in the hegemonic model, the site of struggle where consent must be negotiated in the face of opposition and resistance. Skinner openly rejects the political and cultural values of the dominant bloc. He refuses to be impressed by the trappings of municipal power in the Guildhall or by Michael's aspirations to middle-class values. He understands the futility of the peaceful marches that both Michael and Lily believe in for their different reasons, and he knows that large-scale action on the part of a unified majority is the only way to achieve significant and positive changes for the disempowered. Yet Skinner articulates his activism through a popular cultural discourse of irreverent and self-mocking humor, breaking out of it only to confront Lily with his politicized view of her life: "for the first time in your life you grumbled and someone else grumbled and someone else, and you heard each other, and became aware that there were hundreds, thousands, millions of us all over the world, and in a vague groping way you were outraged" (154).

With this political rhetoric and through his command of a range of institutional discourses, such as electioneering ("And that's why I appeal to you, when you go into that polling station, put an X opposite my name," 155), committee meetings ("You have before you an account of last week's meeting," 159), and establishment authority ("Because you presumed, boy. Because this is theirs, boy, and your very presence here is a sacrilege," 140). Skinner reveals that he is closer to the dominant bloc than either Michael or Lily. Far from being working-class, as some critics have categorized him,[9] Skinner's language and his name, Adrian Casimir Fitzgerald, indicate that he belongs to a more middle-class section of society. Skinner therefore represents that affront to hegemonic power, the class traitor. Instead of working to promote hegemonic consent, as Michael does so willingly from his subordinate position, Skinner actively seeks to challenge it through irreverent humor and antisocial behavior: "He had been in trouble many times, my lord. Petty larceny, disorderly behaviour — that sort of thing" (109).

The problem for Skinner is that the hegemony of the state is ultimately too powerful for him to initiate change without the strength of a fully developed counterhegemony behind him. "According to Gramsci," says Strinati, "the revolutionary forces have to take civil society before they take the state, and therefore have to build a coalition of oppositional groups united under a hegemonic banner which usurps the dominant or prevailing hegemony. Without this struggle for hegemony, all attempts to seize state power will be futile" (Strinati 1995:169–70). Given the complexities of modern civil society, Skinner's efforts alone are no more likely to effect revolutionary change than are Michael's law-abiding marches. Instead, his antiauthoritarian gestures are easily absorbed and contained by the ruling hegemony, mainly in the form of the police. Skinner is no

9. For example, Andrews (1995:130) says, "The three central characters represent working-class, Catholic Derry."

more a threat to the prevailing order than Lily or Michael, and he himself acknowledges this in his "public" speech, when he admits that he and his supporters never took the state authorities seriously enough and that "to match their seriousness would demand a total dedication, a solemnity as formal as theirs" (150). In other words, the hegemony of the state can be challenged only by a counterhegemony that is at least its equal in seriousness and dedication.

All these different discourses, public and private, work to remind us of the power of hegemony to reproduce dominant "truths" and so maintain consensus. But there is still the exercise of coercive forces in the play, and it is the presence of these, as well as the discursive operations of hegemony, that make the play so disturbing. The visible signs of the soldiers and weapons of the British army exemplify Gramsci's concept of coercive control exercised by the state, acting alongside the consensual power of hegemony. The presence of both kinds of mechanisms for social control within the play constructs an "overdetermined" version of consensus, one that must not only be negotiated through discourse but also be physically enforced by violence. This in turn constructs a view of Northern Ireland as a society in crisis, one that is so far from being stable that the ideologies and practices of the dominant bloc cannot be maintained by hegemonic strategies alone. Through the characters of the three victims, who must be seen to some extent as metonyms for the disempowered and disaffected people of Northern Ireland, the play graphically demonstrates that the recourse to coercion by violence represents the failure of the dominant bloc to govern by consensus and, therefore, its failure to justify its cultural leadership in a society characterized by inequality and discrimination.

Without claiming that the play is in any way a form of propaganda, which would be overstating its purpose, I think it is possible to read *The Freedom of the City* as a stylized and dramatized example of hegemony in action. The play sets up a situation in which a disempowered section of the community confronts the dominant bloc in an already unstable society. Through the use of hegemonic discourses and some concessions to the subordinate classes, such as the civil rights marches and the funeral ceremony, in addition to the further application of coercion by the legitimate forces of the political state, a precarious consensus is restored and the dominant ideology is reasserted. By focusing on issues of power, Friel reconfigures the traditional binary oppositions used to structure representations of Irish society — Gaelic and English, Catholic and Protestant, nationalists and unionists—to show that dominant ideologies dismantle these "natural" divisions within the social fabric and reerect them around locations of institutional power.

Such an interrogation of assumed alignments within the structure of Northern Irish society has a particular relevance for the language debate in Ireland. Because hegemonic power is related to institutions rather than to language alone, hopes that a resurgence of the Irish language would automatically further a nationalist agenda need to be reassessed. Just as power and the lack of it can be articulated within the English language through a range of discourses, so too can the Irish language encode both hegemonic power and its opposite. If, as modern linguists claim, the current revival of Irish is primarily led by the middle classes (Ó Murchú 1992:46–47), would its reappearance as a dominant language assist in the empowerment of the socially disadvantaged? Institutions of power, such as government, law, and the media, will maintain their power through discourse, regardless of which language they happen to be using, whereas the discursively disempowered in any language group will remain socially and culturally dispossessed.

These issues pertaining to language and power show the kinship between *The Freedom of the City* and Friel's later play *Translations*. The operations of hegemony through consensus and coercion throw a particular light on the nineteenth-century decline of Irish, for example. Interrogating the argument that the Irish voluntarily abandoned their language, *Translations* shows how the British hegemony, represented by the military, co-opts the Irish institutions of church and education into a consensual agreement that Irish speakers will benefit from the change to English. It is the hedge-schoolmaster, Hugh, acting on behalf of hegemonic consensus, who equates English with progressiveness and prepares to teach English to his pupils in order to save Irish culture from stasis and decay. But the play also depicts unease and ambivalence, through the characters of Máire Chatach, Owen the collaborator, and even Yolland, the British officer nostalgic for a romantic "Celtic" past, the symbol of the very traditions from which Hugh has decided to retreat. In constructing these ironies of sentiment and pragmatism in the play, Friel presents the Irish language as a casualty, even a necessary one, of modernization, itself a hegemonic operation. Thus, in a variety of ways, *Translations* continues to articulate Friel's consciousness of language as a crucial aspect of the political and social landscape of Ireland.

In *The Freedom of the City*, the revival or survival of the Irish language is irrelevant to the struggle for political and cultural autonomy, which happens at the level of economic class. The distribution of characters along a hierarchy of institutional power, rather than on either side of an English-Irish language divide, clearly implies that hegemonic consensus will be maintained whether through Irish or through English. Lily's consent to her own economic, social, and personal subjugation is as "voluntary" as the decision to stop speaking Irish appears to have been in the nineteenth century, but both decisions were made as a result of the processes of hegemonic consensus. The real pathos and irony of *The Freedom of the City* lie in the different discourses of the Guildhall characters, who are divided not only from other English-speaking groups in the play but from each other as well. Whereas *Translations* offers us the knowledge that a culture disappeared along with the Irish language, *The Freedom of the City* seems already aware that cultural survival depends not on access to a particular language but on access to the discourses of power.

To say that the message of the play is the corruption of authority or the hypocrisy of the church or the triumph of the individual is to depoliticize the complex social relations dramatized in the play. As a political text, its message expresses the heat and passion of its author: a society that is so divided that it requires coercion to reinforce hegemonic consent is a society governed by a dominant bloc whose leadership has failed. As a literary text, the play enacts the power of discourse to construct and maintain a dominant view of "reality" that can absorb and contain all but the most sustained challenges to its authority.

Works Cited

Andrews, Elmer. 1993. The fifth province. In *The achievement of Brian Friel*, ed. Alan Peacock, 29–48. Gerrards Cross: Colin Smythe.

———. 1995. *The art of Brian Friel: Neither reality nor dreams*. New York: St. Martin's.

Bellamy, Richard, and Darrow Schecter. 1993. *Gramsci and the Italian state*. Manchester: Manchester University Press.

Bennett, Tony. 1986. Introduction: Popular culture and "The turn to Gramsci." In *Popular culture and social relations*, ed. Tony Bennett et al., xi–xix. Milton Keynes: Open University Press.

Dantanus, Ulf. 1988. *Brian Friel: A study*. London: Faber and Faber.

Deane, Seamus. 1985. *Celtic revivals: Essays in modern Irish literature, 1880–1980*. London: Faber and Faber.

Edwards, John. 1984. Irish and English in Ireland. In *Language in the British Isles,* ed. Peter Trudgill, 480–98. Cambridge: Cambridge University Press.

Fairclough, Norman. 1989. *Language and power*. London: Longman.

Femia, Joseph. 1981. *Gramsci's political thought: Hegemony, consciousness, and the revolutionary process*. Oxford: Clarendon.

Friel, Brian. 1984. *Selected Plays*. London: Faber and Faber.

Glass, Frances Devlin. 1996. Deconstructing history and heroism: The theatre languages of O'Casey, Friel, and Davis. In *Irish-Australian studies: Papers delivered at the Eighth Irish-Australian Conference,* ed. Richard Davis et al., 113–23. Sydney: Crossing.

Gramsci, Antonio. 1971. *Selections from the prison notebooks*. Ed. and trans. Quintin Hoare and Geoffrey Nowell-Smith. London: Lawrence and Wishart.

———. 1994. *Further selections from the prison notebooks*. Ed. and trans. Derek Boothman. London: Lawrence and Wishart.

Hall, Stuart. 1982. The rediscovery of "ideology": Return of the repressed in media studies. In *Culture, society, and the media,* ed. Michael Gurevitch et al., 56–90. London: Routledge.

Hindley, Reg. 1990. *The death of the Irish language*. London: Routledge.

Joll, James. 1977. *Gramsci*. London: Fontana.

Jones, Nesta. 2000. *Brian Friel*. London: Faber and Faber.

Kiberd, Declan. 1995. *Inventing Ireland*. Cambridge: Harvard University Press.

———. 1998. Romantic Ireland's dead and gone: The English-speaking Republic as the crucible of modernity. *Times Literary Supplement,* 12 June, 12–14.

Lynch, Patricia. 1997. A stylistic approach to Irish writing. *Irish University Review* 27:33–54.

Mills, Sara. 1997. *Discourse*. London: Routledge.

Ó Murchú, Máirtín. 1992. The Irish language. In *The Celtic connection,* ed. Glanville Price, 30–64. Gerrards Cross: Colin Smythe.

O'Toole, Fintan. 1993. Marking time: From *Making history* to *Dancing at Lughnasa*. In *The achievement of Brian Friel,* ed. Alan Peacock, 202–14. Gerrards Cross: Colin Smythe.

Peacock, Alan. 1993. Introduction to *The achievement of Brian Friel,* ed. Alan Peacock, i–xix. Gerrards Cross: Colin Smythe.

Pine, Richard. 1990. *Brian Friel and Ireland's drama*. London: Routledge.

Ransome, Paul. 1992. *Antonio Gramsci: A new introduction*. New York: Harvester Wheatsheaf.

Richards, Shaun. 1997. Placed identities for placeless times: Brian Friel and postcolonial criticism. *Irish University Review* 27:55–68.

Richtarik, Marilynn. 1994. *Acting between the lines: The Field Day Theatre Company and Irish cultural politics, 1980–1984*. Oxford: Clarendon.

Simon, Roger. 1982. *Gramsci's political thought: An introduction*. London: Lawrence and Wishart.

Storey, John. 1993. *An introductory guide to cultural theory and popular culture.* New York: Harvester Wheatsheaf.

Strinati, Dominic. 1995. *An introduction to theories of popular culture.* London: Routledge.

Turner, Graeme. 1992. *British cultural studies: An introduction.* London: Routledge.

JEREMY LOWE

Contagious Violence and the Spectacle of Death in *Táin Bó Cúailnge*

Does *Táin Bó Cúailnge* (*The Cattle Raid of Cúailnge*)[1] celebrate heroism and acts of martial valor? Many have thought so, believing that the tale embodies the traditional heroic ideal in action, exemplified by the premier Irish warrior, Cú Chulainn. It is easy to conceive of the *Táin* as a straightforwardly heroic tale, celebrating the feats of valor and the martial prowess of the young boy-hero. Cú Chulainn defends his tribe, which lies prone and defenseless against the threat of an aggressive invading force, because of a mysterious "debility" (*ces noínden*),[2] and so the tale seems to offer us an uncomplicated vision of a society dependent on its heroes. In this essay I attempt to examine the "darker side" of the *Táin,* in the belief that the tale as we have it dramatizes the destabilizing effects of warfare, even as it celebrates feats of heroism. Violence in the *Táin* is invasive, immediate, and disruptive, offering a challenge to human order on a bodily, as well as social, level. In the terms outlined by the present collection, therefore, I am more concerned with *displacements* than continuities. Rather than focus on the social systems that legitimize violence in the tale, I intend to look at the way that such violence is represented as a threat to order and bodily integrity. Conflict punctuates the narrative, emerging as a raw force that subverts rigid boundaries and established hierarchies. In particular, the *Táin* seems to depict warfare not as the ultimate social act, whereby noble warriors defend their tribe and define its customs and ideals, but as a profoundly antisocial one.

---

1. *Táin Bó Cúailnge* (*The Cattle Raid of Cúailnge*) is the central narrative of the Ulster Cycle, a principal cycle of medieval Irish heroic literature. The tale concerns a raid instigated by the Connacht queen Medb into the lands of the Ulstermen (henceforth Ulaid, their name in the tale). Here I will refer to Medb's army as the "Connachtmen," the name they are first given in the tale. The text also calls Medb's army *fir Érenn,* 'the men of Ireland', because Medb draws her warriors from every province in Ireland. Cúailnge is modern-day Cooley.

2. Tomás Ó Broin (1961–63) discusses the nature of the *ces noínden.* See also comments by Tomás Ó Cathasaigh (1993) concerning the mysterious debility. The ces noínden is traditionally understood to be a consequence of the curse of Macha, who, when pregnant, was forced to race against the horses of the king of Ulster.

Cú Chulainn's feats have become legendary, and his role as a hero of the tribe is celebrated in the General Post Office in Dublin, where the famous statue of him stands as a memorial to the Easter Rising of 1916. As Maria Tymoczko (1999) has demonstrated, the idea that the *Táin* reflects the ideals of heroism has its origins partly in late-nineteenth- and early-twentieth-century treatments of the tale. She argues that the interpretation of the *Táin* as a heroic epic reflects the efforts of Irish patriots to represent it as a literary symbol of Irish national identity at a time of struggle. Tymoczko points to the way in which the figure of Cú Chulainn came to represent a particular ideal of Irish heroism to the nationalist movement leading up to the Rising in 1916; the result was a heroic paradigm that permitted nationalist identification with a fierce martial hero, identification that "glorified both individualism and action on behalf of the tribe" (Tymoczko 1999:79). The desire to read the *Táin* as an unproblematic affirmation of the heroic ethos and its contribution to society still informs modern scholarship on the tale. The conception that violence in early Irish literature reflects the codes of a heroic society, thus functioning as an instrument of the social order, was articulated most famously by Marie-Louise Sjoestedt (1949), who portrays the warrior as society's leader, the "hero of the tribe." From her early formulation, through to influential essays by Joseph Nagy (1984), Tomás Ó Cathasaigh (1986), and others, we have a clear sense of the role that heroes play in performing deeds of valor on behalf of society.[3]

Yet, the *Táin* does not merely reflect the warrior's role as a "hero of the tribe" but also reveals the disruptive aspect of the warrior function, exploring the chaos of violence unleashed by heroes who fight on behalf of their society, as I have already indicated. My chief focus here is on the disturbing aspects of warfare in the *Táin*, rather than an "official" portrait of idealized warfare conducted by noble men and women: to show how the *Táin* questions and subverts the heroic ethos, rather than uncritically celebrating it. The medium of this subversion is violence, which is explicit in the tale, a spectacle arrayed for the fascinated onlooker. Yet, it is also intrinsic: the very narrative is woven around a succession of death tales

3. These ideas have also been challenged in the critical literature. For example, Bart Jaski (1999) questions some of Ó Cathasaigh's conclusions, arguing that Cú Chulainn is a fosterling of the Ulaid, an adopted son rather than a proper member of their tribe, because only his mother, Deichtire, is one of the Ulaid, whereas his mortal father, Sualtam, is an alien. Jaski's argument challenges the notion that Cú Chulainn is a "hero of the tribe" and suggests that Cú Chulainn's status as hero is more complex and marginal.

that are at turns exciting, spectacular, grotesque, humorous, and banal. In the absence of plot, character, or even narrative structure, very often there is only the violence, which cannot be kept at a distance and which does not refer to anything beyond itself. This spectacle, in the words of Steven Shaviro in his discussion of film violence, "destroys customary meanings and appearances, ruptures the surfaces of the flesh, and violates the organic integrity of the body" (Shaviro 1993:102).

In the *Táin*, warfare is a fluid and chaotic state that threatens social borders rather than defining them. The "heroic" encounters that take place between warriors similarly involve violence that destabilizes the human body, warping and mutilating it beyond recognition. Above all, violence is ever present in the tale, hovering over Medb's army in the form of the Nemain, the goddess of war who takes the form of a raven, and spreading like a contagion from one warrior to another. Nemain, whose name means 'battle-fury, warlike frenzy, strife', assails Medb's host five times in the tale (ll. 210, 2085, 3537, 3942, 4033).[4] She always visits them at night and throws the host into confusion; her repeated visits suggest the confusion and horror of war. Notably, the war goddess does not act as an instrument of the invading army but as its enemy, suggesting that war undermines and assails those who practice it. Cú Chulainn is similarly assailed by another war goddess, the Morrígan, 'nightmare queen', who attacks him in the guise of an eel, a wolf, and a red heifer during his battle with Lóch (ll. 1982–2027). The *Táin* depicts a *state* of war and the effect that this state has on systems of order and structures of meaning. Although the story ends with the seeming cessation of conflict, the *Táin* focuses for much of its length on the shattering violence that threatens to engulf everything.

Within the *Táin*, violence is not recuperated by society but continually threatens its borders, a point reinforced by the so-called *macgnímrada*, 'the boyhood deeds', of Cú Chulainn, which the exiled Ulaid warriors

4. The *Táin* exists in three separate versions or recensions. I will be discussing the oldest version of the tale, recension 1, edited and translated by Cecile O'Rahilly (1976), and all line references and translations are taken from this source, unless otherwise noted. Recension 1 is found in four separate manuscripts, the most famous of which are "Lebor na hUidre" ("The Book of the Dun Cow"), dating from ca. 1100, and the Yellow Book of Lecan, a composite manuscript dating from the fifteenth or sixteenth century. O'Rahilly (1967) also edited and translated recension 2, a complete but embellished version of the tale found in the twelfth-century Book of Leinster. Thomas Kinsella's (1969) readable modern translation draws from both main recensions of the tale and also contains the "pre-tales" (*remscéla*) that help explain the origins of the conflict in the *Táin*. Line references in this essay refer to O'Rahilly's edition and translation of recension 1.

narrate to the frightened Connacht army.[5] In one way the macgnímrada demonstrate Cú Chulainn's status as the premier Ulaid warrior, but they also reveal the disruptive effects of the hero's actions as well as their ameliorative benefits.[6] In the macgnímrada Cú Chulainn challenges and bests the boytroop of the Ulaid, to whom by rights he should, as an outsider, defer. He defies and outwits Conchobar, the king of the Ulaid, in order to obtain arms and armor. He bowls over the respected warrior Conall, who guards the perimeter of the Ulster lands, and then transgresses those borders in his chariot. He becomes so excited by his adventures that he returns to the Ulaid fort, Emain Macha, seemingly bent on continuing his destructive wild ride, aiming at the Ulaid themselves, and his battle fury is diverted only when the Ulaid send forth bare-breasted women to greet him.

In terms of Cú Chulainn's heroic identity, these stories reveal the warrior's growing independence and authority and his gradual emergence as an adult figure capable of representing his tribe and defending its frontiers. Within the structure of the *Táin*, however, these tales offer a glimpse of the chaos and disruption attendant on Cú Chulainn, a hero whose deeds pose a continual threat to harmony and order. As I have argued elsewhere (Lowe 2000), in the macgnímrada Cú Chulainn does not merely behave as the "hero of the tribe" but also unleashes disturbing and unstable forces that are a consequence of violent action and that even threaten his own people. Within the framework of the action of *Táin* itself, the disruptive effects of the macgnímrada, rather than their socially legitimate aspect, attain an even greater significance.

We see an example of the disruption in the episode in which the Connacht army has just arrived at the ford where Cú Chulainn has slain four warriors and impaled their heads on tree branches. As the heads sway above the host in the deepening gloom (ll. 333–35), Fergus tells about the unearthly character the Connachtmen are destined to face and about his past feats of valor, while the army sits confronted by the spectacle of Cú

---

5. The *macgnímrada* of Cú Chulainn occupy just over four hundred lines of recension 1 of the *Táin* (ll. 398–824). They are an account of Cú Chulainn's early career, as the name suggests, giving the audience an idea of the powers he must have at his disposal now that he is a man.

6. See, for instance, Nagy 1984 on the "heroic destinies" of two warriors, Finn and Cú Chulainn, and Melia 1974 for a discussion of parallel versions of the macgnímrada. See also Breatnach 1990, who offers a cautionary critique of such structuralist readings of early Irish material in his review of Nagy's *Wisdom of the Outlaw* (1985).

Chulainn's immediate victims.[7] The heads literalize the threat that Cú Chulainn poses and that all martial conflict poses, offering a graphic representation of death that cannot be ignored in the present or assigned a comforting place in the past.

The figure of Cú Chulainn in these stories embodies a contradiction inherent in the warrior figure that remains immediate and undeniable throughout the *Táin,* suggesting a culture aware of the ambivalence of the heroic ethos and the fact that warlike action remains difficult for any society to assimilate.[8] The ideals of heroism, far from being seen as ennobling or beneficial to society, often bring about sorrow, misfortune, or confusion on a personal and a social level. The individual heroes within the tale may behave with great pomp and splendor, but their actions very often end in ignominy and shame. Similarly, although the deaths in the narrative are sometimes tragic, the frequent mutilations and bodily inversions that mark the combats undermine the sense of pathos. Warfare in the *Táin* has little dignity, only wastefulness and sorrow, pain and humiliation: fosterbrother fights fosterbrother, status is inverted, and the rules of conduct are flouted or ignored.

The *Táin* is founded on the notion that warfare is a threat to social stability rather than an expression of society or its ideals. The story concerns a cattle raid, an act of piracy as much as war, involving the incursion of one group into the territory of another to do damage and cause mayhem, at times seemingly indistinct from an *orgain,* or 'ravaging'.[9] As though symptomatic of this destabilizing threat, the raid is led by a woman, which alone suggests an upheaval in the hierarchy of values.[10] The story itself takes place on the borders of Ulaid lands, and the frequent battles between Cú Chulainn and the Connachtmen are fought at fords, streams, hills, and mountain passes. The tale has no center, no locus: the

7. Fergus, fosterfather of Cú Chulainn, is the leader of the exiled Ulaid who march with Medb's army. Fergus's status as an exile is traditionally connected with the story of Derdriu and the sons of Uisliu, told in *Loinges mac nUislenn* (*The Exile of the Sons of Uisliu*) (cf. Kinsella 1969:8–20).

8. See McCone 1984 for a discussion of the destabilizing aspect of the warrior function, which draws on the analysis of Georges Dumézil (cf. Dumézil 1970).

9. The genre of the *orgain* is still another type of tale occurring in early Irish literature that deals with violence and destruction, in particular with the threat to stable society from an invading force.

10. Patricia Kelly, for example, sees Medb's role as a commentary on "the dangerous potential of the sovereignty goddess myth to privilege the female at the expense of the male" (Kelly 1992:87). We can also note that the Ulaid are defended by a boy on the verge of manhood, another instance where heroic tradition is undermined.

Connacht army is almost perpetually on the move, while the Ulaid themselves appear in force only well into the final quarter of the narrative. With traditional structures subverted or absent, conflict spreads unchecked: there is a sense that no one is in control and that nothing is sacred.

Thus, one of the recurring patterns in *Táin Bó Cúailnge* is the failure of social systems to control or structure this violence. The *Táin* does not negotiate the ideology of the heroic ethos so much as it exposes the insufficiency of such social systems to organize violence that is a natural force intrinsic to human nature. In this respect the tale is reminiscent of Georges Bataille's (1987) analysis of the rules of warfare, which he describes as the arbitrary assertion of a model of conduct that bears no relation to the frenzy of violence that it is meant to moderate. Bataille argues that "man has built up the rational world by his own efforts, but there remains within him an undercurrent of violence" (40). Humanity attempts to impose a rational order on nature, according to Bataille, and to suppress all violent impulses, but these impulses emerge from within, unbidden, to overthrow such arbitrary systems. Violence and death can never be expelled completely because they are not opposed to life but part of the very forces of life. The construction of rational systems can never separate the social realm from the realm of violence absolutely; there is "nothing that can conquer violence" (48).

In early Irish literary texts, one such rational system intended to provide rules of combat or to structure the ethical behavior of warriors when they encounter one another is the concept of *fír fer* (literally 'truth of men'; more colloquially, 'rules of fair play'). Philip O'Leary (1987) has written about the operation of fír fer in the *Táin* and in the Ulster Cycle as a whole, pointing out that individual combat in these tales appears to be governed by an accepted system of rules that represents an ideal that each hero could strive to attain. O'Leary argues that the society depicted in the Ulster Cycle had "taken a significant step in its ethical development by internalizing a standard of conduct regulating one of the most emotionally charged activities of its members, single combat." He goes on to acknowledge, however, that "the fact that the principle of *fír fer* was often flouted or that it was upheld in letter only while the spirit was, from a modern perspective, outrageously violated, does nothing to diminish its significance as an indication of an evolving ethical sophistication" (13).

In fact, the rules of fair play are so consistently transgressed in the *Táin* that they become insufficient to explain the nature of the battles that take place. The concept of fír fer repeatedly fails to define the contests between warriors: it does not reveal the presence of a prevailing ideology so much as demonstrate how the rules do not work. Even among the nobler figures in the tale, efforts to invoke fír fer seem doomed to failure. The attempts of Fergus to insist on the practice of fair play seem to have little or no effect on Medb, who goes so far as to call for the rules to be broken. Whether or not her authority counts for more than Fergus's is hard to ascertain. Medb encourages the seven Maines, the warriors who attack Cú Chulainn before Lóch, to assault the Ulaid warrior vigorously, saying "brister fír fer fair" ("let terms of fair play be broken against him," l. 1885), but the other four instances when fír fer is transgressed (ll. 915, 1552–53, 2031–33, and 2494) do not follow her specific instructions: the rule itself appears to be arbitrary. As O'Leary points out, even when Cú Chulainn explicitly does fight fair in his encounter with the Connacht warrior Nad Crantail, he "manages to bend the rules just short of the breaking point" (O'Leary 1987:11), collapsing the boundaries of what is actually meant by "fair." Lugaid upholds the rules when he comes to meet Cú Chulainn (l. 1178), and the text acknowledges his sense of fair play, but it is far from clear that the combatants are obeying an actual law in this instance. After all, Fergus and Cú Chulainn make a similar deal to "fight fair" when they eventually face each other without invoking fír fer. The rule has only semantic, not actual, force in these encounters. That characters so often bring fír fer forward as a model of action only demonstrates its failure to govern the behavior of individual warriors and leaders: the disruptive nature of war continually exceeds the limits placed on it by society.

Indeed, conflict itself seems to represent the most significant point of continuity in the tale. Violence is contagious: it seems to beget itself, so that the only things assured in the *Táin* are the capacity violence has to recur and the power it has to destroy without moderation. The prophetic words of Fedelm, a female seer, at the beginning of the tale, "atchíu forderg, atchíu rúad" ("I see it bloody, I see it red," l.50, repeated at ll. 55, 60, and 65), serve both as a commentary on the immediate fate awaiting Medb's host and on the consequences of the cattle raid as a whole.[11] They are echoed by Cú Chulainn's words at the end, "Conscar bara bith" ("anger destroys the world," l. 4076) and "tuigthir fuil firu" ("men are covered

11. Fedelm has prophetic powers, and her dreadful cry serves as a dire warning of the doom that awaits the Connachtmen for embarking on the cattle raid.

in blood," l. 4084), which reflect a fear that conflict, if allowed to rage unchecked, will eradicate all human society. This refrain runs through the *Táin*, voiced elsewhere by Ailill and Dubthach. Ailill utters the prophetic warning "fuilglassa de fulib méderath" ("there will flow streams of blood from headless necks," l. 1107), and Dubthach speaks long, rhetorical prophecies anticipating the slaughter in the imminent battles (ll. 189ff., 2371ff., 3527ff.).

Dubthach's prophecies of doom, like the visits of the Nemain to the Connachtmen or those of the Morrígan to Cú Chulainn, suggest the immediacy of death and its perpetual presence in the tale. They remind us that men stand precariously over its abyss: death lies all around them and beneath them. Warriors are therefore intimately connected to death in the *Táin:* they bring it to others and wait for it to claim themselves. They are infected by violence, which spreads from them, engulfing others. Cú Chulainn kills the warrior Orlám and brandishes his head, which in turn provokes Lon, Ualu, and Díliu to fight him. Their deaths, or possibly the murder of Fer Tedil the charioteer, then provoke Lethan. Bloodshed begets more bloodshed.

As violence proliferates, it begins to eradicate the boundaries that separate individuals and the social ties that bind them to one another: like a disease that infects an organism, it breaks down walls and reduces everything to base matter. The emergence of the Ulaid from their ces noínden is a dramatic demonstration of this principle. While they suffer their debilitation, the Ulaid lie inseparable and indistinguishable from one another, and their society exists only in memory, through the stories Fergus tells of Cú Chulainn's early exploits. Their moribund state mimics the effects of violence, leaving them infected, without boundaries or social order, just as death is faceless and formless.[12] Their affliction effectively preserves them from the bloodshed around them: until their pangs come to an end (l. 3455), they remain untouched by warfare, because in their stricken state they are to all intents and purposes *already* dead.

When the Ulaid do finally emerge, long individuated descriptions of the chief Ulaid warriors precede their arrival at the battle (ll. 3589–3861), as though to distinguish them from their previous state. For this brief space the warriors stand absolute and intact, like chess pieces, with their relative

---

12. Neil Buttimer also draws attention to the ces noínden as a state without boundaries or social order in an unpublished paper entitled "Noínden Ulad: Private and Public," delivered at the Annual Symposium of the Dublin Institute for Advanced Studies in 1995.

powers and individual qualities, before they are once more sucked into the chaos of battle and so surrender their individuality. This sequence of events demonstrates the ambivalence of the warrior function: it is based on individuality and the trappings of glory and status, but it actively pursues the chaos and anonymity of death. The Ulaid warriors awake from a kind of death, only to pursue death itself.

Individuated descriptions also introduce the Connacht host at the beginning of the *Táin* (ll. 9–19), and Lóeg, Cú Chulainn's charioteer, frequently describes Connacht warriors in detail before they encounter his master. In each case, it seems, subjectivity can be preserved only outside the context of battle: the chaos of war destroys all boundaries. The shattered and mutilated bodies of the heroes in death stand in stark contrast to the dazzling descriptions of the warriors before they enter the fray. The social coding of status and the human artifice of armor and splendid decoration mask the brutal reality of war and simultaneously draw attention to it: as the conflict begins, violence distorts and overthrows such irrefutable certainties.

The *Táin* therefore depicts both the individual glories of warriors and the destruction that they unleash, a duality played out most graphically on the bodies of the warriors themselves. In the encounters that take place between Cú Chulainn and the Connachtmen, we witness the dismemberment and mutilation of the human body, a graphic representation of warfare as the ultimate destabilizing act. For instance, when Cú Chulainn faces Etarcomol, who approaches him under the protection of Fergus, Cú Chulainn tries to persuade the Connacht warrior to abandon the fight, first by inverting the ground beneath his feet and then by removing his clothes and cutting off his hair. Cú Chulainn reduces the hapless Etarcomol to the status of a denuded body, the absolute ground zero. Finally, because the churl was "importunate" and "persistent" (l. 1359), Cú Chulainn splits him in two from head to toe with his sword, utterly destroying Etarcomol so that Fergus is forced to drag him back to camp, tied to the back of the chariot by his heels. Etarcomol's body divides whenever the chariot goes over rocks and recombines when the path is smooth, a macabre detail that seems to foreground the absolutely inhuman nature of Etarcomol's final status. A proud warrior becomes dismembered flesh.

Such violence is not merely irrational and overwhelming but also spectacle, a graphic realization of the warrior function and therefore a consequence of its ideals. The mutilation of Etarcomol represents a logical conclusion of the heroic ideal taken to excess. Nagy remarks that "what Cú Chulainn does to Etarcomol with his deft swordplay is to render him a sign of the fate he is blindly courting" (Nagy 1996:148). In seeking fame above honor, Etarcomol turns his back on his promises, and his duplicity is graphically represented by the splitting of his body in two. The disorganization of Etarcomol's body reflects the threat that his pursuit of heroic deeds poses to the social order. Nagy (1996:148) points out that Etarcomol's fate is partly brought about by his "inability or unwillingness to read the verbal signs on the wall": he misreads Fergus's verbal warnings and Cú Chulainn's physical ones. Such failures are revealed to be a component of war in the *Táin*, a process that begins with Medb's refusal to heed Fedelm's prophecy and the Connacht host's inability to heed Cú Chulainn's warnings at the ford.

These themes are highlighted when a succession of warriors comes forward to fight Cú Chulainn, engaging him on false terms. Nad Crantail refuses to fight a "beardless boy" (l. 1450); in response Cú Chulainn smears a fake beard on himself, so as to mislead Nad Crantail into fighting with him. The Connachtman is pierced by a spear, then beheaded and split into four pieces (ll. 1476–81): the arrogant warrior becomes less than the sum of his parts. Mand similarly refuses to treat Cú Chulainn as a warrior, regarding him as a "beardless imp" (l. 2531). Mand therefore appears unarmed to the fight, and Cú Chulainn responds by shattering him to pieces against a rock (ll. 2544–45). Nad Crantail and Mand are both superior in age and presumably in status to Cú Chulainn, and so he must trick them into fighting with him. It is their insistence on the external appearance of the warrior that makes this subterfuge possible: in effect, Cú Chulainn allows his opponents to dictate the terms of their encounter and gives them precisely what they ask for. The mutilated bodies literalize the heroic careers of the warriors, taking their desires to a logical — and absurd — extreme.

Another warrior whose eventual fate reflects his heroic persona is Láiríne. Láiríne's arrival is heralded by his brother Lugaid, who uses his own friendship with Cú Chulainn to encourage him to spare Láiríne's life. Consequently, when Láiríne comes to meet Cú Chulainn, rather than kill him outright, Cú Chulainn decides to shake him until the excrement comes out of him, so that the ordure flies everywhere (ll. 1838–41). After that time, the narrative tells us, Láiríne's innards never recovered: he was never without a chest illness; he never ate without pain (ll. 1842–43).

Láiríne survives, but he pays the price: his body collapses, and his humiliation becomes a spectacle witnessed by all. In heroic society, sometimes
surviving is worse than dying, for a warrior whose body speaks its own
defeat is hardly a warrior at all.

Perhaps this is why the Ulaid hero Cethern, who survives a "hard fight"
(*caladgleó*) and emerges with a body riddled with wounds, decides to
reenter the fray until he is finally overcome. His wounds from the "hard
fight" give visible evidence of his experiences; they literally permeate him
so that Cethern becomes inseparable from his injuries. Each injury refers
back to the warrior who inflicted it, and from Cethern's descriptions Cú
Chulainn is able to identify the assailants: the wounded body speaks its
own overthrow, and violence becomes a form of communication. Cethern's body no longer exists as an intact, discrete entity: violence shatters it
and overwhelms it, pushing it toward what Gilles Deleuze and Félix Guattari (1998) call a "state of becoming." In order to reenter the fray, Cethern's body has to be rebuilt with the marrow of cow bones (l. 2300) and
the ribs of a chariot frame (l. 2303), so that it becomes a fusion of human
and nonhuman elements. The integrity of the body does not survive, all
boundaries are gone, and there is no way to tell where the body ends and
the prosthetics begin. Cethern's body gives graphic evidence of the fluidity
of violence, the way it challenges stable order and erodes the boundaries
that separate the human body from its environment.

In the *Táin* other bodies are overwhelmed from within. Cú Chulainn
attacks both Lóch and Fer Diad with the *gae bolga*,[13] which may pierce the
anus and, in the case of Fer Diad, seems to divide and enter the very veins
in his body. The effect is catastrophic — Anne Dooley calls it "the greatest
debasement of the male gendered heroic person" (Dooley 1994:127) —
apparently producing an effect little short of an overthrow of the entire
body. The fact that the two warriors are said to have "hornskin" (*con-
ganchnes;* ll. 2027, 2747) surely bears some significance. Both Lóch and
Fer Diad seem to have rigid, armored bodies when in combat, as though
they are designed specifically to resist the destabilizing, subversive effects
of violence. The harder they come, the harder they fall: the ultimate
weapon does not pierce from without but from within, exposing the rigid
boundary of the body as a sham. As Bataille points out, we may try to
establish fixed limits on our world, separating ourselves from nature, but

13. The gae bolga is Cú Chulainn's special weapon, the "warrior feat" that he alone can
effect. Its precise meaning and form are unclear, but its effects are catastrophic.

violent forces will eventually emerge and, when the frenzy is loosed, it knows no bounds (Bataille 1987:78). The hornskin of Lóch and Fer Diad literalizes the heroic dependence on a firmly structured outward persona: their faith in its arbitrary structures proves their undoing. The attack of the gae bolga strikes at the fundamental basis of the hero's existence. No matter how glorious, well defined, and autonomous these heroes are, violence reduces them all to broken pieces, to permeated flesh. The gae bolga goes even further than traditional weapons: it is a nameless horror, an indefinable assault because it strikes from the inside out, not merely subverting the heroic identity but inverting it.

The gae bolga is Cú Chulainn's defining weapon because as a shape-shifter he is perfectly placed to challenge the very core of the heroic ethos. He is a boy-man, beautiful but fierce, a defender of the Ulaid but not entirely of the Ulaid, and he stands guard at the edges of society. Perhaps because he is fluid,[14] when violence emerges from within him, as it does in the form of the "warp-spasm,"[15] the effects, though catastrophic, do not result in his destruction. As the warp-spasm strikes Cú Chulainn, violence flows like a ripple through him, turning him inside out, bringing his organs up through his mouth, turning his limbs back to front, and causing blood and fire to burst from his head. The warp-spasm is the literalized spectacle of unchecked violence, operating beyond society, beyond restriction, and beyond the norms of the body. Cú Chulainn survives, but in monstrous form, and a more radical expression of how he is not like other warriors could hardly be imagined. Through the figure of Cú Chulainn, the *Táin* offers us a radical challenge to the heroic ethos: traditional warriors with fixed identities and rigid boundaries are destroyed, whereas the boy whose body is fluid conducts the forces of violence and survives.

Thus, although characters within the *Táin* are at pains to distinguish inferior warriors such as Etarcomol and Láiríne from Cú Chulainn, Cú Chulainn himself embodies — on an extreme level — the conflicted nature of the warrior function. Ó Cathasaigh argues that it is "impossible not to see in *Táin Bó Cúailnge* a celebration of the martial heroism of Cú Chulainn; of his courage and ingenuity, his mastery of the martial arts, his

---

14. See Lowe 2000 for a more extensive discussion.

15. The "warp-spasm" — to use Kinsella's (1969) English term for Cú Chulainn's *ríastrad*, 'distortion' — is a battle fury producing a horrific transformation in Cú Chulainn, offering a graphic spectacle of the warrior's devastating rage and aggression.

unswerving loyalty" (Ó Cathasaigh 1986:156). Yet, it also seems impossible to ignore the fact that the warp-spasm represents precisely those forces
of violence unleashed by acts of martial heroism which are only ever
conditionally under control and which threaten to escape at the slightest
provocation.[16] Cú Chulainn does not merely represent the ideal hero; he
represents those ideals taken to excess. The noble persona that he reveals
to the women, poets, and *áes dána,* 'people of arts', on the day after his
warp-spasm (ll. 2336ff.) reflects society's mastery of irrational forces: at
such times Cú Chulainn truly is the "hero of the tribe." Yet, this socially
acceptable face of heroism can never be divorced from the carnage that
surrounds it. As the ultimate warrior, Cú Chulainn acts as the locus of the
struggle to contain violence that continually threatens to escape its bonds,
and so he represents the essential ambivalence of the warrior function.

To Deleuze and Guattari (1988), war is one of the events that overwhelms stable structures and, thus, reveals the proliferating flow of forces
that permeate life. Although human systems demand order, definition,
and stasis, natural forces such as violence are fluid and versatile, instantiating what Deleuze and Guattari term a "state of becoming," as we have
seen. Like Bataille, Deleuze and Guattari insist that warfare is not contained within the social apparatus; instead, it brings a furor to bear against
society because war operates through "relations of becoming" (352): it
destroys the boundaries that humanity erects and reveals the natural
forces of life and death that such boundaries repress.

Following Deleuze and Guattari, I would argue that the *Táin* embodies
a state of war, representing a continual challenge to order on both a bodily
and a social level, expressed through the warrior function. This is not to
say, however, that the story charts the movement of a society heading
toward dysfunction, revealing the breakdown of traditional structures
and relationships, as Joan Radner (1982) suggests. Nor do I agree with
Dooley's argument that the *Táin* reflects a society in crisis, where the many
bodily inversions within the tale (exemplified by Cú Chulainn's use of the

16. Kim McCone (1983) discusses the unstable nature of the hero in relation to another
Irish tale, *Scéla Muicce Meic Da Thó (The Story of Mac Da Thó's Pig).* The tale exploits the
ways in which the heroic body is disrupted through violence, although the tale itself is comic.
The proud warrior Cet mac Magach humiliates those who challenge him for the position of
honor at the carving of the pig by describing the wounds he has inflicted on them in the past.
As in the *Táin* the violence distorts the organic integrity of the body and simultaneously
undermines the heroic status of the warriors. Violence, the prime activity of the martial hero,
therefore contains the seeds of its own destruction, a fact graphically realized in the bodily
mutilations that run through early Irish heroic literature.

gae bolga) stem from "male terror of the devouring female," a concept that can be associated in turn with "deep anxiety about the instability of male gendering and identity" (Dooley 1994:127). My argument, rather, is that the way that violence permeates and distorts both social and physical systems in the *Táin* reveals a society deeply aware of the consequences of martial heroism. The *Táin* is the product not of a society in decline but of one that questions the traditional ideals that ostensibly define it.

In addressing related questions, Ó Cathasaigh stresses that although "evidence of the breakdown of social order is all about us in *Táin Bó Cúailnge*," it is "the strength of kin-love which ultimately defeats the destructive forces which are unleashed upon Ulster" (Ó Cathasaigh 1986:156). His argument is crucial in reminding us that violence does not go unchecked and that, despite the ravages that occur in the tale, the *Táin* ends with the resumption of order. Ó Cathasaigh believes that the actions of the loyal Fergus demonstrate that it is a social bond, *condalbae*, 'love for kin', which encourages Fergus to turn aside his sword in the final battle. Thus, the "collapse of the social order is stemmed and ultimately reversed" by the family ties that connect Fergus and Cú Chulainn both to their tribe and to each other (ibid.).

The *Táin* does not bear witness to the end of all values, then, but instead reveals how social systems remain continually under threat from violent conduct and hints at the abyss that lies beneath any society defined by its martial heroes. The encounters between Cú Chulainn and Lóch, Fer Diad, and Fer Báeth (who comes to fight him at ll. 1737–1806) reflect this threat: they are all fosterbrothers of Cú Chulainn, Ulaid warriors in exile bribed by Medb into challenging their former comrade. Despite Cú Chulainn's appeal to the bond that should connect them as brothers, they choose to fight, with inevitable consequences. As Bart Jaski remarks, their deaths "highlight the destructiveness of warfare, which rips through bonds of brotherhood and comradeship" (Jaski 1999:27). The conflict in this instance subverts the ties of fosterage and turns one fosterbrother against another; yet again the social category cannot contain the violence that manipulates and perverts it.

Society is also under threat even when familial bonds are upheld, as in the case of Cú Chulainn's encounter with his supernatural father Lug, who visits him during the battle (ll. 2088ff.). Lug comes to the aid of his son and heals his wounds, but he fails to uphold his promise to fight in Cú Chulainn's place while the warrior sleeps. Consequently, the boytroop is forced to enter the fray, whereupon it is annihilated. This episode inverts the hero's role: here the salvation of Cú Chulainn leads to the destruction of many, where elsewhere the hero absorbs the threat to his society. The encounter between Cú Chulainn and Lug is an interesting reflection of the contradictory nature of the warrior, which, in this scene at least, brings inadvertent harm to the society that the warrior supposedly protects. In addition, the meeting between the two characters highlights that part of Cú Chulainn's nature that leads him away from society, the semidivine essence that renders him permanently marginal. Despite Cú Chulainn's great power, he cannot entirely be trusted: his encounters with forces on the edges of society can lead him away at a time of great need, just as such encounters can bring powerful forces back to society's borders in the form of violence and destruction. In this way, Cú Chulainn pushes the heroic ideal to its extreme, revealing that the heroic ethos demanding individual endeavor at the margins of society is ultimately counterproductive, undermining the collective responsibility on which social structures are founded. The healing of Cú Chulainn may spring from more benign impulses than the behavior of Lóch, Fer Diad, and Fer Báeth, but the consequences of their actions for society are wastefulness and death.

The social order is eventually restored at the end of the *Táin* (although we do not see its restoration), but the tale also reminds us that this peace can only ever be conditional. The heroic ethos — in which warriors thrive and which highlights their glory — also draws society toward a maelstrom of violence that threatens its borders and structures. The *Táin* does not simply celebrate heroism, then, or see the career of the hero as an ideal, a force for social betterment. Warriors bring about the primal violence of war that suffuses the epic: they liberate its destructive power but can never contain or define it. Warfare unleashes forces that escape the control of each individual character, even the greatest hero of them all, Cú Chulainn. In the act of pursuing society's aims and defending its rights and territories, warriors introduce its greatest threat. It does not diminish the power of Ireland's ancient heroic tale to say that it casts heroism in such a conflicted role but helps us to acknowledge the text's complexity. In the world of the *Táin,* as in any warlike society, violence becomes the medium of expression for the hero and therefore the medium of society's potential destruction.

In summation, we should not believe that early Irish "heroic literature" offers an uncritical celebration of warfare, but, rather, acknowledge that the early tales continually subject heroic values to scrutiny. It is through the medium of such stories that we can continue to investigate the culture of early Ireland, because throughout the body of the literature traditional values are represented, defined, and continually explored and interrogated. I have argued that *Táin Bó Cúailnge* reveals the ambivalent nature of the heroic acts it describes, both through language and through representations of graphic spectacle. As anyone who lives in a society afflicted by violence must know, the glorious achievements of warriors coexist with the sufferings of death, mutilation, and social upheaval. The *Táin* reminds us all that glory and horror are both attributes of the hero of the tribe and that Ireland has been aware of this ambivalence for more than a thousand years.

Works Cited

Bataille, Georges. 1987. *Eroticism.* Trans. Mary Dalwood. London: Marion Boyars.

Breatnach, Pádraig A. 1990. Review of *The wisdom of the outlaw,* by Joseph Falaky Nagy. *Éigse* 24:155–67.

Deleuze, Gilles, and Félix Guattari. 1988. *A thousand plateaus: Capitalism and schizophrenia.* Trans. Brian Massumi. London: Athlone Press.

Dooley, Anne. 1994. The invention of women in the *Táin. Ulidia: Proceedings of the First International Conference on the Ulster Cycle of Tales,* ed. J. P. Mallory and Gerard Stockman, 123–33. Belfast: December Publications.

Dumézil, Georges. 1970. *The destiny of the warrior.* Trans. Alf Hiltebeitel. Chicago: University of Chicago Press.

Jaski, Bart. 1999. Cú Chulainn, *gormac* and *dalta* of the Ulstermen. *Cambrian Medieval Celtic Studies* 37:1–31.

Kelly, Patricia. 1992. The *Táin* as literature. In *Aspects of the "Táin,"* ed. J. P. Mallory, 69–102. Belfast: December Publications.

Kinsella, Thomas, trans. [1969] 1970. *The Táin.* London: Oxford University Press.

Lowe, Jeremy. 2000. Kicking over the traces: The instability of Cú Chulainn. *Studia Celtica* 34:119–30.

McCone, Kim. 1983. Scéla muicce Meic Dathó. In *Léachtaí Cholm Cille XIV: Ár scéalaíocht,* ed. Pádriag Ó Fiannachta, 5–38. Maynooth: An Sagart.

———. 1984. *Aided Cheltchair Maic Uthechair:* Hounds, heroes and hospitallers in early Irish myth and story. *Ériu* 35:1–30.

Melia, D. F. 1974. Parallel versions of "The boyhood deeds of Cú Chulainn." *Forum for Modern Language Studies* 10:211–26.

Nagy, Joseph Falaky. 1984. Heroic destinies in the *macgnímrada* of Finn and Cú
  Chulainn. *Zeitschrift für celtische Philologie* 40:23–39.
———. 1985. *The wisdom of the outlaw: The boyhood deeds of Finn in Gaelic
  narrative tradition.* Berkeley: University of California Press.
———. 1996. Daring young men in their chariots. In *A Celtic florilegium: Studies in
  memory of Brendan O Hehir,* ed. Kathryn A. Klar, Eve E. Sweetser, and Claire
  Thomas, 144–51. Lawrence, Mass.: Celtic Studies Publications.
Ó Broin, Tomás. 1961–63. What is the "debility" of the Ulstermen? *Éigse* 10:286–
  99.
Ó Cathasaigh, Tomás. 1986. The sister's son in early Irish literature. *Peritia* 5:128–
  60.
———. 1993. Mythology in *Táin bó Cúailnge.* In *Studien zur "Táin bó Cúailnge,"*
  ed. Hildegard L. C. Tristram, 114–32. ScriptOralia 52. Tübingen: Gunter Narr.
O'Leary, Philip. 1987. *Fír fer:* An internalized ethical concept in early Irish litera-
  ture? *Éigse* 22:1–14.
O'Rahilly, Cecile, ed. and trans. 1967. *"Táin bó Cúalnge" from the Book of
  Leinster.* Dublin: Dublin Institute for Advanced Studies.
———, ed. and trans. 1976. *Táin bó Cúailnge: Recension I.* Dublin: Dublin In-
  stitute for Advanced Studies.
Radner, Joan Newlon. 1982. "Fury destroys the world": Historical strategy in
  Ireland's Ulster epic. *Mankind Quarterly* 23:41–60.
Shaviro, Steven. 1993. *The cinematic body.* Minneapolis: University of Minnesota
  Press.
Sjoestedt, Marie-Louise. 1949. *Gods and heroes of the Celts.* Trans. Myles Dillon.
  London: Methuen.
Tymoczko, Maria. 1999. *Translation in a postcolonial context: Early Irish litera-
  ture in English translation.* Manchester: St. Jerome Publishing.

SALLY K. SOMMERS SMITH

Interpretations and Translations of Irish Traditional Music

The first thing to note, obviously enough, is that Irish music is
not European.

—Seán Ó Riada, *Our Musical Heritage*

Any music must be studied in the context of the culture that produces it. In
the case of a traditional music, it is even more necessary to understand and
appreciate the environment in which the music is made. If the term *traditional* carries with it the meaning of something old, something handed
across generations, something honored both in its transmission and in its
practice, then a traditional art form will connect a people and a culture
through time. In this essay I focus on traditional Irish music, relating it to
its environment, using Irish music to interrogate and evaluate a number of
current views and controversies about the fundamental nature of traditional music and tradition itself.

An analysis of popular misconceptions about traditional music by
Bruno Nettl (1973), the dean of American ethnomusicology, offers a convenient starting point. Study of the meaning of a traditional music is, like
the music itself, subject to misunderstanding. Nettl has defined several
pervasive misconceptions about traditional music; these misconceptions
often reveal preconceived notions about the people who make the music
as well as the music itself (Nettl 1973:1–16). Such misconceptions include
the notion that a traditional music rises, almost like a smoke, from the
collective consciousness of a people; it therefore has no individual composers of note. In this misconceived view, the individual voice characterizes neither a musical piece nor a performance. A second false expectation
identified by Nettl is that a traditional music is a national music, implying
that traditional music carries a political subtext, understood as such by its
performers and its audience. As Nettl indicates, however, the concept of
nationality can transcend and, in some cases, prefigure the political sense

of that term, reflecting the earliest sense of *nation,* as identifying a people or ethnic group, rather than a political state. A third popular misconception discussed by Nettl is the belief that a traditional music must be of rural rather than urban origin. A presupposition of this view is that an urban sensibility may imply a sophistication in the structure of music or professionalism in the performance of music that cannot be found (or honored) in a rural setting. Traditional music is therefore a music born of poverty and isolation, according to this notion.

Nettl argues that the most pervasive stereotype about traditional music is that it serves a purely practical purpose within society. Thus music may be made for ritual or for dancing, to express nationalistic fervor, or to tell the tales of the culture. In any of these cases, however, music is not normally associated with what are taken to be the more refined pastimes of entertainment or listening for pleasure, for in this framework the very concept of entertainment implies that sufficient leisure time exists to devote to the study and enjoyment of music, a concept at odds with the assumption that traditional music is made by and for a rural laboring class. This last attitude strongly implies that traditional music occupies a place outside normal life and normal time: that it is reserved for the sacred, rather than profane, practices of a culture.[1]

Nettl did not include Ireland and Irish traditional music in his analysis and in his refutations of these misconceptions. In fact, he lumped Irish music together with English and Scottish music, which itself perhaps reflects a political as well as cultural assumption.[2] When Nettl's analysis of stereotypes about traditional music is applied to Irish music, however, it provides a fascinating glimpse into assumptions about Irish life and culture constituting the context that is so crucial to the understanding of the music. Notions about Irish life from the post-Cromwellian period, during

1. The ethnomusicologist David Neuman characterizes such implications as examples of "interpretive musical history," which views the history of a culture as parallel to its music and musical culture. Interpretive musical history can serve as a means of reinforcing the interpretation of a traditional music as sacred, for it consciously places music and musical evolution outside the context of daily life and events (Neuman 1993:269).

2. Nettl's lapse here is in part explained by the late development of the study of Irish traditional music. Ethnomusicology of Irish traditional music was pioneered by uilleann piper Breandán Breathnach in his seminal *Folk Music and Dances of Ireland* (1971). It had been given an impetus by the musical revival begun in the mid-1950s. In the 1950s, Donal O'Sullivan (1952:59) could lament, "Until the present year, no research [about Irish traditional music] has ever been done under the auspices of a university or similar body, nor do any voluntary societies exist for the promotion of the serious study in the subject and the publication of results."

the height of English imperialism in Ireland, through the Great Famine, and to the present have been formed with relation to the traditional music that is such a splendid part of Irish heritage.

Irish traditional music is difficult to analyze using standard models of traditional music. Ireland's heritage is Western, but it is also affected by England's colonization of Ireland. Until recently Ireland has been largely rural, although it is possessed of a vibrant urban culture as well. Music has been recognized as the stamp of Irish culture since at least the twelfth century, when Giraldus Cambrensis wrote admiringly of the skill of Irish harpers, even while disdaining the culture that produced them (Giraldus 1951:87–88).[3] Although the Irish harping tradition clearly predates Giraldus's comments, what we recognize today as Irish traditional music does not have nearly so lengthy a life span. Many listeners presume that Irish traditional music has an ancient lineage, yet much of the repertoire of dance music is at most two hundred years old. Traditional dance music is easily identified by modern listeners as Irish, but inclusion of the music as an Irish form of expression has occurred in ethnomusicology only in the last fifty years.

Irish traditional music refutes every one of the misconceptions about traditional music characteristic of ethnomusicology discussed by Nettl, thereby confirming his critique. In Ireland traditional songs and dances do generally have individual composers; indeed, composers are often memorialized in the names of tunes or in the versions that have been crafted from individual variations of the melodies. After playing *Joe Cooley's Hornpipe,* for example, a performer will frequently note both that the tune was composed by Paddy O'Brien, the great accordion player from Tipperary, and that it commemorates the playing of the master accordion player from Galway after whom it was named. Breandán Breathnach (1996:126–31) relates the story of how one Cork clergyman, the Reverend E. Gaynor, reacted unfavorably to the publication of the largest collection of the traditional dance music of Ireland ever assembled, the Francis O'Neill Collection of 1903. Father Gaynor virulently opposed O'Neill's work precisely because it contained airs written by an Irish composer whose work Gaynor did not consider sufficiently Irish or sufficiently traditional. If traditional musical pieces do not have individual compos-

---

3. Giraldus's work is often quoted as the earliest and most authoritative commentary on native Irish music, but it may be neither (Ó hAllmhuráin 1998:16–19; cf. Grattan Flood 1927:46–53).

ers, then Gaynor's objections, although perhaps misguided, could never have carried weight with his audience.[4] Although the composers of many tunes have been forgotten, it is incorrect to assume that simply because an Irish tune is written in the traditional style, it has no composer of note. Traditional Irish music clearly does not rise from a collective consciousness but rather from a system of remembering—as much as possible—excellent musicians and singers who have contributed to the body of the tradition.[5]

The national character of Irish traditional music is also a rather problematic construction. Indeed the term *Irish music* embraces at least two very different forms of music from very different eras. The music of Irish harpers praised by Giraldus Cambrensis was music made for an aristocratic class. Medieval harpers were musicians of great skill who occupied positions of trust and prestige in noble households (Breathnach 1971:2–7, 65–69; O'Neill [1913] 1987:23–28; Ó hAllmhuráin 1998:16–27). This musical tradition survived until the end of the eighteenth century as an entertainment for the wealthy, preserved by well-trained musicians whose repertoires included a mixture of older pieces, contemporary ballads, and newer tunes, sometimes composed in honor of their patrons. Its popularity among the wealthier classes and its performance by trained and often literate musicians has led some to define this Irish harp music as a native form of art music, as opposed to folk music (Moloney 2000:7).[6] As

4. Sometimes a composer for a particular tune is not listed, say, on a recording because the composer is not known. Moreover, mistakes do happen. Sometimes a tune sounds so "traditional" that it is assumed to be old and the name of the composer to have been lost. Dating traditional tunes is a tricky business, however, and O'Sullivan (1952:8) cautions against the presumption of antiquity simply because a melody sounds old; "extrinsic evidence" is necessary before assigning dates to songs or dance tunes. Such highly regarded living composers as accordionists Martin Mulhaire and Joe Derrane recall hearing tunes that they had composed attributed later to the venerable source of "tradition" (personal communication with Martin Mulhaire, 14 November 1994).

5. It is curious in this regard, therefore, to read O'Sullivan's (1952:7) characterization of a folk music: "Every country has its body of folk music and verse, and they are all, in some mysterious way, an emanation of the people: the result, no doubt, of a corporate urge for self-expression. Nobody knows who composed them . . . none of them bears the impress of individual genius." Breathnach (1996:121) points out that O'Sullivan was writing for the Cultural Relations Committee of Ireland and that his views may have had more to do with the establishment of traditional music as part of a national identity than with the historical treatment of the origins of a folk expression. In his introduction to *Folk Music and Dances of Ireland,* however, Breathnach also defines a folk music as anonymous (1971:1–2).

6. A selection of Irish harp music—mainly contemporary, but with a smattering of older tunes—was transcribed in 1792 and published by Edward Bunting, in an attempt to preserve the Irish harping tradition from extinction. Sadly, efforts to keep the tradition alive by

used at present, the term *Irish traditional music* does not commonly include the Irish harp music but designates music for dancing, as well as a vast repertoire of song that may be ancient or of quite recent vintage. Although Irish dance music and song are usually easily identifiable as such by listeners, they share stylistic features with the folk music of Scandinavia, Brittany, and Scotland, as well as England.

Indeed, for all the nationalist weight placed on it by patriots,[7] Irish traditional music is not the product of an isolated island population. Rather, it derives from a rich history of musical exchange with European music, especially popular dance music. This was music demanded and appreciated by urban Irish audiences from the eighteenth century to the present. As Seán Connolly points out in his study of pre-Famine Irish society, travelers' accounts from eighteenth-century Ireland chronicle the movement of popular European dances and the music that accompanied them from the urban centers of Ireland where they made their first appearance to the more rural areas of Ireland (Connolly 1996:88–90). Minuets, country dances, cotillions, and quadrilles were recognized by these travelers. Not all accounts speak positively about finding European dances in a rural Irish setting. Connolly quotes one of the travelers, the English Reverend J. Burrows, as being horrified at hearing French dance music played at a celebration for Irish tenants and laborers; he called it "perfectly ridiculous" (91).

With respect to the preconception that traditional music serves functional purposes, Connolly finds evidence in Ireland for the use of music in recreational activities, such as dances, that were shared between landholders and their tenants in the eighteenth and early nineteenth centuries. The practice of shared dances suggests a mechanism for the incorporation of European popular musical forms into the existing body of Irish traditional music: dances and music may have been introduced by landlords and eagerly taken up by their tenants, who changed the tunes to fit their preferred rhythms and steps. Breandán Breathnach notes that the quadrille probably arrived in Ireland with soldiers returning from the Napo-

---

establishing schools for the training of young musicians were failures, and harpers became stage entertainers in the nineteenth century. Patrick Byrne, "the last of the great Irish harpers," died in Dundalk in 1863, "unwept, unhonored, and unsung, within a few miles of the capital of his native land" (O'Neill [1913] 1987:82).

7. For the treatment of traditional music as a symbol of Irish national identity, see Sommers Smith 1998 and Trachsel 1995. White (1998:36–52) offers a comprehensive view of Irish nationalism and politics as reflected in the music of the nineteenth century.

leonic Wars. It was then, he asserts, adapted to the quicker rhythms of established Irish dance music such as the jig and the reel (Breathnach 1970:117). Clearly, the music we today characterize as Irish traditional dance music is neither exclusively Irish in its origin nor exclusively rural. Seán Corcoran contests the pervasive "traditional as rural" notion, arguing that modern attempts to collect Irish traditional sources falsely assume the rural nature of the music. Although many people who give songs or tunes to collectors at present live in rural areas, the songs or dance tunes themselves often have their origin in an urban situation of the seventeenth or eighteenth century (Corcoran 1991:5).

A further assumption about traditional music implicit in the idea that it springs from a rural origin is that transmission of the music is exclusively aural — that the people who make and pass along the music are illiterate, at least in musical terms. Many traditional musicians, both past and present, read and write music quite well. Yet strangely, as Mary Trachsel points out, the transcription of traditional music in written collections in the nineteenth century transformed the music heard by the collectors into texts that were considered more "authentic" than the original aural sources (Trachsel 1995:38). In fact, when music is aural, changes may be introduced into the music by individual performers. As a result of this practice of innovation in traditional music, in the transcription of traditional music, the question arose as to which version of a musical piece should be considered "authentic." In effect, writing down previously unwritten music lent the written text a legitimacy not achievable by those who play and learn "by ear"; the written music became a historical, unchanging, and consumable record of the rural past rather than a vigorous and living (but mutable and, therefore, flawed) form of expression. Here a basic misunderstanding of the process and practice of traditional music results not from comparison with the actual aural reality of the music but from the presumption that music should be fixed and that aurally transmitted music is rough and imprecise because of its fluidity. Ironically, therefore, authenticity of folk expression in Ireland came to be associated with written documents.

Perhaps the most interesting area of Nettl's argument concerns the uses and functions of traditional music in society. He carefully separates the functions of music in a traditional society from those which predominate in modern Western cultures. One of the common misconceptions he identifies sees traditional music as powerful precisely because it fulfills the task or tasks prescribed for it by the culture (Nettl 1973:13). In performing those tasks, music becomes an activity reserved for special times and places, and thus it is removed from normal experience. Traditional music performance is, according to this line of reasoning, a sacred activity. Although music for entertainment may transmit to its listeners the idea that the workday is over and it is time for leisure, in such a view, because of its sacred associations, traditional music may also tell its audience that something special is about to happen. In other words, a traditional music has the power to tell not just what time it is but also what kind of time it is. There is an aura of the primitive about such an association of traditional music with sacred time and space, perhaps even a superstitious equation of the power of the music with magic.

This notion, when applied to the traditional music of Ireland, suggests much more about attitudes toward Ireland and its people than about the interpretation of Ireland's music. Irish traditional music was never relegated solely to sacred time. Much of the music was dance music, made expressly for entertainment and listening pleasure. Although some Irish music was clearly reserved for rituals, such as wakes, this was not the distinguishing function of the music.[8]

This analysis of Irish music demonstrates how the origin, nature, and meaning of a traditional music can be misinterpreted and its message misused, indicating as well that such misinterpretations are not confined to the past but continue into the present. Moreover, a musical system within the context of imperialism is often correlated by colonizers with the level of civilization attributed to the colonized. If the colonized culture is thought to be primitive and degenerate, the musical system of that culture may also be interpreted in a similar manner. When England ruled Ireland, it feared rebellion by Irish patriots. The traditional music of Ireland was looked on with suspicion, interpreted as both primitive and subversive, inclined to incitement of violence. Acceptance of Irish melody by British listeners was predicated on its modification, both to suit contemporary dominant taste and to quell the wild politicized element perceived by some of its popularizers and by its would-be British audience. Let us turn to an examination of perceptions of Irish music held by British

---

8. Here Gearóid Ó Crualaoich's (1998) examination of rituals surrounding the Irish wake is instructive, in that he defines the particular forms of music reserved for mourning, in contrast to the more everyday music that accompanied ordinary social activities.

listeners and the remaking of Irish traditional music to suit the tastes of audiences influenced by dominant musical standards in English culture.

One of the earliest collections of Irish traditional music — and one of the most enduringly popular — is the Bunting collection of 1796. This collection consists of Irish airs gathered by Edward Bunting, many in connection with the Belfast Harp Festival of 1792. As is well known, the airs were translated from the harp originals to notation for keyboard instruments. This change in setting reflected not only Bunting's musical strengths (he was an organist) but also concessions to contemporary tastes (White 1998:39–40). The pianoforte was becoming available as a personal instrument during this period, and pianos were beginning to appear in homes of the middle and upper classes in Ireland and England alike. Music for the piano is usually given a harmonized melody, a custom Bunting follows even though the tunes he transcribed from the harpers were unaccompanied melody lines. In his description of what he termed the "ancient" tunes of Ireland, Bunting notes that he was surprised to discover that they easily admitted the addition of harmony and, thus, translation to the keyboard (Bunting 1796:ii; cf. Brown 1998:41). Interpreting Bunting's finding as a rationalization for the changes Bunting introduced to the music, Harry White also notes the significance of Bunting's suggestion that this "ancient" music requires translation in order to be introduced into the homes of the musically literate (White 1998:39–40).

Richard Leppert has analyzed eighteenth- and nineteenth-century notions of proper forms of music; these notions, first pronounced by Jean-Philippe Rameau in the seventeenth century, looked to Greek ideals of mathematical harmony as the basis for every "true" musical system. Those systems which did not make use of what was termed "natural" harmony — as Western music did — were considered degenerate, for the "natural" basis for harmonic music was identified clearly in the Enlightened mentality with "the good" (Leppert 1987:76). Harmonic order in musical systems, then, was considered equivalent to order in a culture, a language, and a society. Leppert cites a pamphlet, written by John Keeble in 1784, that purports to demonstrate the scientific nature and therefore the rational basis of the Greek harmonic system. Although the mathematics that Keeble employs is neither musical nor scientific, he nonetheless arrives at an "argument, embodied in mathematics . . . that the Western system developing from the Greeks is natural and must be obeyed. It is an argument built not on 'pure' reason, but on a subjectively constituted reason at whose base lies the attraction of power and firm conviction . . . that the Western system is the only one able to claim universal validity. . . . [T]he musical order (theoretical systems *and* the values attached to them) . . . is constituted by, and hence reinforces, an identical ideological base of Western self-legitimization" (Leppert 1987:74–75).

In this context, it is instructive to examine British attitudes about the Irish and about Irish traditional music, for they reveal the kinds of assumptions seen in Leppert's study.[9] That the British public held the Irish and their culture in low esteem is well known; caricatures of simian Irish faces in *Punch* are familiar to all. Irish music likewise carried with it a suspicion of the exotic and the dangerous: "in the wake of the rebellion of 1798 . . . to make Ireland a literary and musical subject [for entertainments] involved attendant difficulties, not to say risks. For the music of a primitive people could all too easily be associated with political instability by English audiences. It could call to mind all that made the wild Irish a suspect people. Had they not risen with violent and terrible consequences in 1798 and might they not again?" (Brown 1998:39–40). Collectors and popularizers of Irish music, such as Bunting and Thomas Moore after him, faced difficulties in bringing the wealth of the traditional Irish musical heritage to a wary public.

Thomas Moore, particularly, embraced the challenge of serving Irish traditional music to British audiences in a manner acceptable to their prejudices. He took much of his material from the Bunting collection and shared many of Bunting's ideas about the adaptation of the music to the keyboard. Like Bunting, Moore associated with political rebels; unlike Bunting, he used the music and the lyrics he set to the traditional airs as a means to immortalize activists such as Robert Emmet (White 1998:44–45). In musical circles, however, Moore is remembered more for the alterations he made to the Irish airs he found in the Bunting collection than for his vision of Irish traditional music as a tool to unite and inspire republican sentiments. Moore's alterations were quickly accepted by the Victorian audience, for they offered an accessible and "civilized" means of enjoying the genius of Irish melody, without the "primitive" and even "dangerous" dimensions of the untranslated music.

Liam de Paor characterizes Moore's "civilizing" influence on the music

9. Leppert and McClary (1987) argue that musical conventions often parallel social values, but because music is nonrepresentational, its relationship to society is often overlooked.

as congruent with middle-class Irish aspirations in the nineteenth century: "Moore's gift was that he did in fact represent the sentiment, if not of Ireland, at least of Irish respectability—the English-speaking aspirant middle class coming up in the world. He was nothing so dangerous as a revolutionary or a rebel . . . but he gave an acceptable voice to expressions of carefully modified regret at the suppression of Irish independence, and in the sentimental embroidery which devised for this regret he contributed to the making of the new nationalist myth" (de Paor 1989:6). De Paor is unsentimental about the changes wrought by Moore in his interpretation of Irish airs. He comments on the political and social impact of this altered traditional Irish music, now fit to the very different musical requirements of the parlor pianoforte: "Moore's value [was] to that large and increasing part of Ireland which had made its peace with the cultural values of the English-speaking world. He was outstanding among those who made the origins of native Ireland—the old cultural values—respectable. In doing so of course he distorted them" (11). Moore's *Irish Melodies* not only succeeded in "civilizing" the traditional music of Ireland but also managed to bring the music out of its somewhat threatening original location into more ordinary time and space. If the music of Ireland was not previously fit for the ears of the British and Irish middle class, Moore's musical alterations and his supply of rich and yeasty verse to accompany the melodies made the rough, "primitive" tradition welcome in the parlors of all who aspired to gentility. Mícheál Ó Súilleabháin notes that Moore's re-creation of Irish melody "was of no consequence to Moore's audience. They were more than grateful to be allowed to participate in this urbane reflection of the native tradition" (Ó Súilleabháin 1994:339). That the music could be symbolically brought into the light for the entertainment of people who not only possessed but also cultivated leisure time meant that the music had been rendered orderly, rational, Western, and, therefore, "good."

Despite the sanitizing of Irish music that Bunting and, later, Moore and his contemporaries hoped would bring the traditional music of Ireland into the modern age, there was still a perceived threat in the wildness of the untranslated music that persisted throughout the nineteenth century. In 1893 George Bernard Shaw, for example, commented on the unculti-vated streak of Irishness in Sir Charles Villiers Stanford's *Irish Symphony* (1887):

The success of Professor Stanford's *Irish Symphony* . . . was, from the Philharmonic point of view, somewhat scandalous. The spectacle of a university professor "going Fantee" is indecorous.

The *Irish Symphony,* composed by an Irishman, is a record of fearful conflict between the aboriginal Celt and the Professor. The scherzo is not a scherzo at all, but a shindy, expending its forces in riotous dancing. However hopelessly an English orchestra may fail to catch the wild nuances of the Irish fiddler, it cannot altogether drown the "hurroosh" with which Stanford the Celt drags Stanford the Professor into the orgy.

(Quoted in Murphy 1998:53).

This review was written just prior to the time that English traditional music was championed and incorporated into the compositions of Percy Grainger and Ralph Vaughan Williams, who, not so incidentally, were both students of Stanford. Michael Murphy points out that this inequity in attitude toward English and Irish traditional music was the result of the insular nature of English folkloric studies: "they promoted the study of the English peasant rather than the colonial savage" (Murphy 1998:51).[10]

And if the traditional music of a culture could be transformed into a rational Western system, was it not also possible to infer that its political system could be made subject to and congruent with the British model? Moore's work was aimed at recasting Irish traditional music as the romantic expression of an ancient and splendid Celtic past. He was also clearly aware of the "proximity between music and politics in Ireland" (White 1998:45). It is interesting, therefore, that the enduring popularity of Moore's *Irish Melodies* permitted the political message of the music to be reinterpreted throughout the nineteenth century. If the political subtext of the *Melodies* initially champions Emmet and the romantic ideal of Irish nationhood, from the 1870s through the beginning of the twentieth century, the music was seen as a reflection of the thoroughly acculturated, thoroughly Anglicized Irish society. Harry White chronicles the reinterpretation of Moore's political message: "The transformation of Moore . . . from romantic agent of Irish emancipation (and specifically Catholic emancipation) to hated darling of the Victorian parlour, is one that belongs in the sectarian projection of Gaelic culture, which in part characterized the Celtic revival of the late 1870s. Between 1807 and the advent of

---

10. Blacking (1987:1–27) offers an excellent examination of Percy Grainger's collection and use of English folk music in the first decade of the twentieth century.

the Famine, however, Moore's voice was the conduit of a romanticised
political sentiment which had its origins in the United Irishmen, the failure
of rebellion, and the newly symbolic force of the music itself" (White
1998:44–45).

Moore himself sought to downplay the potentially revolutionary impact of his music and lyrics. Terence Brown notes that Moore was at pains
as his career progressed in the first decades of the nineteenth century to
reassure his readers and auditors "that they had little to fear from him,
however Irish the subject matter of the verses which he set to Irish airs . . .
Irish music will appeal, Moore believes, to the kind of people who can be
depended upon not to be inflamed by political fervor of a dangerous kind"
(Brown 1998:40–41). An integral part of making Irish music acceptable
to the "cultured" ear was therefore to strip it of its political menace. The
message was clear: traditional music translated from the wild harp and
pipes to the safe, "feminine" (Leppert 1987:75) pianoforte — simple me-
lodic music ennobled with rational harmony — was also a music that
ceased to carry a threat of Irish insurrection. It was civilized, sweet, and
proper. It was also traditional music stripped of some of its meaning, a
powerful music declawed.

Interpreting the message of Irish traditional music — its uses, its proper
place, and above all its future in a world of diverse musical choices — is
still an activity that can be readily observed among enthusiasts as well as
players of the music.[11] Two centuries ago Irish traditional music was radically altered to make it attractive to a listening public, and the same
process can be observed in the later twentieth century, as it was adapted to
the needs and tastes of the recording industry and mass-market music, just
as at present it is still experiencing changes to render it appealing to the
CD-buying and concert-going public.[12] What is perhaps surprising about
the current marketing of Irish traditional music is that the same misconceptions that attended its earlier transformations are still being applied
either to justify its modernization or to protest against such updating.

For example, Tony MacMahon, a traditional accordionist and Irish

11. Traditional Irish musicians would much rather play the music than talk about its
direction and future. Colin Hamilton (1999:82), a traditional flute player and ethnomusicologist, notes that the future of the tradition lies in the decisions that this generation of players
makes regarding what is or is not to be admitted to the tradition, decisions made through the
practice and performance of the music itself.

12. This is a very large subject that goes beyond my scope here. See Sommers Smith 2001;
Vallely, Hamilton, Vallely, and Doherty 1999:5.

television presenter of traditional music, suggests that the image of tradi- tional music in Ireland suffers because of its association with a "primitive" past: "I regard Irish Traditional Music as an important part of this [Irish] artistic landscape and it deserves to be taken as seriously as any other sector. I say this because it has been my experience over the years that this body of music and song has generally been regarded as entertainment of a fairly primitive nature" (MacMahon 1999:112). As he decries the notion that equates traditional music with a primitive society, however, he also rails against its association with the modern, prosperous Ireland and its trappings: "What is [music's] value? What can it do for us? Is it an aural carpet, a sort of ear chocolate to soothe our nerves in pubs, traffic jams, or shopping centres? . . . Is it to be reduced, drained of the veiled voices of Ireland, electronically scrubbed clean, packaged and presented as a com- mercial commodity whose value is measured in record sales, TV Tam ratings?" (MacMahon 1999:116). The place of traditional music in a modern world, where value is often determined by sales figures rather than by "the wonder and the beauty of the music that has been given to us" by the past (115), is a serious issue for people who cherish and trans- mit the tradition.

Fintan Vallely clearly sets forth the tension between the continuity of a traditional music and the changing world in which it is played and en- joyed, a world that necessitates adaptation in the tradition. He notes that encroaching modernism has always been a force that reshapes the tradi- tion: "there always had been a commercial life, and music in Ireland was no different to that anywhere else in how it could both provide supple- mentary income and support full-time professionals. The blinders of the Gaelic League's, and, later, the CCE's [Comhaltas Ceoltóirí Éireann] 'means to an end' rule-bound protectionism fell away as it became evident that céilí dance is modern, that costumed dance is the creation of exiles, that 'traditional' standards are strongly influenced by recorded music and radio, and that the music is not just about *what* is played but *how* it is played, and that the priests and the state did not kill house dances — but modernization and the experience of exiles did" (Vallely 2000:151). Val- lely acknowledges that many traditional musicians in Ireland are wary of the current popularity of Irish music, fueled by stage extravaganzas such as *Riverdance* and often expressed via the professional pub session. Some critics such as Séamus Tansey (1999) perceive the currently fashionable fusion of Irish melodies with other forms of popular music as a threat to the integrity of the tradition.[13] There is concern over whether traditional means of teaching and learning the music will survive the age of the CD, whether master players will continue to be remembered in the playing of their tunes, whether unique repertoires and styles will persist or fade into extinction.

These fears can perhaps be best appreciated by remembering that the general acceptance of the genius of Irish traditional music is a hard-won understanding. The misconceptions and the prejudice surrounding Irish music in the not-too-distant past may have had a distinct effect on the way its most ardent practitioners view its current popularity. Traditional musicians of today have been given a priceless heritage. The tunes themselves — and the style in which they are played — convey unmistakable messages about Ireland and its people. In the eighteenth and nineteenth centuries, those messages were interpreted in ways that cast the Irish as degenerate and their splendid music as dangerously wild. Is it any wonder that musicians who have given their lives to the study and teaching of Irish traditional music would view its sudden worldwide popularity with suspicion?

The characteristics of Irish traditional music explored here also shed light on current controversies about the very concept of tradition itself. In a well-known argument, Eric Hobsbawm (1983:8) attempted to make a distinction between *custom* and *tradition*. Arguing that custom implies a continual practice, Hobsbawm maintains that custom is a purposeful and practical approach to the needs of the people who create and maintain it but that it does not preclude change or adaptation. Tradition, on the other hand, is a synthetic cultural formation adopted for the purpose of maintaining an invariant practice. Custom may be flexible, but tradition cannot be changed, and it therefore becomes a ritualistic or sacred activity. Clearly what Hobsbawm says about the flexible nature of customary practices accords with the characteristics of Irish traditional music that I have been exploring, and his delineation of the invariant nature of other more synthetic cultural practices touted as heritage fits with the common misconceptions about traditional music against which Nettl warns. His terminology, however, flies in the face of the terms used by scholars and practitioners alike of Irish traditional music.

13. Examples include the music of the very popular Afro-Celt Sound System or the delightful stylings of Niall Keegan. There is some feeling, however, that this may be a passing fashion. See Wallis 2001:24.

Not even a traditional music can be preserved in the form in which it was played two hundred years ago. This must be understood if the music is to be dealt with on its own merits and not as subject of continuing misconception. Perhaps the music of Ireland is too close to its musicians and the community that supports it to escape completely the creation of a mythos surrounding its origins, meaning, and preservation. It is clear, however, that if traditional music can survive the interpretations, transformations, and translations of the past, it can surely survive the commercial success of the present.

Works Cited

Blacking, John. 1987. *A common-sense view of all music: Reflections on Percy Grainger's contributions to ethnomusicology and music education*. Cambridge: Cambridge University Press.

Breathnach, Breandán. 1970. The dancing master. *Ceol* 3, no. 4:117–21.

———. 1971. *Folk music and dances of Ireland*. Cork: Mercier.

———. 1996. *The man and his music: An anthology of the writings of Breandán Breathnach*. Ed. Seán Potts, Terry Moylan, and Liam McNulty. Dublin: Na Píobairí Uilleann.

Brown, Terence. 1998. Music: The cultural issue. In *Music in Ireland, 1848–1998*, ed. Richard Pine, 37–45. Cork: Mercier.

Bunting, Edward. 1796. *A general collection of the ancient Irish music*. London: Preston.

Connolly, Seán. 1996. Approaches to the history of Irish popular culture. *Bullán* 2, no. 2:83–100.

Corcoran, Seán. 1991. What is traditional music? In *Traditional music: Whose music?* ed. Peter MacNamee, 2–9. Belfast: Institute of Irish Studies.

de Paor, Liam. 1989. *Tom Moore and contemporary Ireland*. Cork: Irish Traditional Music Society, University College Cork.

Giraldus Cambrensis. 1951. *A topography of Ireland*. Trans. John O'Meara. Dundalk: Dundalgan Press.

Grattan Flood, W. H. 1927. *A history of Irish music*. Dublin: Browne and Nolan.

Hamilton, Hammy [Colin]. 1999. Innovation, conservatism, and the aesthetics of Irish traditional music. In *Crosbhealach an Cheoil, 1996, The Crossroads Conference: Tradition and change in Irish traditional music,* ed. Fintan Vallely, Hammy Hamilton, Eithne Vallely, and Liz Doherty, 82–87. Cork: Ossian Publications.

Hobsbawm, Eric. 1983. Inventing traditions. In *The invention of tradition,* ed. Eric Hobsbawm and Terence Ranger, 1–14. Cambridge: Cambridge University Press.

Leppert, Richard. 1987. Music, domestic life, and cultural chauvinism: Images of

British subjects at home in India. In *Music and society: The politics of composition, performance, and reception,* ed. Richard Leppert and Susan McClary, 63–104. Cambridge: Cambridge University Press.

Leppert, Richard, and Susan McClary. 1987. Introduction. *Music and society: The politics of composition, performance, and reception,* ed. Richard Leppert and Susan McClary, xi–xix. Cambridge: Cambridge University Press.

MacMahon, Tony. 1999. Music of the powerful and majestic past. In *Crosbhealach an Cheoil, 1996, The Crossroads Conference: Tradition and change in Irish traditional music,* ed. Fintan Vallely, Hammy Hamilton, Eithne Vallely, and Liz Doherty, 112–20. Cork: Ossian Publications.

Moloney, Colette. 2000. *The Irish music manuscripts of Edward Bunting (1773–1843): An introduction and catalogue.* Dublin: Irish Traditional Music Archive.

Murphy, Michael. 1998. Race, nation, and empire in the Irish music of Sir Charles Villiers Stanford. In *Music in Ireland, 1848–1998,* ed. Richard Pine, 46–55. Cork: Mercier.

Nettl, Bruno. 1973. *Folk and traditional music of the western continents.* New Jersey: Prentice-Hall.

Neuman, Daniel M. 1993. Epilogue: Paradigms and stories. In *Ethnomusicology and modern music history,* ed. Stephen Blum, Philip V. Bohlman, and Daniel M. Neuman, 268–77. Urbana: University of Illinois Press.

Ó Crualaoich, Gearóid. 1998. The "Merry wake." In *Popular Irish culture: 1650–1850,* ed. James S. Donnelly Jr. and Kerby A. Miller, 173–200. Dublin: Irish Academic Press.

Ó hAllmhuráin, Gearóid. 1998. *A pocket history of Irish traditional music.* Dublin: O'Brien.

O'Neill, Francis. [1913] 1987. *Irish minstrels and musicians.* Reprint, Louth, Lincolnshire, England: Moxon.

Ó Súilleabháin, Mícheál. 1994. "All our central fire": Music, mediation, and the Irish Psyche. *Irish Journal of Psychology* 15, nos. 2–3:331–53.

O'Sullivan, Donal. 1952. *Irish folk music and song.* Dublin: Colm Ó Lochlainn.

Sommers Smith, Sally K. 1998. Landscape and memory in traditional Irish music. *New Hibernia Review* 2, no. 1:132–44.

———. 2001. Irish traditional music in a modern world. *New Hibernia Review* 5, no. 2:111–25.

Tansey, Séamus. 1999. Irish traditional music—the melody of Ireland's soul: Its evolution from the environment, land, and people. In *Crosbhealach an Cheoil, 1996, The Crossroads Conference: Tradition and change in Irish traditional music,* ed. Fintan Vallely, Hammy Hamilton, Eithne Vallely, and Liz Doherty, 211–13. Cork: Ossian Publications.

Trachsel, Mary. 1995. Oral and literate constructs of "authentic" Irish music. *Éire-Ireland* 30, no. 3:27–46.

Vallely, Fintan. 2000. The making of a lifelong companion: An editor's memoir. *New Hibernia Review* 4, no. 2:141–52.

Vallely, Fintan, Hammy Hamilton, Eithne Vallely, and Liz Doherty, eds. 1999. *Crosbhealach an Cheoil, 1996, The Crossroads Conference: Tradition and change in Irish traditional music.* Cork: Ossian Publications.

Wallis, Geoff. 2001. Compact discord. *Journal of Music in Ireland* 1, no. 5:24–27.

White, Harry. 1998. *The keeper's recital: Music and cultural history in Ireland, 1770–1970.* Notre Dame: University of Notre Dame Press.

Interpreting Ireland:
Literary and Historical Perspectives on
the Role of Interpreters in Ireland

Translation has been a feature of the relationship between language and tradition for centuries on the island of Ireland. Often the discussion of the tradition of translation itself has focused on the sentences on the page rather than on the words in the mouth. Here I will discuss not the physical traces of translation in translated texts, the "relics" described in my earlier book *Translating Ireland* (1996), but translation as part of the talk and conversation of villagers, town-dwellers, and political powers in troubled times. In other words, I will look at how to interpret *interpreting* (the term used to describe oral translation) as part of historical experience in Ireland.

There is an inherent paradox in the project. Because interpreting is an oral activity, except in exceptional circumstances it does not leave written records. Indeed, the oral dimension to the activity has often been used as a convenient reason for ignoring it altogether. As with oral cultures generally, then, any historical work must use the documentary evidence of the *scripta* to reconstruct the importance of the *verba*. Given that the Irish repeatedly came into contact with speakers of foreign languages both on the island and abroad, there is no gainsaying the importance of the manipulators of *verba* in more than one language in Irish history. In exploring aspects of the history of interpreting in Ireland, I want to investigate a number of notions, including the idea of embodied agency, the relative ethics of fidelity, the shift from recruiting native interpreters to training imperial ones, and the representative dynamics of interpreting encounters. In this essay I will examine these ideas in the context of certain specific historical situations, primarily the Anglo-Norman invasion of Ireland, the Tudor reconquest of the island, the French expedition of 1798, and court interpreting in nineteenth-century Ireland.

One of the primary characteristics of interpreting is that no appreciable time lag exists between the act of translation and the moment of reception. The interpreter translates for the listener at the same time as the person is speaking (simultaneous interpreting) or as soon as the person has stopped speaking (consecutive interpreting). The message and messenger are coterminous in time so that they are easily conflated. Although translation has a long list of martyrs and victims from William Tyndale to the Italian and Japanese translators of Salman Rushdie,[1] textual translation always potentially provides the possibility of anonymity. Moreover, the point of textual production is almost invariably remote in time and space from the point of textual reception. The applications of modern technology in the form of video interpreting and telephone interpreting have freed interpreting from spatial constraints, but for much of the history of humanity and indeed throughout much of the world to this day, interpreting is an exercise in bodily proximity. This proximity is why the conditions and context of utterance are always of a real and primordial concern to interpreters and are inseparable from the contents of the utterance. The interpreter is not free to say what he or she likes.

Interpreters in Irish history have not always been fallen angels, hopelessly compromised by circumstances. As narratives about interpreters illustrate, the monopoly of the scarce resources of language can confer on the interpreter the prestige and authority normally reserved for myth and majesty. This elevated status is apparent in one of the most important works in French to be produced in Ireland, the long verse chronicle commonly known as *The Song of Dermot and the Earl*.[2] The chronicle was composed around the year 1200 and eulogizes the exploits of Dermot mac Murrough and his Norman allies. The beginning of the chronicle has been lost, and the surviving text begins with a reference to the person who is the main informant for the story of Dermot's activities:

> . . . Par soen demeine latimer
> Que moi conta de lui l'estorie
> Dunt faz ici la memorie.
> Morice Regan iert celui,
> Buche a buche parla a lui

---

1. Willim Tyndale was executed in Antwerp in 1536 for his activity in translating the Bible into English. The Japanese translator of Salman Rushdie's *Satanic Verses* was murdered in 1991, the same year that saw the serious wounding of the Italian translator of the novel in a stabbing incident.

2. The text was given its title by Goddard H. Orpen, who was responsible for editing the chronicle in 1892.

Ki cest jest endita.
L'estorie de lui me mostra.
Icil Morice iert latimer
Al rei Dermot, ke moult l'out cher.
Ici lirrai del bacheler,
Del rei Dermod vus voil conter.

(Orpen 1892:ll. 1–11)

. . . by his own personal interpreter [literally *latimer*]
who related to me the account of him
which I record here.
This was Morice Regan,
who face to face spoke to him,
and related this tale.
He taught me the history of him.
This Morice was the interpreter
of King Dermot who held him dear.
Here, I shall quit talking about the squire
for I wish to tell you about King Dermot.

(Adapted from Picard 2003:74)

The word *latimer* originates in the Latin word *latimarius* < *latinarius*. The substantive derives from the Latin verb *latinare* meaning 'to translate into Latin'. As Jean-Michel Picard notes, "By 1086, when the forms *latinarius* and *latimarius* appear in the *Doomsday Book,* the latimer was a professional secretary and interpreter, translating and writing down in Latin the speeches and letters dictated to him in various languages" (forthcoming). Morice Regan, a native Irish speaker from Munster, is clearly designated as enjoying the close friendship of the Irish king, "ke moult l'out cher" ("who held him dear").

We are also told in the chronicle that a latimer is entrusted with the important mission of going to Wales to recruit soldiers and knights to fight for Dermot.

Dunc fit le conte passer
Un son demeyn latimer,
Al gros Reymund fist nuncier
Qu'i tost a lui venist parler,
Si li durreit a uxor
Le gentil conte sa sorur.

(Orpen 1892:ll. 2994–99)

This can be translated literally as

> Then the count sent
> One of his own latimers
> to tell Raymond le Gros
> that he should quickly come talk with him
> and that indeed he would give him as wife
> his own sister, sister of the noble count.
>
> (My translation)

Although it is not specifically indicated in the passage, one can surmise that it is Regan who is sent to enter into negotiations with the Norman notable Raymond le Gros. The language used in the negotiations is not mentioned, but it is presumably either French or Latin. Regan's activities are not confined to Hiberno-Norman tractations, as indicated in lines 1626–61, where he is involved in negotiating the surrender of the people of Dublin in the siege of 1170. The Scandinavian king of Dublin is named as Esculf Mac Turkil, and talks would presumably have been conducted in Irish, a language spoken by both Regan and Mac Turkil.

The interpreter in this chronicle is not an anonymous, shadowy figure. Instead, he is explicitly named, and his central role in what were momentous historical events in Irish history is made abundantly clear. The perception of the interpreter as potential spy or betrayer of secrets is a powerful source of suspicion of interpreters,[3] but here, in a sense, Regan plays on his role as informant not to jeopardize but to enhance his reputation, as well as that of his patron. In *The Song of Dermot and the Earl,* it is the interpreter who is presented as informing the narrative, and he is thus able to emphasize his own centrality to the events that he describes. His role as informer is therefore not tainted with the opprobrium of double-dealing; on the contrary, the chronicler makes him credible as a witness. In addition, the narrator of the *Song* emphasizes the dual function of orality in the case of Morice Regan. We are told, after all, that, "Morice Regan iert celui, / *Buche a buche parla a lui* / Ki cest jest endita" ("This was Morice Regan, / *who face to face spoke to him,* / and related this tale"; emphasis added). The most obvious function is, of course, interpreting itself, which is defined by its constitutive orality. But the intrinsic orality of interpreting leads us to the second function, which is the *testimonial* function of interpretation. It is the fact that the interpreter is obliged by the nature of

---

3. In the case of historical figures such as Cortés's interpreter, la Malinche, the suspicion has given rise to active hostility (Mirandé and Enríquez 1979:24).

the interpreting activity to be physically present at the important moments of mediation recounted in the chronicle that makes the interpreter particularly important as a source of historical information. Here, it is the intrinsic orality of interpreting that will confer authority on the literacy of the textual account.

The authors of the chapter "Interpreters and the Making of History" in *Translators through History* make the following observation: "The spoken word is evanescent. Our knowledge of the past performance of interpreters tends to be derived from such sources as letters, diaries, memoirs and biographies of interpreters themselves, along with a variety of other documents, many of which were only marginally or incidentally concerned with interpreting" (Bowen et al. 1995:245). The assertion is self-evidently true in *The Song of Dermot and the Earl*. We know about Morice Regan's activities through the text of the chronicle. On the other hand, it would be mistaken to establish a hierarchy of precedence where the oral is seen as invariably subordinate to the textual, its transience depriving it of lasting value. What is highlighted by the thirteenth-century Hiberno-French text is that Regan's influence as a historical figure relies precisely on the oral nature of his work that brings him into direct contact with the main protagonists of late-twelfth-century Ireland, protagonists who are Irish, Welsh, Normans, and Scandinavians. It is the oral engagement of the interpreter rather than the textual traces of the chronicle that significantly determines the outcome of events. It is because Regan is an interpreter, not despite the fact, that his influence is enduring. His embodied agency that makes him uniquely susceptible to physical containment or destruction accounts as well for his particular power in directly using languages to effect change at a crucial point in Irish history. His presence also indicates the importance of Irish as having equal status to the other languages in late-twelfth-century encounters.

Regan's knowledge of Latin confers status on him, but knowledge of the same language makes interpreting a more problematic activity in Tudor Ireland. In a letter to the Gaelic chieftain O'Carroll, Lord Deputy Bellingham intimates his unease at the use of Latin as a medium of communication between English and Irish speakers: "And where you would have answher in latyn, remember you lyve under a englyshe kyng, which requirythe in so gret a cyrcut of countrey as you occupy to have sum honest man whom you myght trust to wryte your letters in englyshe, and I lykewhyse trust to expounde myn sent unto you."[4] Latin was suspect not so much because of the intrinsic nature of the language itself — after all it remained a staple of English public school and university education — but because its most able practitioners were Catholic priests whose loyalty to Reformation England could not be counted on. The difficulty with an "answher in latyn" was that it might fall into the hands of someone who was not an "honest man," most probably a priest, and therefore likely to be hostile to the Crown's interest. Bellingham's suspicions were not, of course, wholly unjustified. Access to education and sojourns on the European continent meant that the Irish Catholic clergy of the sixteenth and seventeenth centuries would find themselves acting as important language mediators in times of conflict. The conflicts themselves ranged from minor administrative difficulties to important affairs of state.

One such figure was Hugh McCaghwell (Aodh Mac Aingil; also Aodh Mac Cathmhaoil), a Franciscan priest who was appointed archbishop of Armagh on 27 April 1626 but who died unexpectedly on 22 September of the same year while still in Rome, awaiting his departure to Ireland. As a theologian of some distinction and a lecturer in theology at the Ara Caeli, the principal Franciscan house in Rome, his knowledge of Latin was extensive (Giblin 1995:64). Born in County Down in 1571 into an Irish-speaking family, he was author of *Scáthán Shacramuinte na hAithridhe* (*The Mirror of the Sacrament of Penance*), one of the Irish texts printed in 1618 by the Franciscan press in Louvain in the Spanish Netherlands. As tutor to the two sons of Hugh O'Neill, Hugh and Henry, McCaghwell became a close confidant of the earl of Tyrone and was sent as a legate on O'Neill's behalf to Spain with O'Neill's son Henry in 1599. They settled in Salamanca, where McCaghwell attended lectures and acquired Spanish during this period. It was in Salamanca that he decided to enter the Franciscan order (Ó Cléirigh 1985:48). In 1610 he was appointed guardian of St. Anthony's College in Louvain to succeed Donagh Mooney (McCaghwell had arrived in Louvain in June 1607). McCaghwell's command of English is evident as early as 1609 from his work trying to negotiate terms with the English government and the English king on behalf of the earl of Tyrone. On 3 July 1614, a letter from Whitehall written by Robert, earl of Somerset, urges William Trumbull, the English representative in Brussels,

___
4. Quoted in Jackson 1973:21.

to have no further dealings with McCaghwell: "It is his majesty's pleasure that you forbear from further treaty with the friar or any other touching Tyrone, in expectation of being received to his majesty's grace upon those terms of restitution to his dignity and lands in Ireland, because that would disjoint the whole course which his majesty hath been so careful to settle in that country" (quoted in Jennings 1964:354).

McCaghwell's linguistic abilities meant that while he was negotiating with the English, he was also giving an account of Irish affairs to Guido Bentivoglio, the papal nuncio to Flanders; McCaghwell was supplying information to the Spanish court as well. In a letter to Cardinal Borghese, dated 3 May 1608, Bentivoglio refers in passing to his valuable informant:

> Per quanto ho inteso a quest'hora il Conte di Tirone deve esser in Roma. . . .
> So senz'altro, ch'egli e partito forzato da gli Stati del Re. E lo so dalle cose
> passate tra qual Franciscâno e me come piu volte significai pienamente a
> Vostra S. illustrissima.   (Quoted in Giblin 1995:84)

> As far as I know at this time the Earl of Tyrone should be in Rome. . . . I
> know for certain that he was forced to leave the King's States. And I know of
> things that happened through this Franciscan as I fully indicated several
> times to your Holiness.   (My translation)

Though the memoranda of Bentivoglio's conversations with McCaghwell went from Flanders to the Holy See in Italian, it would appear that they conversed in both Spanish and Latin. In 1613, when McCaghwell, along with Eugene Matthews, archbishop of Dublin, and Christopher Cusack, president of the Irish College at Douai, presented Bentivoglio with a document that included details on the military needs of the native Irish, the document was drawn up in Latin (Giblin 1995:84).

In the fraught world of the early-seventeenth-century Irish diaspora, McCaghwell is interpreter in the richly ambiguous sense of the term, his role both linguistic and hermeneutic. He not only brings information, perceptions, and sentiments across the Irish, Latin, English, and Spanish (and, later in Rome, Italian) languages but also interprets the meanings of events and plans for Trumbull, Bentivoglio, O'Neill, his contacts in the Spanish court, and all who fall within the ambit of his multilingual activism.

It is noteworthy as well that McCaghwell's interpreting activities were not confined to the destinies of nations but that he exercised his skills in a variety of domains. When the Spanish Infanta sent her confessor to Louvain in 1610 with the intention of moving the English Augustinian Canonesses Regular of the Lateran from their house and replacing them with another order of nuns, McCaghwell was appointed as the confessor's interpreter. The English nuns were distraught at their likely fate and pleaded with the confessor through McCaghwell that they be allowed to stay. McCaghwell reassured the religious women that he would ensure that the Infanta's confessor did intercede on their behalf with the Infanta, and it was the Irish interpreter who eventually brought them the welcome news that they would be allowed to remain in the house (Hamilton 1904:75). McCaghwell was also involved in persuading the town council of Douai on 18 February 1616 that the planned foundation of English Franciscans in the town would not place any extra burden on the inhabitants of Douai and its environs (Lepreux 1875:266–71).

In both instances McCaghwell is to the fore in promoting the interests of his English coreligionists so that in his work as interpreter/mediator, religious loyalties clearly transcend ethnic or linguistic differences. McCaghwell's role as interpreter cannot be seen as purely a matter of linguistic dexterity. To function as interpreter at the level he did, he needed to have a thorough understanding of the politics and culture of the different parties in the Irish conflict. His sympathy for and understanding of native Irish culture is borne out not only by his writings in Irish but also by his support for the scholarly activities of his Louvain colleagues who would in part help to refashion the Irish language itself through their publishing activities (Cronin 1996:59–65). McCaghwell's knowledge of English politics is alluded to in the strange episode of George Ligonius, an alumnus of the English College in Rome. Ligonius moved to Louvain in 1615 where he resided with the Jesuits. He then decided to write a book to demonstrate to King James I the harm he was doing to English Catholics. Before he set sail for England armed with his opus, the Jesuits, fearful of the damage he might cause, had him arrested and his book confiscated. Ligonius appealed to the internuncio in Brussels and the Holy See, asking that a prominent theologian be allowed to inspect the contents of his book. The theologian he named was Hugh McCaghwell, because he claimed McCaghwell was a man of notable piety, a famous professor of theology, and a man exceptionally well versed in English affairs (Giblin 1995:90). That a relative outsider such as Ligonius should have such a favorable view of McCaghwell's familiarity with English political life meant that it was not only Trumbull who viewed McCaghwell as a worthy mediator with whom he could do business.

The strategic value of interpreting to the colonization process in six-
teenth- and seventeenth-century Ireland is evident in the succession of
named interpreters who are in the employ of both the colonizers and the
soon to be colonized. Given that only a small fraction of the Irish population spoke English when the reconquest of Ireland began in earnest under
the Tudors, it was inevitable that Ireland would become the theater for a
very real war of words. Submission, for example, was meaningless unless
it was intelligible. Consider the 1567 account of a visit by O'Connor Sligo
to Elizabeth I in London: "and there in his Irish tongue, by an interpreter,
declared to her Majesty that the chief cause of his coming was to see and
speak to the illustrious and powerful Princess, whom he recognised to be
his sovereign Lady, acknowledging that both he and his ancestors had
long lived in an uncivil, rude and barbarous fashion, destitute of the true
knowledge of God, and ignorant of their duty to the Imperial Crown of
England."[5] If it was symbolically expedient to understand those willing to
accept the new dispensation, it was even more important to understand
those who were not. As the Gaelic Irish leaders naturally dealt with their
followers through Irish, it was necessary to engage the services of inter-
preter/informants who would practice, in somewhat less exalted circumstances than McCaghwell, the antique trade of spying or intelligence
gathering.

It is interesting to note that ethnic intermarriage has a particular role to
play in the evolution of interpreting networks. For example, in a letter
from Lord Deputy Sidney to his successor, Grey de Wilton, in 1580,
Sidney urges de Wilton to spare no expense in the recruitment of spies. He
mentions three informants as particularly valuable: Thomas Masterson,
Robert Pipho, and Robert Hartpole, all of whom were English speakers
who had married Irish-speaking women (Egerton 1968:71). An English-
speaking male who married an Irish-speaking woman could use the language skills of his spouse to help him acquire information on the political
or military activities of the native Irish. This is what I have termed elsewhere a *heteronomous* interpreting strategy, whereby the colonizers have
recourse to the services of the natives to interpret for them (Cronin 2002).
Alternatively, the Anglophone male could have recourse to an *autonomous* interpreting strategy whereby he learns Irish from his spouse and
puts his own knowledge of the language to use in espionage. In this in-

5. Quoted in Jackson 1973:22; cf. Palmer 2001:193.

stance, it is the colonist himself who acquires the language of the native through a relationship with the natives. The recurrent danger of the heteronomous strategy was, of course, that the native's loyalties would revert back to the natives.

As William Jones observed in his *Grammar of the Persian Language* (1771), for British officials "it was found highly dangerous to employ the natives as interpreters, upon whose fidelity they could not depend" (quoted in Niranjana 1992:16). The Elizabethan adventurer Captain Thomas Lee would have agreed with Jones, though in Lee's case the infidelity was closer to home. Lee had the ambition of establishing a "principality" for himself on the borders of the two Irish counties of Kildare and Wicklow. He married the Irish-speaking daughter of a local landholder in the area and then set about extending his own holdings through the ousting or elimination of both his English and Irish rivals in the area. Donald Jackson notes that Lee's exploitation of his wife's interpreting abilities had an unforeseen outcome: "[Lee] employed his Irish-speaking wife as an intermediary in a plot to dispose of one of the most dangerous of the local Irish rebels. Unfortunately, it turned out her sympathies were with the rebel, to whom she betrayed the plan" (Jackson 1973:24). Fidelity for interpreters in situations of conflict, as Lee would discover to his cost, is a relative rather than absolute notion.

One way of maintaining loyalty is to regularize the situation of interpreters and give the activity some form of public recognition. This was the tactic adopted by the Spanish Crown in Latin America, where, in the *Recopilación de Leyes de las Indias* (*Compendium of the Laws of the Indies*) between 1529 and 1630, we find fifteen laws governing the activities of interpreters. The 1529 law gives the *lenguas*, 'interpreters' (literally 'tongues'), the formal status of auxiliaries of "Governors" and "Justice"; by 1563 the laws recognize a professional hierarchy of interpreters, establish specific compensation for particular language tasks, and enunciate a general set of ethical principles. In return for this newfound status, interpreters were forbidden from requesting or receiving jewels, clothes, or food from the native peoples (Bowen et al. 1995:262–63).

There was an incipient professionalization in the Irish situation with the creation in the mid–sixteenth century of the official post of "interpreter of the Irish tongue," attached to the establishment of the lord deputy in Dublin. William Dunne held the position in the early period of Elizabeth's reign, and he is explicitly mentioned as interpreter in a docu-

ment from 1570 where an Irish saying is described as having been "interpreted by Christopher Bodkin, the Archbishop of Tuam, and Mr. Dunne"
(Hughes 1960:24). Thomas Cahill would later occupy the same position
in 1588. The long-term survival of a cadre of official interpreters, however, depended on the languages of the island of Ireland being accorded
equal status, which did not happen. Though there were inconsistencies in
English-language policies in Ireland and a tension between the evangelical
commitment of Protestantism to the vernacular and the cultural wars of
the Crown, Irish had been effectively removed from the official, public life
of the country by the end of the seventeenth century (Cronin 1996:47–
90). In these circumstances, although interpreters would still be employed
in the law courts, as we shall see, there would be no retention of interpreters in the new Ascendancy administration. Interpreters who were to
prove so useful in furthering the aims of conquest through intelligence
operations and negotiations would paradoxically become victims of their
own success. Once the regime was fully in place, to have a body of official
interpreters would be to offer recognition to a language that was seen as
indissociable from sedition and disloyalty. Indeed, when official interpreters emerged once more in Ireland, it would be as a measure to give
Irish comparable official status to English, though by this stage, it was
English, not Irish, that was the majority language of the country (Daltún
1983:12–14).

As Jean Delisle notes in his introduction to Ruth A. Roland's *Interpreters as Diplomats,* "language has always been more than a simple
communication tool: it has also been a mark of national prestige, and
interpreters have brought this prestige to the international arena" (Delisle
1999:2). The presence of an interpreter is not simply a matter of expedi-
ency but confers as well a particular status on a language and suggests a
symmetrical dimension to political relationships. This dimension of status
was especially relevant in Tudor Ireland, where conquest had not only to
do with territorial acquisition and military supremacy but also with the
progressive acculturation of the native Irish.[6] The practice of interpreting
facilitates communication by removing the obstacle of language, but
through the person of the interpreter, it also establishes the *distance of
difference.* In other words, the use of an interpreter by Hugh O'Neill in his

6. See the most recent authoritative survey of the period, Nicholas Canny's *How Ireland
became British* (2001).

dealings with Elizabeth I (even though he himself spoke English) was a way of initiating dialogue that nonetheless marked the cultural and political distance and difference between the two parties, thereby constructing interpreting as an activity of both interaction and resistance. Crucially, the change from the seventeenth- to the eighteenth-century practices of interpreting in Ireland is a shift in what R. Bruce W. Anderson calls the "arena of interaction" (1976:209). Although interpreting practices were present in the political and legal arenas of interaction in Ireland in the sixteenth and seventeenth centuries, the greater part of the eighteenth century would see the exclusion of interpreting from the political arena of interaction. Thus, though interpreters would still be used in the courts, their absence from the public sphere of politics signaled a decisive change in the fortunes of Irish, the uncoupling of the language from structures of power and prestige, that would have such damaging long-term consequences for the Irish language.

The reentry of interpreting into the politico-military arena of interaction in Ireland at the end of the eighteenth century was the result of dramatically changed political conditions. French support for the armed insurrection of the United Irishmen in 1798 materialized most memorably in the landing of French troops at Killala, County Mayo, under the leadership of General Jean-Joseph Humbert. A problem that had been anticipated by the French in their preparations for the Irish expedition was that of language. Humbert in particular was persuaded of the urgent necessity of recruiting an interpreter who had mastered both French and Irish and knew some English as well. He was eventually introduced to an Irish-speaking officer in the French army, Henry O'Kane, initially referred to as "MacKeon" (Bertaud 1990:225). The officer in question was in fact a Mayo-born priest who had emigrated to France and in 1788 had become a curate in the parish of Saint Hermand, near Nantes in Brittany. Obviously attracted to the radical new ideas that were current in late-eighteenth-century France, O'Kane became a member of an Irish freemason lodge in France known as Les Irlandais du soleil levant (Keogh 1993:182; Hayes 1945:53). On Humbert's instructions, O'Kane was commissioned as staff officer and official interpreter to the French expedition to Ireland. O'Kane proved to be a brave soldier and able interpreter during the Connacht campaign, and in a letter of 1800 "le citoyen Henry O'Keane" was praised by Humbert as having shown commendable bravura and intelligence in

1798.[7] When the insurrection was finally put down by the Crown forces, O'Kane was taken to Castlebar and court-martialed on a charge of high treason. He was sentenced to death, but unlike many of his compatriots, he was fortunate in receiving a reprieve, returning to France, where he served with distinction in the republican and Napoleonic Wars. He was subsequently awarded the Legion of Honour and retired in 1815.

Along with Morice Regan, Henry O'Kane is another Irish interpreter who appears in verse, this time in the lyrics of a song that was especially common in North Mayo in the nineteenth and twentieth centuries. Guy Beiner has transcribed and translated what may be the only surviving full version of the song.[8] The first stanza goes:

> Tá na Franncaig 'teacht thar saile
> fada a gcabhair ó Clanna Ghaedheal
> Tógaidh suas bhur gcroidhe 's bhur n-aigneach
> 's suiblaidh [sic] amach le Corpréal Caen.

> The French are coming over the sea
> Long has been their help from Clanna Gael
> Raise up your heart and your mind
> And step out with Corporal Kane.

The song was most probably a rallying song aimed at encouraging local men in Mayo and further afield to join the Franco-Irish army (Hayes 1979:243). As in *The Song of Dermot and the Earl,* the interpreter again occupies a prominent position — indeed, is the main subject of the song. For the anonymous author of the verses, it is not General Humbert but his interpreter who becomes the incarnation of the cause of the United Irishmen, just as Morice Regan was closely identified with the victory of the Anglo-Normans. One could argue that interpreters in periods of conflict are always potentially open to *metonymic* appropriation.[9]

In the case of interpreters, it is their active engagement as a party to conflict that makes them representative figures. Thus they occupy a metonymic relationship to the cause that they serve and come to embody (in every sense of the word). But the intrinsic duality of the interpreter's task,

7. Letter signed in Paris, 29 Nivose Year 8 (1800), quoted in an unpublished study by Guy Beiner on Henry O'Kane. The author is indebted to Guy Beiner for allowing him access to the original material he has collected on the Irish interpreter.

8. Beiner, unpublished manuscript.

9. By contrast, women, for example, have long featured in figurative representations of Irish resistance to conquest and occupation through the centuries, but they have done so primarily in a *metaphoric* mode. See McPeake 2001 for a comprehensive overview.

mediating between more than one language and culture, complicates any simpleminded or closed sense of allegiance. This dimension is apparent in the statements of O'Kane's political enemies, detailed in their accounts of the events of 1798. The staunchly loyalist Sir Richard Musgrave, for example, noted that O'Keon, as he called the Mayo interpreter, "was humane, having on all occasions, opposed the bloodthirsty disposition of the popish multitude." Musgrave further remarked that O'Kane was "free from the sanguinary spirit which actuated the common herd" and that "more than once he prevented rebels from murdering the Protestant prisoners" (Musgrave 1995:546–47, 560–61, 565). The Protestant Bishop Stock claimed with reference to O'Kane that "his language breathed nothing but mildness and liberality," and he too noted O'Kane's key role in preventing the ill-treatment of local Protestant loyalists (quoted in Freyer 1982:59). If O'Kane's enemies found his presence reassuring, his putative allies, the Gaelic Irish, were less sure. Recounting local 1798 folklore, Dominick McDonnell of Muingrevagh in County Mayo claimed that O'Kane was remembered as a "brave soldier" and a "great talker" and that no one "could handle a crowd like him." However, he was also feared because of his involvement in recruitment efforts, which sometimes involved violent intimidation. As McDonnell put it, "A lot of people hid themselves away, for there was terror on them," and he gave the example of fifty men hiding in the house of Honour McNulty of Knockboha, where, during the course of the search of the house, O'Kane shot the dog (Hayes 1979:219).

In view of the treatment meted out to the native Irish by the British military and yeomen, the reluctance of the former to get involved in the conflict was understandable. Whereas captured French soldiers and officers were treated according to normal conventions governing the treatment of prisoners of war, the Irish soldiers were summarily executed as traitors (O'Donnell 1998:74–76). O'Kane's knowledge of his native language made him well qualified to be a "great talker," an essential attribute of the effective interpreter, and reputed skill with crowds is testimony to his communicative efficacy. It is this skill that must have delighted Humbert with his choice of O'Kane as official French interpreter in Ireland. But it was precisely this ability that also produced ambivalent responses to O'Kane in local folklore. On the one hand, he is the subject of song, praise, admiration. On the other, O'Kane's ability to speak the local language, along with the strong-arm tactics used when persuasion failed, meant that he was a much more disruptive presence in a local community than a French officer, say, with little Irish. O'Kane's knowledge of Irish made the Gaelic Irish much more vulnerable. If some of them tried to hide away physically in a house, it was because there was no hiding from what O'Kane was saying. He spoke their language. They knew exactly what he meant. And the consequences terrified them. In this way the interpreter in song, folklore, and local history comes to represent the very real human dilemmas of a population who find themselves caught up in violent conflict or war.

As mentioned earlier, though interpreters were excluded from the political arena of interaction after the collapse of the Gaelic Order, they did continue to function in the legal system.[10] In a society where even at the beginning of the nineteenth century the majority of the population was Irish-speaking, it was neither practicable nor desirable to try people in a language they did not understand, though this, of course, did happen on occasion. A persistent theme in representations of interpreting practice, whether in literature or legal folklore, is the interventionist nature of the interpreter. The modern notion of the court interpreter as an impartial, self-effacing conduit for the business of the court is noticeably absent.

A typical example is an anecdote relating to Daniel O'Connell attending the Cork assizes. In Irish O'Connell is beseeched by an old man to defend his only son, who is on trial, and he offers the Liberator his life savings, ten guineas, to take the case. O'Connell refuses, explaining that his arrangements with his colleagues and his professional code of conduct would not allow him to renege on other commitments, but he recommends giving the ten guineas to his colleague James Lyons, claiming that Lyons would be just as effective as he in defending the son of the poor farmer.

> At that, the old man burst into tears and joined a despondent group that had watched the interview. When the court rose and O'Connell left the building, he saw across the road a delighted crowd around a handsome youth. Most prominent in the crowd was the old man he had met that morning. The great advocate strode up and held out his hand.
> "The boy is free?"
> "He is, thank God."

10. For a preliminary survey of the role of interpreters in the legal system, see Ní Dhonn-chadha 2000.

"Well, you took my advice then and gave your ten guineas to James Lyons."

"Oh Christ no! I didn't waste it — I gave it to the interpreter."

(McArdle 1995:55)

The clear implication is that the interpreter is not only willing to take a bribe but that he will exploit his knowledge of the two languages and the linguistic ignorance of the magistrates to achieve specific outcomes.[11] In the absence of transcripts of the Irish spoken by witnesses or defendants in nineteenth-century court cases, it is not possible to substantiate or invalidate allegations of interpreter bias. However, one can ask why the image of the interventionist or, indeed, manipulative interpreter persisted in the Irish legal system. It is possible to advance two reasons, one related to language and power and the other connected to tensions between literacy and orality.

The use of legal instruments to further land expropriation in the seventeenth century and the presence of penal legislation in the eighteenth were not designed to inspire Irish Catholic confidence in the British legal system in Ireland. Thus, though the courts might be used to seek redress, they were generally viewed with suspicion. In what would be perceived as a strongly asymmetrical situation from the standpoint of the dispossessed, language was a potential point of strength, a way of tilting the balance in favor of those who were disadvantaged not only in the legal arena but in many other realms of Irish public life of the period. In such a situation — replicated in colonial encounters throughout the world — interpreters are potentially power brokers for the powerless. The adverb here is deliberate: "potentially" because the interpreter may view his or her status as a sign of election and an opportunity to curry favor with the master; the interpreter may either collaborate in the designs of the master or exact a high price (ten guineas) for his or her pliancy. Repeated references to the wily interpreter or the devious defendant who insists on having an interpreter while being able to understand and speak English make interpreters and interpreting suggestive metaphors of politico-linguistic anxieties in nineteenth-century Ireland. As the Irish-speaking population gradually translated itself into English throughout the century (whether at home or abroad), anxieties about the "fidelity" of interpreters and the knowledge of English on the part of defendants or witnesses appear to reflect wider concerns

---

11. Women interpreters appear in Irish courts only in the late twentieth century.

about political discipline and control in post-Union Ireland. In a sense the court interpreter was an uneasy reminder that areas of Irish life and experience were still outside the Anglophone purview. Moreover, interpreting would inevitably be an object of continual suspicion for it acts as an index of Anglicization. The very need to be interpreted shows the limits of the process of linguistic assimilation, but it is the motives of the clients (the duplicitous natives) rather than the paymasters of interpreting that are continually called into question.

In a much-cited incident from a court case at the beginning of the twentieth century, a Clare barrister, Michael McNamara, who also acted as court interpreter in Irish, administered the oath in the following manner to a defendant who was up on a charge of unpaid debts:

> The Counsellor addressed him in Irish: "Listen carefully now to the terms of the oath, and repeat after me — 'If I do not tell the truth in this case — ' "
> "If I do not tell the truth in this case — "
> "May a murrain seize my cattle — "
> "What's that, Counsellor? Sure that's not in the oath?"
> "Go on and repeat your oath: 'May a murrain seize my cattle — ' "
> "Oh! Glory be to God! 'May a murrain seize my cattle — ' "
> "May all my sheep be clifted — "[i.e. fall over a cliff].
> "Yerra, Counsellor, what oath is that your [sic] trying to get me to take? Sure I never heard an oath like that before!"
> "Go on, sir; don't argue with me; repeat your oath: 'May all my sheep be clifted — ' "
> "Oh! God help us all! 'May all my sheep — ' yerra, Counsellor, are you sure that's in the oath?"
> "Go on, sir!"
> "Oh! God! 'May all my sheep be clifted — ' "
> "May my children get the falling sickness — "
> "Arrah, Counsellor, tell his Honour that I admit the debt, and I only want a little time to pay!"   (Healy 1939:152–53)

Leaving aside the somewhat unorthodox practice of the prosecuting lawyer doubling up as interpreter, the humor of the episode lies partly in the inappropriate use of particular kinds of language in a formal or legal setting. The ritual curse that McNamara puts into the mouth of the unfortunate defendent is taken from the oral culture with which the defendant is familiar. It is the curse of the defendant's unwritten, oral culture that McNamara, "who had a great dread the defendant would swear himself out of the debt by barefaced perjury," knows to be considerably more potent than the formal oath of the court's literate culture (Healy 1939:152).

Unlike written translation, interpreting is by definition an oral encounter; thus, differences between an orality overdetermined by literacy and an orality that retains many of the features of primary oral culture will be strongly marked.[12] It is a general failure to recognize such differences that explains in part the notion of the dissembling native in nineteenth- and early-twentieth-century interpreting stories. In listing characteristics of orally based thought and expression, Walter J. Ong mentions the redundant or "copious" nature of oral discourse. In writing the mind can concentrate on moving ahead in a linear fashion because the written text is there to remind it of what has already been said. In oral discourse the situation is different because there is nothing to refer to outside the mind, the oral utterance vanishing as soon as it has been uttered. Therefore, in primary orality, "the mind must move ahead more slowly, keeping close to the focus of attention much of what it has already dealt with. Redundancy, repetition of the just-said, keeps both speaker and hearer surely on track" (Ong 1998:40). In addition, acoustic problems in addressing large audiences, where it is necessary to repeat what has been said so that everyone gets a chance to hear, and in dealing with the fatal threat of hesitation in oral delivery by continuing to say more or less the same thing while thinking of something else to say, mean that "oral culture encourages fluency, fulsomeness, volubility" (ibid.). The copiousness of speech is evident in the Clare interpreting story — the curse is repeated in a number of different formulations and could be extended indefinitely were it not for the panic-stricken admission of guilt.

For those in a position of authority, where authority itself is invested with the legitimacy of literacy through laws, decrees, and legal instruments, the speech of those from primarily oral backgrounds with no access to literacy in their own language will appear when interpreted as "blarney" or "blather," a wordy, whimsical subterfuge.[13] The assumption readily made by literates is that "fulsomeness" and "volubility" are suspect deviations from plain speech. Interpreters, then, by remaining *faithful* to the *copia* of their clients in Irish, would paradoxically present them as somehow being *unfaithful* to the truth. In a way, what is asked of interpreters in these situations is to make a dual translation, from oral

12. This is not to argue that orality has no place in discussions of written translation. On the contrary, as Maria Tymoczko (1990) has convincingly demonstrated, it is often of paramount importance.

13. The Irish language, of course, had its own traditions of literacy which informed oral culture in Ireland, but the absence of literacy in Irish as a realistic option for the vast majority of Irish speakers meant strong residual primary orality in Irish. See Ó Ciosáin 1997.

mode to literate mode and from one language to the other. Interpreters are faced with a double bind. If they do not make the switch from oral to literate mode, there is the recurrent difficulty of a systematic misrepresentation of the motives and nature of speakers of a language coming from a predominantly oral culture. Conversely, if they do make the switch, the risk is another form of infidelity, a failure to represent adequately the epistemic wholeness of an oral worldview.[14] There is a sense in which, professional ethics notwithstanding, the interpreters' guineas in preindependence Ireland were indeed hard-earned.

Though interpreters do not feature anywhere as a recognizable group in literary and historical surveys of Ireland, their enduring presence is a most graphic testimony to the changing political fortunes of the island over the centuries. The fortunes are still changing as Ireland has shifted from being a country with historically high levels of emigration to becoming a destination for immigrants.[15] Thus, interpreters are now being called on to provide services for asylum seekers and political refugees who have either no English or a limited grasp of the language. Once again interpreters are at the forefront in negotiating the new plurilingual and multicultural realities of Ireland as they have done so often in the past.

Works Cited

Anderson, R. Bruce W. 1976. Perspectives on the role of interpreter. In *Translation: Applications and research,* ed. Richard W. Brislin, 208–28. New York: Gardner Press.

Beiner, Guy. 2001. To speak of '98: The social memory and vernacular history of Bliain na bhFrancach. Ph.D. diss. University College Dublin.

Bertaud, Jean-Paul. 1990. Forgotten soldiers: The expedition of General Humbert to Ireland in 1798. In *Ireland and the French Revolution,* ed. Hugh Gough and David Dickson, 220–37. Dublin: Irish Academic Press.

Bowen, Margareta, David Bowen, Francine Kaufmann, and Ingrid Kurz. 1995. Interpreters and the making of history. In *Translators through history,* ed. Jean Delisle and Judith Woodsworth, 245–77. Amsterdam: John Benjamins.

14. For the questions this dilemma raises for ethnography and anthropology, see Sturge 1997.
15. In 2000 almost twenty thousand work permits and visas were issued to foreign nationals, and between 2001 and 2006 it is estimated that two hundred thousand immigrant workers are needed to meet the demands of the domestic Irish labor market.

Canny, Nicholas. 2001. *How Ireland became British*. Oxford: Oxford University Press.

Cronin, Michael. 1996. *Translating Ireland: Translation, languages, cultures*. Cork: Cork University Press.

———. 2002. The empire talks back: Orality, heteronomy, and the cultural turn in interpreting studies. In *Translation and power*, ed. Maria Tymoczko and Edwin Gentzler, 45–62. Amherst: University of Massachusetts Press.

Daltún, Séamas. 1983. "Scéal rannóg an aistriúcháin." *Teangeolas* 17:12–17.

Delisle, Jean. 1999. Introduction to *Interpreters as diplomats: A diplomatic history of the role of interpreters in world politics* by Ruth A. Roland, 1–6. Ottawa: Ottawa University Press.

Egerton, Peter, ed. 1968. *Life of Lord Grey of Wilton*. 1847. London: Camden Society.

Freyer, Grattan, ed. 1982. *Bishop Stock's "narrative" of the Year of the French*. Ballina: Irish Humanities Centre.

Friel, Brian. 1981. *Translations*. London: Faber and Faber.

Giblin, Cathaldus. 1995. "Hugh McCaghwell, O.F.M., archbishop of Armagh (†1626): Aspects of his life. In *Dún Mhuire Killiney, 1945–1995: Léann agus seanchas*, ed. Benignus Millet and Anthony Lynch, 63–94. Dublin: Lilliput.

Hamilton, Adam. 1904. *The chronicles of the English Augustinian Canonesses Regular of the Lateran at St. Monica's in Louvain*. Vol. 1. Edinburgh: Sands and Co.

Hayes, Richard. 1945. Priests in the independence movement of '98. *Irish Ecclesiastical Record* 25:45–59.

———. 1979. *The last invasion of Ireland: When Connacht rose*. Dublin: Gill and Macmillan.

Healy, M. 1939. *The old Munster circuit*. Cork: Mercier.

Hughes, J. L. J., ed. 1960. *Patentee officers in Ireland, 1173–1826*. Dublin: Irish Manuscripts Commission.

Jackson, Donald. 1973. The Irish language and Tudor government. *Éire-Ireland* 8, no. 1:21–28.

Jennings, Brendan, ed. 1964. *Wild geese in Spanish Flanders, 1582–1700*. Dublin: Irish Manuscripts Commission.

Keogh, Dáire. 1993. *The French disease: The Catholic Church and Irish radicalism, 1790–1800*. Blackrock: Four Courts Press.

Lepreux, Jean. 1875. Documents relatifs à l'établissement à Douai des Récollets anglais. *Analectes pour servir à l'histoire écclésiastique de Belgique* 12:266–79.

McArdle, J. 1995. *Irish legal anecdotes*. Dublin: Gill and Macmillan.

McPeake, Margaret. 2001. Embodying Ireland: Representing woman as nation and community in Irish writing. Ph.D. diss., University of Miami.

Mirandé, Alfredo, and Evangelina Enríquez. 1979. *La Chicana: The Mexican-American woman*. Chicago: University of Chicago Press.

Musgrave, Richard. 1995. *Memoirs of the different rebellions*. 4th ed. Enniscorthy: Round Tower.

Ní Dhonnchadha, Máire. 2000. Irish language interpreting in the courts since the 1850s. Master's thesis, Dublin City University.

Niranjana, Tejaswini. 1992. *Siting translation: History, post-structuralism, and the colonial context.* Berkeley: University of California Press.

Ó Ciosáin, Niall. 1997. *Print and popular culture in Ireland, 1750–1850.* New York: St. Martin's.

Ó Cléirigh, Tomás. 1985. *Aodh Mac Aingil agus an scoil nua-Ghaeilge i Lobháin. 1935.* Dublin: An Gúm.

O'Donnell, Ruán. 1998. *1798 diary.* Dublin: Irish Times Books.

Ong, Walter J. 1988. *Orality and literacy: The technologizing of the word. 1982.* London: Routledge.

Orpen, Goddard H., ed. and trans. 1892. *The song of Dermot and the earl: An Old French poem from the Carew manuscript no. 596 in the Archiepiscopal Library at Lambeth Palace.* Oxford: Clarendon.

Palmer, Patricia. 2001. *Language and contest in early modern Ireland.* Cambridge: Cambridge University Press.

Picard, Jean-Michael. 2003. The French language in medieval Ireland. In *The Languages of Ireland,* ed. Michael Cronin and Cormac Ó Cuilleanáin, 68–81. Dublin: Four Courts.

Sturge, Kate. 1997. Translation strategies in ethnography. *Translator* 3, no. 1:21–38.

Tymoczko, Maria. 1990. Translation in oral tradition as a touchstone for translation theory and practice. In *Translation, history, and culture,* ed. Susan Bassnett and André Lefevere, 46–55. London: Pinter.

Triangulating Opposition:
Irish Expatriates and Hagiography
in the Seventeenth Century

In 1623 two Irish Franciscan priests were traveling from the Irish College in the university town of Louvain, in the Spanish Netherlands, to Rome to participate in a general chapter of the Franciscan order. En route they stopped in Paris at the Irish College there. One of them was Hugh Mc-Caghwell (Aodh Mac Cathmhaoil or, later, Aodh Mac Aingil, 1571–1626), the guardian of the Irish College of St. Anthony in Louvain and definitor general of the Franciscan order. His companion was Father Patrick Fleming (1599–1631), a young Franciscan in his midtwenties who had been sent off from Ireland when he was thirteen to be educated on the Continent, in order to insure the preservation of his Catholic faith, and who had joined the Franciscans in Louvain at eighteen. In Paris these two Franciscans met another, Hugh Ward (Aodh Mac an Bhaird, 1593–1635), who was on his way to Louvain from the Irish College in Salamanca. Ward was five or six years older than Fleming, but the two had been in Europe for about the same amount of time.

These three Franciscans, along with the many other Irish clerics abroad at that time, might be described as latter-day *peregrini*, clerical émigrés following in the footsteps of Columbanus and the other Irish monks abroad more than one thousand years earlier in the Merovingian and Carolingian eras. It was the upheaval of the Reformation that brought the seventeenth-century peregrini from Ireland to the Continent. Paradoxically, however, their journey took them into the heart of the religious controversy of the age rather than away from it.

In Ireland, until the arrival of Oliver Cromwell's army in 1649, the religious upheaval of the age was experienced for the most part without bloodshed. The Church of England, with the monarch at its head and a usage that moved further and further from Roman Catholic tradition, was

established as the only sanctioned church.[1] For many of the Irish, however, laypeople living far from the Anglicized area around Dublin, this
transformation at the top was a barely noticeable tremor. But it made a
real difference to Catholic priests and aspiring priests with a strong attach-
ment to the ways of the old religion, at least to those with any sort of
intellectual pretensions. Such men could neither study nor preach openly
in Ireland after about 1560, and their situation became even more difficult
after 1605, when "seminary priests" were expelled from Ireland by royal
proclamation. It became fairly common practice during this period for
young men from intellectual recusant families to leave Ireland for the
Continent. Many of them took up residence in "Irish colleges" that were
established at universities throughout the Catholic parts of Europe — Italy
and Spain, France and the Low Countries — from about 1590 on.[2] In
Europe these Irishmen were inevitably far more acutely aware of the issues
of doctrine and practice that divided Protestant from Catholic than they
would have been at home, and they would have been more acutely aware
as well of the ways in which the Catholic church had responded to the
challenges of Protestant reform at the Council of Trent (1545–63).[3]

Another paradox of expatriation was that these Irishmen, abroad in
the European archipelago of monasteries and Irish colleges, had the opportunity to form connections with countrymen whom they would probably never have met had they stayed at home. Those who felt the need to
leave Ireland in the late sixteenth and early seventeenth centuries were not
merely Catholics, but Catholics of a particularly intellectual bent — those
who wanted to study and to teach Catholic philosophy and theology.
They came, by and large, from families with a tradition of learning. Our
three Franciscans certainly belonged to this group.

Hugh McCaghwell, an Ulsterman born in Downpatrick and educated
early on in Wales, became tutor to the sons of Hugh O'Neill of Tyrone,
one of Ireland's last great Gaelic chieftains. McCaghwell left Ireland for
the Continent in 1599, but he was not driven by religious persecution,
which hardly reached into O'Neill country at the time. Rather, he went as

1. The Reformation may be said to have come to Ireland with the Act of Uniformity
passed by the Irish Parliament in 1650 and the Twelve Articles (of Belief) in 1566. For
general background on the Reformation in Ireland, see Bradshaw 1978; Canny 1979; Corish
1985:63–122; Ford 1985; and Moody, Martin, and Byrne 1978.
2. For general background on the Irish colleges on the Continent in the seventeenth
century, see Walsh 1973 and Hogan 1870–71.
3. On the Roman Catholic response to the Protestant Reformation, see Luebke 1999.

companion to one of his pupils, Henry O'Neill. They were on an embassy to the Spanish court in quest of support for Hugh O'Neill's armed resistance to the Elizabethan administration of Ireland—the embassy that would ultimately lead to the arrival of a Spanish naval force at Kinsale and to O'Neill's defeat there in 1601. McCaghwell, in other words, was both a learned man and a man of the world, involved in the most consequential Irish politics of his time. But he never returned from that embassy to Spain. Instead, he joined the Franciscan order in Salamanca and earned a degree in theology.[4]

Hugh Ward was a scion of the Mac an Bhaird family of Tír Conaill (otherwise known as Donegal). His family were hereditary bards to the O'Donnells, chieftains of Tír Conaill and sometime rivals, sometime allies, of the O'Neills. Hugh's elder brother was Eoghan Ruadh (Owen Roe) Mac an Bhaird (ca. 1570–1630), *ollamh*, or chief poet and professor of poetry, to Red Hugh O'Donnell. O'Donnell, in turn, was the son-in-law and comrade in arms of that same Hugh O'Neill whose sons were the pupils of Hugh McCaghwell. In fact, Eoghan Ruadh joined Hugh O'Donnell's son Ruaidhrí O'Donnell and Hugh O'Neill when they left Ireland for good in 1607. The sort of hereditary bardic family that Hugh Ward came from had a profound tradition of historical learning—they were the keepers of the genealogies of their patrons, of the history of Ireland, of the history of their own province in particular, and of the stories about the legendary origins of the Irish. Although Hugh Ward embraced the study of theology and philosophy rather than of poetry and history, he was by background no stranger to scholarship.[5]

Patrick Fleming's family had come to Ireland with the Normans in the twelfth century, and he had relatives among the aristocracy in Louth, where he grew up. One of his uncles, Father Christopher Cusack, is said to have been not only the administrator but also the patron of a number of Irish colleges in Flanders; it was to this uncle that Patrick was sent for his education when he was thirteen. In Ireland, Fleming belonged to the world of the so-called Old English, a group that numbered many recusant Catholics among its members.[6] These descendants of the earliest English incursions into Ireland were of particular concern to the English in the late sixteenth and seventeenth centuries, with their new and intense sense of

4. On McCaghwell the most detailed work is Ó Cléirigh 1935.
5. On Hugh Ward see Hogan 1870–71:56–77.
6. On Patrick Fleming see Hogan 1870–71:193–215.

"Englishness." It was more threatening to the new order that such families should resist the reform of religious practice and adhere to the authority of Rome, rather than ceding supremacy in ecclesiastical matters to the English monarch, than that the utterly alien and barbarous Irish should do so. Consequently, although Patrick Feming's background was relatively privileged, for him and his family recusancy was more dangerous than it was for McCaghwell and Ward.

It is unlikely that all three would have met in Ireland. McCaghwell and Ward, men of learning attached to the households of the two most powerful chieftains in the North, might conceivably have encountered each other, but neither would have come across Fleming. Nor would either of them have been likely to encounter Father Thomas Messingham, a secular priest and rector of the Irish College in Paris. Messingham was the editor of *Florilegium insulae sanctorum* (*Anthology of the Isle of the Saints*), a collection of Irish saints' lives culled from printed sources that would be published in Paris the following year, 1624. In Paris, however, all these Irishmen did encounter one another.

The four clerics are representative of the Irish nation in miniature — a nation defined by its adherence to Catholicism in the face of the Reformation — that was taking shape in Europe in the early seventeenth century on a smaller scale but a bit earlier than it did in Ireland itself.[7] This expatriate nation, composed for the most part of clerics, would do a great deal to define Ireland for itself and for the world in the coming years. Their instruments included the printing press, which was a tool of early modern nation building everywhere in Europe, and the glories of a heroic history. They also employed media that might seem at first glance to belong to the past, to the Middle Ages, rather than to an emerging future dominated by distinctive nation-states — the Latin language and fantastic stories of miracle-working saints.

Our three Franciscans constituted just one little band in a larger Ireland abroad, but they were not an unimportant little group, and it is their enterprises that I propose to follow. What came of their meeting in Paris in 1623 was a monumental project of collecting and publishing the lives of Irish saints. The idea — which seems to have originated with Fleming, the gentleman of Old English stock, and Ward, the scion of a long line of Gaelic bards — was this: in the monastic libraries of Europe were to be

7. The alliance of "Old English" with Gael on the basis of religion was a feature of the late 1630s and 1640s.

found manuscript copies of lives of Irish saints, who, by virtue of being so many, had earned for Ireland long since the epithet *insula sanctorum,* 'Isle of Saints.' The three Franciscans agreed to locate as many of these documents as they could in their travels through the network of European monasteries. Copies of these texts they would send back to Paris to provide Father Messingham with material for a second volume of Irish hagiography. This pious enterprise might seem to be of little consequence to the formation of Irish national identity, which was to a very considerable extent a seventeenth-century development, but I will argue that it constitutes an important chapter in that process.

Two great Irish-language works compiled in the seventeenth century are unquestionably the most important monuments of Irish nationalism in that era, namely, Geoffrey Keating's *Foras Feasa ar Éirinn* (*History of Ireland*) and *Annála Ríoghachta Éireann* (*Annals of the Four Masters*). Both of these — the former in narrative mode, the latter annalistic — represent the history of Ireland as fully as their sources permit, from the earliest times to the coming of the Normans in 1170 in Keating's case and in the *Annals of the Four Masters* to about 1600. Both respond to accusations of Irish barbarism, immorality, irreligion, and "incivility" — the absence of political institutions capable of maintaining peace and administering justice — made during the sixteenth and early seventeenth centuries by English writers such as Stanihurst, Spenser, and Moryson.[8] The Four Masters and Keating answer those accusations with implicit and explicit claims for the antiquity, historicity, and continuity of Irish tradition and for the heroism, sanctity, and erudition of the Irish character. Their engagement with the Tudor accounts of Ireland constitutes a dialogue that is central to our understanding of the beginnings of Irish nationalism in the response of the subjugated to their representation by the conqueror.

Keating's *History* and the *Annals of the Four Masters* presented Irish history and Irish achievement within a frame that was insistently and exclusively Irish, as the reference to *Éire,* the Irish-language name of Ireland, in both titles — *Foras Feasa ar Éirinn* and *Annála Ríoghachta Éireann* — suggests. That is, it was precisely and emphatically as *Irish* Ireland, the society vilified in so much English writing, that Keating and the

8. The principal texts in the dialogue between the Gaelic Irish and the English on Irish civility are the following: Richard Stanihurst, *De rebus in Hibernia gestis* (1584); Edmund Spenser, *A View of the Present State of Ireland* (1596); Fynes Moryson, *Of the Commonwealth of Ireland* (1620); Geoffrey Keating, *Foras Feasa ar Éirinn* (ca. 1634); and the *Annals of the Four Masters* (1632–36).

Four Masters celebrated their nation. Important as it was for the Irish to embark on this discourse of nationhood, in these texts they were talking to themselves. In fact, even the English who had provoked them could not have read these books, written in Irish, had they wished to. There was no full printed edition of the *Annals of the Four Masters* until the mid-nineteenth century or of Keating's history until the early twentieth. They circulated in manuscript—Keating far more widely than the *Annals*—among their Irish audience.

The representation of Ireland to the larger world required a different language from that of the *Foras Feasa* and the *Annals of the Four Masters*. Neither the Irish language nor the rhetoric of nationalism could succeed in making Ireland fully present on the European stage. For that purpose in seventeenth-century Europe, Latin was the appropriate medium. In his groundbreaking study of the early foundations of Irish nationalism *Mere Irish and Fíor-Ghael,* Joep Leerssen emphasizes the importance of the Irish language to expatriate Irish intellectuals of the Counter Reformation (Leerssen 1997:259–64). He cites long lists of devotional and catechetical works published on the Continent in Irish and links them, quite properly, to the grammars of Irish produced within the same circles, works that lent to the Irish language the dignity of an ancient and complex tongue worthy to take its place beside Latin as a grammatical language, capable of systematic analysis. As the bardic tradition became less and less productive under the pressures of English plantation and recomposition, the Irish language was becoming less and less effective as the medium in which identity might be mirrored, fabricated, and enhanced. Bonaventura Ó hEoghusa and other writers were working hard to reverse that trend, not only by celebrating the dignity of the language but also by attempting to raise the level of literacy in Irish among its speakers.[9] Nevertheless, in attending to this important work of shoring up the edifice of the Irish language at a moment of irreversible crisis for the traditional bardic institutions that for

9. Gilbride O'Hussey (Giolla Brighde [Bonaventura] Ó hEoghusa, d. 1614) was the brother of Eochy O'Hussey (Eochaidh Ó hEoghusa, d. 1612), *ollamh,* "chief poet," to Hugh McGuire (Aodh Mac Uidhir), chief of Fermanagh. Thus, his original milieu was the same world of northern Irish poets and intellectuals in which Hugh Ward and Hugh McCaghwell were rooted. Like Ward and McCaghwell, Gilbride O'Hussey, although he composed a number of bardic poems, both religious and secular, left Ireland to study on the Continent. He entered the Franciscan order at Louvain, taking "Bonaventura" as his name in religion. He published a Latin grammar of Irish, *Rudimenta Grammaticae Hibernicae (Rudiments of Irish Grammar),* and also *An Teagasg Críosdaidhe,* an Irish-language catechism.

centuries had served as its guardians, we ought not fail to consider the implications of the use of Latin in the seventeenth century.

Latin, of course, had remained the universal language of European intellectual life, and its prestige was enhanced by the efforts of Renaissance humanists to elevate the standard of Latin style to a level more nearly approximating the refinements of Classical Latin than had been common in the Middle Ages. Struggles were afoot as early as the sixteenth century to validate the use of the vernaculars in highbrow literary endeavors, but there is no doubt that Latin remained the language of learning. It was not only the linguistic badge of Roman Catholicism in an era when religious reform advocated the use of vernacular languages as the means by which divine truth might reach ordinary people, but also the language of humanistic scholarship, the language of Erasmus (ca. 1466 – 1536) and of much of the writing of such innovative thinkers as Giordano Bruno (1548–1600), Francis Bacon (1561–1626), Johannes Kepler (1571–1630), and René Descartes (1596–1650).

Not surprisingly, then, Ireland defended itself against sixteenth- and seventeenth-century English assaults on its civil and moral dignity in Latin as well as in Irish. Philip O'Sullivan-Beare, an erstwhile Cork aristocrat in self-imposed exile in Spain and Portugal after the Battle of Kinsale, published a "Catholic history" of Ireland in Latin, *Historiae Catholicae Hiberniae* (Lisbon, 1621), focusing on the Elizabethan wars in which he and his family had participated. Although far less learned than and greatly inferior in style to Keating's *Foras Feasa*, O'Sullivan-Beare's book was a kind of Latin analogue to it, as was the *De regno Hiberniae sanctorum insula commentarius* (*Commentary on the Kingdom of Ireland, the Island of Saints,* 1598; published in Louvain in 1632) by Peter Lombard, an alumnus of the Irish College in Louvain who became archbishop of Armagh.

What is surprising is the extent to which this flurry of Latin literary activity in defense of Ireland's dignity seems to have been inspired first and foremost not by Elizabethan *English* attacks on Irish civility but by resentment of the claims made by Thomas Dempster (ca. 1579–1625) on behalf of the antiquity and dignity of *Scotland*. Dempster, son of an impoverished Scottish gentleman, was a peripatetic, contentious, prolific, and irascible intellectual who lived at various times in Louvain, Tournai, Douai, Paris, Poitou, Toulouse, Montpellier, London, Rome, Pisa, and Bologna. He was himself among the peregrini of the Counter Reformation. In *Scotia illustrior* (*The More Illustrious Scotia,* 1620) and *Menologium*

Scotorum (*A Record of the Scots,* 1621), Dempster had perpetrated an act of blatant etymological imperialism. In the earlier Middle Ages, the Latin terms *Scotia, Scotus,* and *Scotti* might refer either to Scotland and its Gaelic inhabitants or — and this was in fact the more common usage — to Ireland and the Irish. There were less ambiguous terms, based on *Hibernia* for Ireland and things Irish, and on *Alba* and *Caledonia* for things Scottish. But Scotia was a perfectly ordinary and respectable name for either country. Dempster, however, culled references to Scotia and the Scotti from old books, asserting that every use of these terms referred not to Ireland but to Scotland proper. Next, he claimed for Scotland every holy man and woman, every wandering monk, every scholar, that Ireland had ever produced. Unlike the writings of Stanihurst, Spenser, Camden, and Moryson, Dempster's books were not directed primarily against Gaelic Ireland in support of English civility. They were, rather, a gathering of old stones from an ancient monument to build a fanciful Scottish castle, in the process casually removing those stones from the heap of materials from which the Irish might construct their own national identity. Even though *Scotia illustrior* was placed on the Vatican's *Index librorum prohibitorum* (*Index of Forbidden Books*) in 1623 because of its factual inaccuracies, it aroused tremendous anxiety and ire among Irish expatriate patriots. This is apparent in the titles of the some of the books produced in Ireland's defense, such as Bishop David Rothe's *Hibernia resurgens,* that is, *Ireland Resurgent, or An Antidotal Mitigation of the Bite of the Ancient Serpent in which is Temperately Dashed to Bits the Intemperate Maundering of Thomas Dempster . . .* (1621), or even the volume that was the long-delayed first fruit of that meeting in Paris in 1623, John Colgan's *Acta sanctorum, The Lives of the Saints of the Older and Greater Scotia, or Ireland the Island of Saints,* published in 1645.[10]

Dempster's books elicited such vehement responses from the Irish on the Continent because, by couching his assault on their national history in Latin, he had moved the topic of Irish dignity onto the stage of European intellectual life. The insular dialogue of Gaelic and colonized Ireland with English-speaking England, her colonizer, became a conversation open to all. The third language created a new arena for the debate, one in which

---

10. *Hibernia resurgens, sive refrigerium antidotale adversus morsum serpentis antiqui in quo modeste discutitur, immodesta parecbasis Thoma Dempsteri a Muresk Scoti de repressis mendicabulis* (Rouen, 1621); *Acta sanctorum veteris et maioris Scotiae seu Hiberniae sanctorum insulae* (Louvain, 1645).

the Irish did not labor under the political disadvantage inevitable to an opposition of the Irish language and the hegemonic language of the colonizer, English.

To return to our three Franciscans and their project of collecting Irish saints' lives for publication on the Continent, we can see how Dempster's claims rankled Fleming in a letter he wrote to Hugh Ward from Rome in September 1623. "It would grieve me," he writes, "if . . . this present opportunity should be lost to us, which, perhaps for years, may not occur again. The present time is specially favorable to us: for the Sacred Congregation has imposed a precept on Dempster to abstain in future from treating of such historical matters, and whilst this precept lasts, it would be important to us to set forth our state of the question; wherefore, whatever you may have in Louvain send it without delay to Paris to Messingham and, hereafter, if God gives us the means, we can republish the same documents more elegantly and accurately" (quoted in Hogan 1870–71:196–97).

Thus, it was in the context of Dempster's Scottish chauvinism that the project of collecting and publishing Irish saints' lives was conceived. The fruits of the Irish hagiographic project would be published in Latin, for reasons both simpler and more various than those which motivated Dempster himself to use Latin. First of all, the nature of early medieval hagiography virtually ensured that the documents discovered would be Latin. Even much of the hagiographic material collected for the project in Ireland was written in Latin. In 1626 Ward sent Brother Michael O'Clery (Mícheál Ó Cléirigh) back to Ireland to collect and compile the records of Irish history as well as to search out documents pertaining to the Irish saints. The principal achievement of O'Clery and his three collaborators was the *Annals of the Four Masters,* which constitutes, along with Keating's *Foras Feasa,* part of a body of Irish-language texts that would shape a sense of Irish national identity, as I have discussed. But a great deal of hagiographic material was collected as well by the Franciscans who had returned to Ireland to rescue Irish traditions by copying manuscripts. There were vernacular texts among those collected in Ireland, but the ones that were eventually included in the two volumes that the Franciscan hagiographic project produced were first translated into Latin. Latin was the language of their texts, notes, and prefaces as well.

A year after the project of collecting Irish saints' lives was conceived, its center had shifted from Paris to the Irish Franciscan College in Louvain, and Ward had replaced Messingham as the prospective editor. In a letter from him in Rome to Ward in Louvain, dated 27 July 1624, Fleming complains about Messingham's having failed to keep his promises and proposes that under Franciscan editorship the published lives of the saints will avoid the prolixity of those which he had printed.[11] In the event, however, Fathers Fleming and Ward both died before their hagiography project began to bear fruit in print. Fleming was murdered in 1631, and Ward died in Louvain in 1635. The direction of the work was undertaken at that point by John Colgan (Seán Mac Colgáin, 1592–1658), another Irish Franciscan from a learned family on the Inishowen Peninsula in Donegal. It was Colgan who oversaw the preparation and production of the only two volumes ever published by the Louvain project. The first of these, published in 1645, was a collection of about 270 lives of saints whose feasts fall in January, February, and March, with the notable exception of Saint Brigit (February 1) and Saint Patrick (March 17). It bore the title mentioned earlier, *Acta sanctorum veteris et maioris Scotiae seu Hiberniae sanctorum insulae* (*Lives of the Saints of the Older and Greater Scotia, or Ireland the Island of Saints*). The second volume, published in 1647, was devoted entirely to lives and other texts pertaining to the three national patron saints of Ireland, Patrick, Columba (Colmcille), and Brigit, a strategy made necessary by the sheer quantity of material on these three. It is called *Triadis thaumaturgae, seu divorum Patricii, Columbae et Brigidae, trium veteris et maioris Scotiae, seu Hiberniae sanctorum insulae, communum patronorum acta,* or *Lives of the Three Wonderworkers or Divines, Patrick, Columba, and Brigit, The Three Common Patrons of the Older and Greater Scotia, or Ireland the Island of Saints,* generally known as the *Trias thaumaturga*.

Saints could hardly be a neutral subject in seventeenth-century Europe, let alone the Low Countries where the Catholic Spanish Netherlands abutted on and coexisted tensely with the United Provinces where Calvinism had become the state religion in 1622. The publication of a collection of acta sanctorum celebrating traditional Christian saints in Latin asserted a Roman Catholic refusal to discard saints as vestiges of primitive superstition; to that extent the publication was a gesture of resistance to the principles of Protestantism. At the same time, Colgan's volumes represented a response to and an engagement with Protestant principles in their

11. See Jennings 1934:213–14; Hogan 1870–71:199.

reliance on the authority of textual traditions, which can be interpreted as a characteristically Protestant reliance upon the authority of the Word. Indeed, the underlying idea of the Jesuit Bollandist effort to gather, edit critically, and publish lives of all the saints of the Catholic church, not just those associated with one smallish island—as it was first conceived by Heribert Rosweyde (1569–1629) and as it has been carried on for four hundred years in what was the Spanish Netherlands[12]—was to remove the encrustations of legend, rhetoric, and "error" from the records of historical human persons, so that they might, as it were, shine forth in their genuine sanctity.

Catholic apologists sought to establish the textual authority of the lives of the saints as a kind of ancillary scripture, in contrast to Protestants, who by and large rejected the notion of such subsidiary texts, insisting on the absolute uniqueness of the Word of God as recorded in the Bible. It was the absence of any basis for a cult of the saints in Scripture that caused most Protestants to reject such veneration as idolatry and superstition. The Roman Catholic Council of Trent (1545–63) countered by affirming the value of invoking the saints and of venerating their relics, but there was a perceptible effort in the seventeenth-century Catholic church to control that process and to emphasize the "heroic virtue" of missionary saints and the founders of religious orders rather than the miracle-working powers that are so often what devotees look for in a saint.[13] Robert Bellarmine (1542–1621), the Jesuit architect of a great deal of Catholic Counter Reformation teaching, considered medieval lives of the saints something of an embarrassment; he observed that they are full of things that are "unsuitable, trivial, and improbable, likelier to induce laughter than edification" (quoted in Delehaye 1920:13, my translation). So from a certain perspective, the collection and publication of early saints' lives at this moment in history was primarily a gesture of resistance to change. In the face of a cultural landscape in upheaval, the celebration of traditional Christian saints asserted an intention to preserve old ways of mapping the sacred past. Thus, the Franciscan hagiography project, to an even greater extent than O'Sullivan-Beare's *Historiae Catholicae Hiberniae,* not only moved the topic of Irish national identity onto the inter-

12. See the *Acta sanctorum* of the Societé des Bollandistes (1643–).

13. See Peter Burke, "How to Become a Counter-Reformation Saint," in Luebke 1999: 130–42.

national stage by employing the medium of Latin but also marked the international stage in question as unambiguously Roman Catholic.

By weighing in on the side of saints, the Irish Franciscans at Louvain made a unique claim for Ireland. The compilation of its saints' lives, an effort duplicated at the time by no other nationally or geographically exclusive enterprise, was an assertion of Ireland's claim to be the *insula sanctorum*, 'isle of saints', a term first applied to Ireland as early as the eleventh century and in fairly common use from the twelfth century on, as Richard Sharpe (1991:3–5) has shown. For Colgan, as the preface to the *Acta sanctorum* makes clear, Ireland's history of sanctity is to be read against the Norman Conquest and the contemporary suppression of Roman Catholicism by the heirs of that conquest. In the European context the work of this "nation" of expatriate Irishmen elaborated and confirmed a very particular representation of Ireland: as holy, as Catholic, as deeply rooted in the past.

Of course, Latin was not only the language of humanistic learning but also the language of the "universal" Roman Catholic church, a sign and medium of its difference from national churches that employed vernacular languages for a variety of theological, pastoral, and political reasons. Thus, it was vital to the project of the Counter Reformation that it sustain the tradition of Latin in its promotion of Catholicism. The fact that most of the saints' lives gathered in Louvain were in Latin made them serviceable to the purposes of the Counter Reformation, and the fact that the gathering of saints' lives was almost by definition a Counter Reformation project also prescribed Latin as the most appropriate language for them. On the Continent, at the geographic heart of the controversies of the Reformation, veneration of medieval saints was overwhelmingly a mark of Catholic sympathies. The work that Fleming, Ward, and Messingham undertook to perform in 1623 may have been motivated by Dempster's assault on the history of Ireland, but it was inevitably implicated in the Catholic work of the Counter Reformation by the nature of the texts and the climate of the times in Catholic Europe. The Irish saints belonged not only to Ireland but also to a particular international Christian tradition, and they were of potential interest to European literati whose interest lay not in Ireland, or in Ireland's relationship to England, but in its Roman Catholic culture. The sheer abundance of holy persons of Irish birth whose lives were documented by texts of considerable antiquity helped to win for Ireland privileged status in the European network of Catholic monarchies and institutions. The status, however, was inextricably associated with Roman Catholicism and with Ireland's early Christian past. It was these aspects of Irish history, rather than the heroic struggle against English oppressors that O'Sullivan-Beare had celebrated in his *Historiae Catholicae Hiberniae,* or even the more encompassing history of martial glory, learning, and sanctity that Geoffrey Keating had woven out of Irish tradition, that would shape Irish identity as it was perceived on the Continent. Latin afforded the means by which Irish apologists could reach an audience beyond Britain, and Catholic veneration of the saints afforded the opportunity to do so. Ireland achieved a national identity in the European mind, but that identity was constructed of very particular materials, ancient and decidedly Catholic.

Latin was simultaneously a universal language for European intellectuals and the marked language of the Roman Catholic church; it could serve these two disparate purposes because of its deep roots in the past. By contrast, print was a relatively new technology, yet it too had both a neutral universal aspect and a particular sectarian association: as Latin was identified with Roman Catholicism, printing had a Protestant connotation. It was the printing press that enabled the religion of the Word, the effort to put a Bible into everyone's hands. Protestant evangelism, in turn, contributed significantly to the spread of the printing press. Because Protestants made such effective use of the new technology, Catholic apologists had to respond in kind. During the Counter Reformation the press was an important arena of combat between the Roman and Protestant churches. Consequently, it was natural that the Irish Franciscans at Louvain should seek to publish their collection of saints' lives in printed editions, even though the *Annals of the Four Masters* and Keating's *History of Ireland* would circulate in manuscript for several hundred years. It was through their participation in the world of the European Counter Reformation that the Louvain Franciscans were able to present the lives of Irish saints in printed Latin editions to a world beyond that of Ireland and England. This use of the medium of print was another factor in defining Ireland for Europeans as the "isle of saints" and a bastion of Roman Catholicism.

Colgan's volumes were not the first printed collections of Irish saints' lives. I have already mentioned Messingham's *Florilegium* of lives, the "pilot project," if you will, that got the whole enterprise rolling. Nor was Messingham the first to publish Irish hagiographic texts; the lives in his

Florilegium were derived in turn from other printed sources of the fifteenth and sixteenth centuries. What distinguished the Louvain books was their scope and size. The first volume includes acta for more than 270 saints; the sheer number reflects the encompassing, one might say even national, scope of the project. Like the Irish colleges that made the enterprise possible, that first volume of the *Acta sanctorum* is a kind of representation of Ireland abroad. It is a consciously crafted representation, too, that by the sheer critical mass of holy people offered to the world's inspection seeks to counterbalance the assertions about Irish ignorance and immorality that filled the writings of the Tudor "ethnographers."

Moreover, what distinguishes the second volume, the *Trias thaumaturga,* is not the plenitude of saints but the plenitude of texts about the triad of saints dealt with in the volume. The juxtaposition of their numbers — seven lives of Patrick, five of Columba, six of Brigit — makes us feel that all the available texts pertaining to the three principal national saints must be included. This is not, in fact, the case, but the combined actuality of the number of texts gathered here and the impression of fullness that they give defines the volume as a definitive dossier of each of the three national saints. These ample collections mark Patrick, Columba, and Brigit as holy persons of considerable status, worthy to take their places beside other saints of the universal church. The two volumes thus make a claim on behalf of the Irish church to rightful inclusion among the great Catholic nations.

It was important that the Louvain volumes were printed, but there was nothing in them that could not have been encompassed in a manuscript, at least in theory. There is a tradition of Irish manuscript anthologies of saints' lives stretching back to the Middle Ages, and the collection of the principal documents of the Patrician dossier in the Book of Armagh approximates in a way the Louvain effort. More often, however, manuscript collections of saints' lives included only one life for any given saint, as did Colgan's own 1645 volume. There is also no evidence that Colgan's books were produced in large runs or that they were widely disseminated. Moreover, they are large volumes, not intended to be distributed widely for the formation of the Irish clergy like many of the devotional and catechetical works that came off the Louvain press. They were rather monuments of the acta sanctorum than manuals of spiritual edification, intended for installation in monastic — especially Franciscan — libraries.

The publication of a collection of Irish saints' lives would hardly have been possible in seventeenth-century Ireland, where the relatively few print shops were licensed by the king for the publication of books that were primarily intended for use in the exclusively Protestant Trinity College Dublin. Yet print was essential to the Irish acta sanctorum project. It was the goal of publication that drove its enormous effort at collection, collation, and annotation. Fleming's and Ward's researchers and copyists were motivated by the prospect of contributing to a monumental collection that would be defined by its publication in print as both cutting-edge and definitive. The apparent capacity of print to establish an unchangeable text enabled the Bollandists' vision of saints' lives that had been pared down to an ancient authenticity; print was the antithesis of manuscript transmission and its attendant accumulation of marginalia. For the Louvain Franciscans, as for the Jesuit Bollandists, it was print that made saints' lives potential weapons in the religious controversies of the age, part of a very current discourse despite their venerable antiquity.

Thus, it was once again the Continental exile of Roman Catholic intellectuals from seventeenth-century Ireland that made possible the engagement of Irish culture with the latest trends and technologies. Shifting the ground of the debates in which Irish national identity was crafted from Ireland and Britain to Europe afforded the Irish some opportunity to emerge from the shadow of the colonizer's definition of their history and to forge alliances with the rest of Catholic Europe. However, the nature of the Louvain project ensured that the representation of Ireland in Europe would be — and would remain for a very long time — that of a nation holy, Catholic, learned in matters divine, and deeply rooted in the past. It was simpler than the way that Ireland constructed itself for itself — as noble, heroic, ancient, and literary, as well as holy, Catholic, and learned. While the more complex version of Irish identity would shape and reshape the ways in which Ireland thought about itself in the eighteenth, nineteenth, and twentieth centuries, it was the *insula sanctorum* that the larger world discovered in the seventeenth century.

A hundred years before the Wild Geese alighted on European shores, an expatriate nation of Irish clerics, through their efforts to collect, catalogue, and publish the lives of the Irish saints, made a major contribution to the definition of Ireland for itself and for the world. Their work would serve for a time as a foundation stone for nonsectarian efforts at nation building in the eighteenth and early nineteenth centuries and as a tool of sectarian self-definition in the late nineteenth and early twentieth centuries.[14] Latin is the language that made the work so important. It is difficult to see beyond the dialectic of Irish and English in a reading of Irish linguistic traditions, and easy to forget that Latin was still a vibrant medium in the seventeenth century. Transcending the political oppositions and cultural hierarchies associated with the dichotomy of Irish and English, Latin spoke to an international and multisectarian audience of intellectuals in the seventeenth century. At the same time, paradoxically, it carried a Roman Catholic connotation that would make Colgan's volumes revered sources for Catholic polemicists of the later nineteenth century.

Works Cited

Annala rioghachta Eireann: Annals of Kingdom of Ireland by the Four Masters, from the earliest period to the year 1616. 1848–51. Ed. and trans. John O'Donovan. 7 vols. Dublin: Hodges and Smith.

Bradshaw, Brendan. 1978. Sword, word, and strategy in the Reformation in Ireland. *Historical Journal* 21:475–502.

Canny, Nicholas. 1979. Why the Reformation failed in Ireland: Une question mal posée. *Journal of Ecclesiastical History* 30:1–27.

Corish, Patrick J. 1985. *The Irish Catholic experience: A historical survey*. Dublin: Gill and Macmillan.

Delehaye, Hippolyte. 1920. *A travers trois siècles: L'oeuvre des Bollandistes, 1615–1915*. Brussels: Bureaux de la Société des Bollandistes.

Ford, Alan. 1985. *The Protestant Reformation in Ireland, 1590–1641*. Frankfurt: Peter Lang.

14. An exclusive identification of Irish saints' lives with the Counter Reformation cause would be a misleading oversimplification of the reality. The Jesuit Stephen White, who became involved in the hagiography project and searched out material both on the Continent and in Ireland, had access to the extraordinary library of James Ussher (1581–1656), the Church of Ireland archbishop of Armagh and primate of Ireland. Ussher was completely and profoundly Protestant in theology, and yet he had a deep interest in the Irish saints. Moreover, he was by all accounts extraordinarily generous to Roman Catholic collectors, including Stephen White and the Franciscan Francis O'Mahony, allowing them to copy his manuscript materials and seeking from them the opportunity to make copies of texts uniquely in their possession. Antiquarian or scholarly values could still take precedence over sectarian agendas, even in the matter of texts that served those agendas. The cooperation of Primate Ussher with the Louvain Franciscan project was a harbinger of the kind of cooperation among antiquarian men of different religious persuasions that would be possible in the eighteenth century, when the project of constructing an Irish national identity would be, for a time, a nonsectarian one and when the Irish saints could be seen as an aspect of a common heritage.

Hogan, Edmund. 1870–71. Irish historical studies in the seventeenth century. *Irish Ecclesiastical Record,* 2d ser.:31–43, 56–77, 193–215, 268–89.

Jennings, Brendan. 1934. Documents from the archives of St. Isidore's College, Rome. *Analecta Hibernica* 6:203–47.

Keating, Geoffrey. 1902–14. *Foras Feasa ar Éirinn, The history of Ireland.* Ed. David Comyn and P. S. Dinneen. 4 vols. London: Irish Texts Society.

Leerssen, Joep. 1997. *Mere Irish and Fíor-Ghael: Studies in the idea of Irish nationality, its development and literary expression prior to the nineteenth century.* Critical Conditions 3. Notre Dame: Notre Dame University Press.

Luebke, David M., ed. 1999. *The Counter-Reformation: The essential readings.* Oxford: Blackwell.

Moody, T. W., F. X. Martin, and F. J. Byrne, eds. 1978. *A new history of Ireland.* Vol. 3. Corrected ed. Oxford: Clarendon.

Moryson, Fynes. 1967. *Of the Commonwealth of Ireland: Shakespeare's Europe.* Ed. Charles Hughes. 2d ed. New York: B. Blom.

Ó Cléirigh, Tomás. 1935. *Aodh Mac Aingil agus an scoil nua-Ghaeilge i Lobháin.* Dublin: Oifig Díolta Foillseacháin Rialtais.

Sharpe, Richard. 1991. *Medieval Irish saints' lives: An introduction to "Vitae sanctorum Hiberniae."* Oxford: Clarendon.

Société des Bollandistes. 1643–. *Acta sanctorum.* 68 vols. Antwerp, Tongerloo, Paris, Brussels.

Spenser, Edmund. 1934. *A view of the present state of Ireland.* London: E. Partridge at Scholartis Press.

Stanihurst, Richard. 1584. *De rebus in Hibernia gestis.* Antwerp.

Walsh, T. J. 1973. *The Irish continental college movement.* Dublin: Golden Eagle.

GORDON MCCOY AND CAMILLE O'REILLY

Essentializing Ulster?
The Ulster-Scots Language Movement

Northern Ireland has become the focus of world attention in its struggle for peaceful mutual accommodation after over thirty years of political violence. However, the militarized conflict in Northern Ireland is being replaced by a symbolic cultural one. Language, long a symbol of Irish nationalist identity, has recently been taken up by a section of the unionist population, using similar means to those of the nationalists for their own cultural and political ends. Nationalists find a potent unifying force in the Irish language; unionists seek a counterpart in Ulster-Scots.

Ulster-Scots is a distinctive speech variety closely related to Scots, which is descended from the Northumbrian dialect of Old English, brought to the north of Britain during the seventh century by the Angles. This speech variety, which differed from that of the Saxons who colonized southern Britain, was influenced by the Old Norse of subsequent Viking invaders. Scots also borrowed from French, Dutch, and Scots Gaelic (see Kirk 1998). Many Scots-speakers came to Ireland during the Plantation of Ulster (1610–25) and during further migrations throughout the remainder of the seventeenth century. Scots-speaking settlers came to the counties of Antrim, Down, Londonderry, and Donegal in north Ulster. Ulster-Scots speech developed in these areas, but the impact of the Scots settlement was felt further afield, as the English accent of the northern part of Ulster came to sound distinctly Scottish.

Since the 1980s a politics of culture has taken root in Northern Ireland, and both nationalists and unionists have come to express their ethnic and political affiliations in cultural terms. Unionists, however, often worry that their own cultural identity seems less exciting than Irish traditional music, language, and games associated with nationalism (Dunn and Morgan 1994:17). Many unionists believe that nationalists have much more cultural capital than they do. The Irish-language revival in particular has had an impact on the politics of culture in Northern Ireland in myriad ways, including promoting the nineteenth-century romantic nationalist ideal

156

that a distinct language is an essential part of any national identity. The same ideal motivates the Ulster-Scots movement, which has attempted to create a place for Ulster-Scots in the identities of the people of Northern Ireland, particularly for parts of the Protestant unionist community.

The politics of culture in Ireland as a whole has been dominated by the Irish-language revival since its inception in the late nineteenth century, and this continues to be the case in Northern Ireland today. In nationalist constructions the politics of language is used to define the existence of a distinct group of people entitled to political self-determination. Nationalists in Northern Ireland frequently point to language as the most pertinent aspect of culture in this respect, and the Irish language continues to be a powerful representation of national identity, both in the Republic and in Northern Ireland. While Irish has undergone a long period of decline,[1] it has also been the focus of revival efforts for more than a century. A new phase of the revival began in Northern Ireland in the early 1980s, which was Catholic in religious orientation and nationalist in political ethos (O'Reilly 1999). The current upsurge of interest in Irish in Northern Ireland is related to the political conflict in the North during the last thirty years, although there is no simple cause-and-effect relationship. Irish-language activities are popular in nationalist areas, including adult classes, Irish-medium schools for children, music events, social evenings, lectures, and plays. The 1991 Northern Ireland census included a question about the Irish language for the first time since Ireland was partitioned in 1921, with 142,003 people claiming to have some knowledge of the language (*Northern Ireland Census* 1993).

Throughout the 1990s the Irish language was increasingly seen as an important expression of nationalist identity, and it came to play a significant role in the political negotiations pertaining to the future of Northern Ireland. Following the Irish Republican Army (IRA) cease-fire in 1994, nationalist leaders called for "parity of esteem" for the nationalist community in Northern Ireland. The language movement increasingly associated its own demands with those of nationalist leaders, thus identifying the accommodation of Irish-language revivalism with that of the nationalist agenda in Northern Ireland. This is reflected in the Belfast Agreement, in which the British government promised to promote the Irish language in Northern Ireland, thus changing its stance on this important cultural

---

1. See O Donnaile 1997 for a brief account of the trajectory of decline.

issue (*Agreement* 1998:19).[2] Subsequent negotiations resulted in the creation of a cross-border implementation body for the Irish language, one of six North-South institutions answerable to a council of ministers from Northern Ireland and the Republic of Ireland.

Although it is clear that the recent Irish-language revival in Northern Ireland has influenced the Ulster-Scots movement, the idea of an Ulster-Scots identity is not entirely new. During the debate on the partition of Ireland in the 1920s, some unionists promoted an Ulster-Scots identity that was seen as drawing on historic, religious, and cultural bonds with Scotland. It was a Presbyterian-centered identity that elided intra-Protestant denominational differences and omitted Catholics altogether (Walker 1997: 94). This Ulster-Scots identity was largely set aside after the island was partitioned and unionists in the northeast were assured of their political future. A "British" identity became dominant among Protestants in the years after partition, with the internal variation encompassed by such an "identity" to be understood. This British identity had a rather arbitrary quality in Northern Ireland, but was often seen as being above the local quarrel; as elsewhere, Britishness was often naturalized as nonethnic and "universal," differences being excluded or absorbed so that "Englishness could stand for everybody in the British Isles" (Hall 1997:22).[3]

Since the 1960s, the self-image of Protestants has been severely challenged. Economic decline, changes in government policies, and the loss of ethnic certitude have resulted in a unionist sense of physical and psychological retreat. In addition to the fear generated by the resurgence of nationalism in Northern Ireland, there has been a growing sense of alienation from Westminster. Up until the late 1980s, Northern Protestants tended to ridicule Catholic claims of political and cultural inequality in Northern Ireland. Many Protestants had considered themselves good workers who would not drain the resources of "their" government and had stereotyped Catholics as "spongers" who exploited government benefits to the full. During the "Troubles," however, many Protestants experienced long-term

2. The 1998 multiparty agreement, commonly referred to as the "Belfast Agreement" by Protestants and the "Good Friday Agreement" by Catholics, concluded four years of negotiations between the main political parties in Northern Ireland. It was endorsed by the governments of Great Britain and the Republic of Ireland. In addition, 73 percent of Northern Ireland's voters approved the agreement in a referendum held on 22 May 1998.

3. For a more detailed discussion of Protestant/unionist identity in Northern Ireland, see Aughey 1989; Bell 1990; Bruce 1994; Buckley 1989; Harris 1986; McCoy 1997; Miller 1978; Moxon-Browne 1991; and Todd 1987.

unemployment for the first time and witnessed the concomitant decline of their own local communities. During the 1990s, Protestants, particularly working-class ones, adopted a culture of complaint of their own, representing themselves as discriminated against in terms of ethnic allegiance, political belief, and public resources. The community that once saw itself as part of the Protestant majority in the British Isles has begun to behave like a beleaguered ethnic minority in a corner of the United Kingdom. In part the Ulster-Scots revival is a response to this sense of alienation and grievance. For many Ulster-Scots enthusiasts, the primary imagined community has become that of Northern Irish Protestants, not the indifferent people of Britain or their treacherous government.

The Ulster-Scots Language Society was formed in 1992. A flyer published by the society indicates the aims of the organization: to encourage an interest in traditional Ulster-Scots literature, to support the use of Ulster-Scots in current speech and in educational institutions, and to encourage Ulster-Scots traditions of music, dance, song, ballads, and storytelling. The society publishes a yearly magazine called *Ullans,* a word which refers to the distinctive Ulster variety of Lallans and which is also an acronym for the phrase "Ulster-Scots language in literature and native speech." The society has produced recordings of Ulster-Scots speech and a grammar of Ulster-Scots, as well as a number of novels and children's books. The Ulster-Scots Language Society is a member of the Ulster-Scots Heritage Council, a wider umbrella body that promotes Ulster-Scots culture in Northern Ireland.

The Ulster-Scots Heritage Council received government funding to set up an office employing three full-time staff. The council organizes a number of activities that celebrate and promote Ulster-Scots culture, including recitations, music, historical research, and Scottish dance.[4] The Heritage Council has made efforts to ensure that Ulster-Scots is relevant to a wide number of people in Northern Ireland.[5] The Ulster-Scots Language Society estimates that there are at least one hundred thousand speakers of Ulster-Scots, who live mostly in parts of Antrim, Down, and Donegal, where the majority of the population is Presbyterian. An educational base

4. Recitations involve public performances of poetry or tales, many of which are humorous.

5. For example, the organization translated the names of local political parties into Ulster-Scots; Sinn Féin, which means 'ourselves' in Irish but is sometimes translated as 'ourselves alone', becomes "Oorselves Worlane," and the Women's Coalition becomes the "Weeminfowk's Click."

for the movement was established in 2001, when the Institute of Ulster-Scots Studies was opened at the University of Ulster with initial funding of three hundred thousand pounds sterling. In such ways the profile of Ulster-Scots has been raised in recent years, leading to widespread media interest and a large number of articles and letters on the subject in local newspapers. Though considerably smaller than the Irish-language revival movement, the Ulster-Scots movement has become a significant force in Northern Ireland's cultural battlefield.

As with Scots in Scotland, the categorization of Ulster-Scots as a language distinct from English is disputed. The boundary between language and dialect is not clear-cut, and it is often as dependent on sociopolitical considerations as on linguistic ones. Some assume that mutual intelligibility between speakers of two speech varieties ensures that they cannot be conversing in two distinct languages, but this is a problematic criterion. For example, using the test of intelligibility, there are only two Scandinavian languages — Continental (Swedish, Danish, and two standard varieties of Norwegian) and Insular (Faeroese and Icelandic); it is politics that has dictated otherwise (Crystal 1993:284). Structural differences and intelligibility must be assessed in making the distinction between language and dialect, but there are other criteria to be considered as well, including functional range and degree of standardization, the self-perceptions of speakers, the status of a speech variety as a mother tongue, its dominance for its speakers, and its historical development through time (Görlach 2000:15).[6] The aphorism "a language is a dialect with an army and a navy" epitomizes the problem of distinguishing languages from dialects, and it is frequently quoted by supporters of the Ulster-Scots movement.

There is no standard orthography for Ulster-Scots. Some writers of Ulster-Scots use a spelling system based on that of English which reflects the similarities between Ulster-Scots and Standard English. Tom McArthur refers to this as the "minimalist approach" of Scots enthusiasts (1998:158). Others prefer an orthography that differs a great deal from English, using, for example, the late-medieval <quh> spelling to realize English <wh> (the "maximalist approach"). Samples of the minimalist

6. Görlach doubts that Ulster-Scots can meet these criteria; he describes it as a *cant*, that is, a second dialect relearned to stress ethnicity, noting that Ulster-Scots is largely parasitical because competence in it largely depends on the prior acquisition of another language of wider communication value, namely, English (2000:24).

and maximalist approaches can be found in the appendix. The maximalist approach aids in validating the assertion that Ulster-Scots is not simply a dialect of English. There are also minimalist and maximalist approaches to the Ulster-Scots lexicon. The latter involves the revival of archaisms, the omission of Romance words and other lexical items shared with English, resemantizing Ulster-Scots words to designate contemporary objects and ideas, and coining neologisms such as *langbletherer* for *telephone,* or *stoursucker* for *vacuum cleaner.* Both approaches are problematic. The minimalist approach can be used by critics of Ulster-Scots to claim that it is simply a dialect of English, but the maximalist approach makes Ulster-Scots inaccessible to many, fueling accusations that it is a novel fabrication. One critic, for example, described the result as "a language without native speakers" (Görlach 2000:22).

The Ulster-Scots Language Society represents Ulster-Scots as either a dialect of Scots, which is taken as a distinct language, or as a separate language in itself. The society is particularly sensitive to accusations that Ulster-Scots is a dialect of English.[7] This issue is important because some European governments recognize and improve the status of indigenous languages, but not dialects. The language movement has the support of the British government in the language/dialect debate, which recognized Ulster-Scots as a variety of the Scots language when it signed the Council of Europe's European Charter for Lesser Used Languages in March 2000. Welsh, Scottish Gaelic, and Irish were included in the provisions of chapter 3 of the charter, which grants a high level of status and protection to the languages listed. The chapter 2 provisions, which grant recognition but a lower level of status, were applied to Scots, Ulster-Scots, and Cornish.

Some critics of the language society claim that they have never heard Ulster-Scots and that therefore it does not exist. The response of enthusiasts is that Ulster-Scots is so stigmatized that native speakers are reluctant to use the language in public, making it very much the speech of the private domain, of friends and neighbors. Sophisticated urban dwellers in particular characterize it as an amusing dialect spoken by elderly and ill-educated people in country districts. The Ulster-Scots movement is reluc-

7. Opponents of the movement denigrate Ulster-Scots as a fabrication or simply a dialect of English. The *Andersonstown News,* for example, described Ulster-Scots as a "DIY language for Orangemen" (cited in *Newtownards Chronicle,* 13 February 1997:15), and a writer in the Dublin *Sunday Times* called it "a recently codified backslang of the Planters" (11 October 1998:19).

tant to use the word *dialect* in relation to Ulster-Scots because of its perceived derogatory connotations and because it usually appears in the
phrase "a dialect of English"; thus promoters of Ulster-Scots are more
likely to use descriptors such as "a regional variety of Scots" than "a
dialect of Scots." Ulster-Scots is often described as a *speech variety, linguistic heritage, tradition,* and *tongue.* Such terms allow the user to appear neutral in the language/dialect debate by avoiding the use of the
negative term *dialect* without validating the claims of the society by refer-
ring to it as a language. The Belfast Agreement of 1998, for example,
deliberately avoids the language/dialect debate in its wording: "All par-
ticipants recognize the importance of respect, understanding and tolerance in relation to linguistic diversity, including in Northern Ireland, the
Irish language, Ulster-Scots and the languages of the various ethnic communities, all of which are part of the cultural wealth of the island of
Ireland" (*Agreement* 1998:19).[8]

Thus far we have focused on sociolinguistic issues and avoided ideological or political ones. Clearly, however, the language/dialect debate is not
a matter of linguistic factors alone. The debate on the standing of Ulster-
Scots in Northern Ireland provides a unique perspective on nationalist and
unionist ideologies, revealing insights into unionist-nationalist horse-
trading in the post-cease-fire period.

The constitution of the Ulster-Scots Language Society states that the
movement is avowedly nonsectarian and nonpolitical. Anyone with an
interest in Ulster-Scots can join the society, and at least one member of Sinn
Féin is a member of the society. When asserting its nonpolitical credentials,
the language society draws attention to its Catholic and nationalist members, indicating that many native speakers of Ulster-Scots are Catholics.
Some Catholics with an interest in cross-community work attend Ulster-
Scots events and classes, both to learn more about Ulster-Scots and to
demonstrate their respect for Protestant culture. As in Irish-language circles, however, there is a difference between the Ulster-Scots movement's

8. When discussing the issue in a class in Newtownards, County Down, one teacher
informed the class that Norse and Swedish are dialects of Old Danish; therefore, Ulster-Scots
can be simultaneously a language and a dialect. He asked the class the rhetorical question, "Is
a daisy a flower or a weed?" and told the class that Ulster-Scots could be considered to be
both a language and a dialect of Scots. Part of the research for this study involved one of the
authors, McCoy, attending Ulster-Scots classes, and examples of classes cited here are from
personal observation unless otherwise noted. McCoy attended classes for eight weeks in
Newtownards in 1996 and further classes in Belfast in 1999, as well as a large number of
debates and other events concerning Ulster-Scots.

rhetoric of inclusivity and the nature and location of activities in practice. For example, most Ulster-Scots activities take place in unionist areas into which nationalists would be reluctant to venture. The headquarters of the Ulster-Scots Heritage Council is on the Shore Road in North Belfast, which is a solidly Protestant working-class area. Most branches of the Ulster-Scots Heritage Council are also in unionist neighborhoods.

Moreover, some unionist organizations have begun to use Ulster-Scots in a symbolic fashion. The South Belfast Historical Society, which promotes Protestant culture in the area, is also known as the Fowkgates Societie o' Sooth Bilfawst, and a loyalist group for former prisoners calls itself Gae Lairn (Go Learn). Most people in Northern Ireland regard Ulster-Scots as a "Protestant" concern, just as Irish is perceived to be a "Catholic" language. Unionists have represented Ulster-Scots as a language that promotes their particular worldview. During a debate on the issue, Jim Shannon of the Democratic Unionist Party (DUP) said, "We are Ulster-Scots, descended from a fiercely independent ancestry — from Scots Presbyterianism. Because we live in Ulster it does not make us Irish. . . . There are two distinct nations on this island — the Gaelic-Irish and the Ulster-Scots. We belong to the latter, and no matter how difficult that may be for some to swallow, it is a fact of life. We have as much right to self-determination as any other nation on earth and nobody should tell us that we have no culture, or rights or that we are afraid of that culture, and afraid of that tradition" (Northern Ireland Forum debates: <http://www.ni-forum.gov.uk/debates/1997/100197.htm>, 28 August 2000). Ulster-Scots is advanced by some unionist politicians as a response to the promotion of Irish by Sinn Féin. In fact, meetings of the new assembly at Stormont were disrupted by language debates in the latter part of 1998. Sinn Féin demanded the right to speak in Irish and the availability of simultaneous translation facilities. An article in the *Belfast Telegraph* noted, "The DUP sees no problem in that, while other unionists have threatened that if Irish is increasingly heard on the floor they will retaliate with unadulterated Ullans" (*Belfast Telegraph,* 27 October 1998:4).

In many respects Ulster-Scots has become a political bargaining chip. In view of the much-vaunted goal to secure "parity of esteem" between the unionist and nationalist communities in Northern Ireland, it should come as no surprise that such terminology has spread to the language movements. Irish-language activists adopted the concept of "parity of esteem" soon after the Downing Street Declaration in 1994, suggesting that support for the Irish language would be a positive step toward parity of esteem for nationalists in Northern Ireland (O'Reilly 1996, 1999). In turn, some Ulster-Scots activists have called for parity of esteem for Ulster-Scots with Irish. In their view, parity of funding for Ulster-Scots implies parity of esteem for the unionist community, which in their perception is losing ground to nationalists.

The Ulster-Scots lobby benefited enormously from unionist support during the peace negotiations. The unionist parties agreed that a cross-border implementation body would be set up for the Irish language, provided that the organization included an agency for the promotion of Ulster-Scots. This was accepted by the Irish and British governments. The initial budget for the Irish-language agency was to be £13 million, with £1 million being allocated to the Ulster-Scots agency; this represented a massive increase in funding for Ulster-Scots activities. The corporate plan of the agency includes a three-year project to record and transcribe the language of native speakers of Ulster-Scots, as well as to prepare a dictionary of Ulster-Scots. Many commentators assumed that the comparatively small Ulster-Scots movement was surprised by its political and financial success; the Scots language movement was certainly bemused to discover that a lesser-known branch had overtaken the parent body financially to such a degree.

The two parts of the language implementation body were to differ in linguistic emphasis. Whereas the Irish-language agency was to deal with language matters alone, the Ulster-Scots agency included cultural matters within its remit, which were defined by the legislation as follows: " 'Ullans' is to be understood as the variety of the Scots language traditionally found in parts of Northern Ireland and Donegal. 'Ulster-Scots cultural issues' relate to the cultural traditions of the part of the population of Northern Ireland and the border counties which is of Scottish ancestry and the influence of their cultural traditions on others, both within the island of Ireland and in the rest of the world" (Bille 1999:47). In an effort to appear fair to nationalists and unionists, some public bodies have adopted a trilingual or multilingual approach. The Linguistic Diversity Branch of the Department of Culture, Arts, and Leisure wished its clients "Merry Christmas," "Nollaig Shona," and "a blythe Yuletide" in its Christmas card, and the Stormont assembly decided to redesign its note-paper to include legends in Irish and Ulster-Scots. The Northern Ireland Health and Social Services Agency advertised for an equality schemes manager in local newspapers in English, Ulster-Scots, Irish, and Chinese (*Belfast Telegraph*, 23 November 1999:20).[9]

Some important opinion makers in Northern Ireland doubt that the Ulster-Scots revival movement will succeed, in part because they view Ulster-Scots as a dialect, but they do not air their misgivings publicly, for they do not wish to appear to be anti-Protestant/unionist and they are reluctant to oppose the spirit of inclusiveness and toleration that is being promoted in the wake of the Belfast Agreement. The policy of linguistic diversity sometimes includes speakers of immigrant languages — as indicated by the advertisement discussed above, which was issued in Chinese — who for their part are torn between resentment of tokenistic inclusion and gratitude for any publicity that will bring attention to their plight. At a Belfast symposium on language rights in August 2000, for example, a spokesperson for the Chinese Welfare Association, after detailing the grievous medical and educational disadvantages suffered by her community because of language issues, complained that her organization was only involved in a multilingual language project "as a second thought" (Watson 2000:99).

There is no shortage of irony in the politics of language and culture in Northern Ireland. Opponents of the Irish-language revival movement have often portrayed it as little more than a front for republicanism. In turn, Irish-language activists often portray the Ulster-Scots movement as politically motivated and less than genuine. As one columnist put it, "Ulster-Scots was an anchor forged to stop Orange Ulster from drifting away in a sea of green" (*Irish Times*, 6 October 1998). Some nationalists claim that prominent enthusiasts of Ulster-Scots cannot speak it because they are not "really" interested in it at all. Thus some Irish-language speakers interpret the Ulster-Scots lobby as a negative identity group, based on opposition to their own. They believe that Ulster-Scots enthusiasts have no positive motives and little or no linguistic capital. Irish speakers often suspect that Ulster-Scots is used to thwart their own projects, as funding agencies considering Irish-language projects may become exasperated with competing Ulster-Scots claims and — linguistically, so to speak — "throw the baby out with the bathwater."

For their part some Ulster-Scots activists argue that they are not seeking

9. The advertisement, which translated "Equality Schemes Manager" to "Eeksi-Peeksie Skame Heid-Yin," aroused widespread ridicule and angered some members of the Ulster-Scots language movement.

"a pound for a pound" regarding the Irish language. They highlight the cultural heritage of Ulster-Scots, rather than its political associations. The emphasis that some enthusiasts place on the academic study of Ulster-Scots and their love of its literature has convinced some skeptics, including suspicious Irish speakers, that some Ulster-Scots aficionados may have "genuine" motivations, rather than "political" ones. Echoing similar claims in defense of the Irish language (see O'Reilly 1999), the language society insists that Ulster-Scots is available to everyone and that it is not the organization's fault if unionists support them whereas nationalists do not. In disavowing accusations about political motivations, Ulster-Scots promoters highlight the Scottish origins of the movement. The Scottish connection of the movement counteracts its image as a partisan offshoot of Northern Irish unionism, for both Protestants and Catholics in Northern Ireland have a sense of affinity with Scotland. However, they view the Scottish connection in different terms. Whereas Irish nationalists perceive the Scots to be fellow "Celts" and approve of the growing independence movement in Scotland, Northern Ireland's Protestants view Scotland as a bulwark of Presbyterianism and an ancestral homeland.

There are inherent limits to the extent that Ulster-Scots can become the symbolic language of unionism. In part this is due to the weaknesses within the language movement itself, which pales in comparison with its Irish-language counterpart. Ulster-Scots language classes are few and far between, and they often consist of discussions in English about the language, leaving enthusiasts with no structured means to learn Ulster-Scots. Moreover, at the time of writing, there was no large-scale community demand for Ulster-Scots language classes. Enthusiasts tended to blame this on the adolescence of the movement, a lack of resources, and the hostility of the educational establishment. The areas in which Ulster-Scots is traditionally spoken are limited and do not include Belfast, the capital city of Northern Ireland. Thus many unionists cannot associate Ulster-Scots with their personal histories or their localized identities. Maximally differentiated Ulster-Scots appears alien to some of them; indeed, in east Belfast loyalists ripped down a bilingual sign which read "Tullyard Way" and "Heichbrae Airt" because they mistook the Ulster-Scots on the sign for Irish (*Irish News*, 18 October 1999).

Not all unionists accept the Ulster-Scots project as part of their political program. Some unionists who identify strongly with Britain consider Ulster-Scots to be too parochial for them. They consider themselves part of a modern progressive British state; in turn, they are sometimes referred to as "Anglocentric" by Ulster-Scots aficionados. Moreover, in general unionists are noted for their utilitarian and modernist approach to culture, and they tend to be dismissive of minority cultures and traditions. Not surprisingly, a number of "unionist" letters and articles in local newspapers condemned the increased funding for Ulster-Scots and Irish-language activities as a pointless exercise that would divert funds from more pressing issues, such as education and health.

Since 1997 there has been some cooperation between the Irish-language and Ulster-Scots lobbies, despite the opposing political views of many of their advocates. Discourses of dialogue and diversity are the order of the day, and both unionists and nationalists seek to accommodate each other. Pluralism and diversity are "in," and narrow monocultural agendas are "out," as unionists and nationalists compete to appear more pluralist than the other. Furthermore, funding bodies are likely to look kindly on collaboration between speakers of Irish and Ulster-Scots, as they favor projects that challenge sectarian divisions. If the Irish-language movement is de facto Catholic and the Ulster-Scots movement Protestant, they can nonetheless exhibit their cross-community credentials by working together. Critics claim that this form of cooperation is superficial and cynical, leading to a number of "shotgun weddings" between mutually suspicious speakers of Irish and Ulster-Scots in search of additional funding. Others explain this process as one of mutual curiosity and benefit, which can only be welcomed in the current political climate.

It is easy to focus on the political aspects of the Ulster-Scots language movement because of its highly politicized context. As well as indicating the particular cultural and political circumstances of Protestants in Northern Ireland, however, the Ulster-Scots revival reflects a worldwide ethnic resurgence that has transformed minority ethnicity from a social liability to a desirable asset. As elsewhere, identity politics involves the objectification of a language and culture that informs and articulates political demands. In Northern Ireland the close relationship between politics and indigenous culture which is characteristic of Irish nationalism became a dominant discourse that many unionists felt they had to answer in its own terms.

Despite the apparent politicization of Ulster-Scots, it is important not to lose sight of the multiplicity of meanings and identities that can be associated with a language. In attending Ulster-Scots classes in New-townards, McCoy encountered few responses to the Ulster-Scots language movement that had overtly political or national interpretations. For many, Ulster-Scots expressed a localized rather than partisan identity, evoking childhood memories, old traditions, and neighborhood affiliations. Locals warmed to samples in Ulster-Scots taken from century-old editions of the *Newtownards Chronicle*. Statements such as "Oh, that's what they used to say in the old days" were common. Indeed, there was often collabora-tion between teachers and native speakers, with the latter suggesting rhymes, meanings of words, and pronunciations that augmented the knowledge of the teachers and other students in the classes, tying the present learning to past experiences, handing over knowledge from the past to the present and the future. That is how language is passed on in communities, instantiating the literal meaning of *tradition*.[10]

It is important to avoid the trap of imputing "real" political motiva-tions to seemingly "innocent" cultural facades. There are always complex and even at times contradictory meanings and intentions behind any act or utterance (Frazer and Cameron 1989). The same speakers may invoke different cultural and political discourses related to Ulster-Scots on dif-ferent occasions to different ends,[11] responding to the demands of the situation without necessarily reflecting a strict hierarchy of beliefs. Al-though on occasion Ulster-Scots emerges as the unionist response to the Irish language — itself a language spoken (often haltingly) by Sinn Féin politicians as a ritualized expression of identity — Ulster-Scots can also be a mode of communication that has little ideological significance. It is the language of hearth and home and bygone years. Ulster-Scots is simulta-neously a symbolic language in ethnopolitical terms, an aspect of the shared heritage and tradition of Catholics and Protestants in Northern Ireland, and a repository of nostalgia. As the politics of culture and iden-tity continue to unfold in Northern Ireland, it remains to be seen what place — or places — Ulster-Scots will eventually take.

10. In the Newtownards classes, learners could be roughly divided into two groups: older native speakers, for whom Ulster-Scots expressed a sense of localized belonging, and younger enthusiasts who had less knowledge of Ulster-Scots when they enrolled, for whom Ulster-Scots expressed an "Ulster" national identity. Nevertheless, it would be erroneous to draw a clear dichotomy between native speakers of Ulster Scots and revivalist ideologues. The local affiliations of native speakers may simply attenuate their political beliefs.

11. The same is true in the case of the Irish language; see O'Reilly 1999.

Appendix

Maximally Differentiated Text in Ulster-Scots and English
(*Belfast Telegraph,* 9 February 1999, "Jobfinder" section)

ULSTER-SCOTS VERSION

Unner-Editor (Inglis an Ulster-Scotch)
fur tha Chaummer o tha Scrievit Accoont (Hansard)
6-month leemited-tairm contraick
Sellerie: £13,737 tae £19,215

It's noo apen fur tae pit in job foarms fur tha ontak o Unner-Editor (Inglis an Ulster-Scotch) wi tha Chaummer o tha Scrievit Accoont (Hansard) o tha New Ulster Semmlie sittin at tha Tolsel Biggins, Stormont, Bilfawst. A start wull be gien fur sax month, wi anither contraick aiblins forbye.

ENGLISH VERSION

Sub-Editor (English and Ulster-Scots) in the Office of the Official Report (Hansard)
6-month fixed-term contract.
Salary: £13,737 to £19,215

Applications are invited for the post of Sub-Editor (English and Ulster-Scots) in the Office of the Official Report (Hansard) of The New Northern Ireland Assembly, which is located at Parliament Buildings, Stormont, Belfast. The appointment will be for six months, with the possibility of renewal of contract.

Minimally Differentiated Ulster-Scots Text
(*Ullans,* Nummer 5, Simmer 1997:7–12)

"Mem'ries o oul Newtownards" by Hugh Robinson

Noo, Ah suppose iverybody haes a hame-toon. A hame-toon or village, or some wee place that in their hairt o hairts they ca hame. The place we were boarn in, the place o sweet chilehuid mem'ries, the friens we grew up wi, an the schuils we gaed tae.

Fer me, thon place is Newtownards, Newton as we ca'ad it, in the sweet Coonty Doon. Ah was boarn here. Sae was my parents, an ma ain weans, and their weans. Yin belovit dauchter, Donna, lies in the cemetery at the oul Movilla Abbey. Aye. There's monie things that binds ma hairt tae this place. . . .

Hitler's war o mass-murder an extermination was still ragin in Europe whun Ah was born in Greenwell Street. Ma faither, Frank, like mony ither brave men o the toon pit on a uniform an went tae fecht for liberty an peace. Like mony ithers, he didny cum bak. His name, an theirs, can be foon on the War Memorial at the oul Bowlin Green in Castle Street.

Works Cited

The agreement: Agreement reached in the multi-party negotiations. 1998. London: Stationery Office.

Aughey, Arthur. 1989. *Under siege: Ulster unionism and the Anglo-Irish agreement.* Belfast: Blackstaff.

Bell, Desmond. 1990. *Acts of union: Youth culture and sectarianism in Northern Ireland.* Dublin: National Institute of Higher Education.

An bille um chomhaontú na Breataine-na hÉireann: The British-Irish agreement bill. 1999. Dublin: Stationery Office.

Bruce, Steve. 1994. *The edge of the union: The Ulster loyalist political vision.* Oxford: Oxford University Press.

Buckley, Anthony. 1989. We're trying to find our identity: Uses of history among Ulster protestants. In *History and ethnicity,* ed. M. Chapman, M. McDonald, and E. Tonkin, 183–97. ASA Monograph 27. London: Routledge.

Crystal, David. 1993. *The Cambridge encyclopedia of language.* Cambridge: Cambridge University Press.

Dunn, Seamus, and Valerie Morgan. 1994. *Protestant alienation in Northern Ireland: A preliminary survey.* Coleraine: Centre for the Study of Conflict, University of Ulster at Coleraine.

Frazer, Elizabeth, and Deborah Cameron. 1989. Knowing what to say: The construction of gender in linguistic practice. In *Social anthropology and the politics of language,* ed. R. Grillo, 25–40. Sociological Review Monographs no. 36. London: Routledge.

Görlach, Manfred. 2000. Ulster Scots: A language? In *Language and politics: Northern Ireland, the Republic of Ireland, and Scotland,* ed. John M. Kirk and Dónall P. Ó Baoill, 13–32. Belfast Studies in Language, Culture, and Politics 1. Belfast: Cló Ollscoil na Banríona.

Hall, Stuart. 1997. The local and the global: Globalization and ethnicity. In *Culture, globalization, and the world-system: Contemporary conditions for the representation of identity,* ed. Anthony D. King, 19–40. Minneapolis: University of Minneapolis Press.

Harris, Rosemary. 1986. *Prejudice and tolerance in Ulster: A study of neighbours and "strangers" in a border community.* Manchester: Manchester University Press.

Kirk, John. 1998. Ulster Scots: Realities and myths. *Ulster Folklife* 44:69–93.

McArthur, Tom. 1998. *The English languages.* Cambridge: Cambridge University Press.

McCoy, Gordon. 1997. Protestants and the Irish language in Northern Ireland. D. Phil. Diss., Queen's University, Belfast.

Miller, David W. 1978. *Queen's rebels: Ulster loyalism in historical perspective.* Dublin: Gill and Macmillan.

Moxon-Browne, Edward. 1991. National identity in Northern Ireland. In *Social attitudes in Northern Ireland, 1990–1991,* ed. Peter Stringer and Gillian Robinson, 23–30. Belfast: Blackstaff.

Northern Ireland census 1991: Irish language report. 1993. Belfast: Her Majesty's Stationery Office.

Ó Donnaile, Antaine. 1997. Can linguistic minorities cope with a favourable majority? In *The Irish language in Northern Ireland,* ed. A. Mac Póilin, 191–209. Belfast: Iontaobhas ULTACH/ULTACH Trust.

O'Reilly, Camille. 1996. The Irish language — litmus test for equality? Competing discourses of identity, parity of esteem, and the peace process. *Irish Journal of Sociology* 6:154–78.

———. 1999. *The Irish language in Northern Ireland: The politics of culture and identity.* Basingstoke: Macmillan.

Todd, Jennifer. 1987. Two traditions in unionist political culture. *Irish Political Studies* 2:1–26.

Walker, Graham. 1997. Scotland and Ulster: Political interactions since the late nineteenth century and possibilities of contemporary dialogue. In *Varieties of Scottishness: Exploring the Ulster-Scottish connection,* ed. John Erskine and Gordon Lucy, 91–109. Belfast: Institute of Irish Studies.

Watson, Anna Man-Wah. 2000. Language, discrimination, and the Good Friday agreement: The case of Chinese. *Language and politics: Northern Ireland, the Republic of Ireland, and Scotland,* ed. John M. Kirk and Dónall P. Ó Baoill, 97–100. Belfast Studies in Language, Culture, and Politics 1. Belfast: Cló Ollscoil na Banríona.

Patrimony: On the *Tête Coupée* in John Montague's *The Rough Field*

Irish poets of John Montague's generation frequently claim the pangs of isolation from their ancestral speech and customs.[1] Their poems often lodge on the understanding that — except for familial ties — the poet has been cut off from Ireland. When phrasing this sense of isolation, each poet has confronted the problem of language, as did Michael Hartnett in *A Farewell to English:* "I have come with meagre voice / to court the language of my people" (1975:35). A decade earlier in 1966, Thomas Kinsella defined the problem of postwar Irish poetry by pleading that "every writer in the modern world . . . is the inheritor of a gapped, discontinuous, polyglot tradition" (Kinsella 1970:66).[2] Now a familiar part of postcolonial discourse, Kinsella's adjectives remain challenging. Despite the endurance of the "Troubles" since 1969 in Northern Ireland, Irish poets have faced down Kinsella's assertions, and John Montague is one of them, as may be told from his *Collected Poems* (1995).

Like Kinsella, Montague has sounded notes of deracination, and he has looked outward to see what tactics and themes he might adopt. Montague's earliest poetry displays influences as different as D. H. Lawrence and W. H. Auden, while in *Forms of Exile* (1958) Montague reaches for American techniques and American subjects. Likewise, even the stronger poems of *Poisoned Lands* (1961) evince a struggle for models and a disciplining theme. Published the year that Montague began the sequences that became *The Rough Field* (1972), *Poisoned Lands* was not then seen as the anticipatory exercise that it proved to be (Skelton 1961). Later, parsing

---

1. I am indebted to Liam Ó Dochartaigh and David Gardiner for details in this essay and to Colin Ireland and Maria Tymoczko for helping me bring it to a sharper focus.
2. Kinsella rehearses the same argument in *The Dual Tradition: An Essay on Poetry and Politics in Ireland* (1995). Montague offers similar commentary in his introductions to his translations from the Irish in *A Fair House* (1972[1973]) and to his *Faber Book of Irish Verse* (1974), as well as in "A Primal Gaeltacht" (1970). Commenting on his translations, Montague admits: "I have leaned heavily on the scholars, from the great Kuno Meyer to David Greene and James Carney" (1972 [1973]:v; see also Montague 1989:50–52, 109–26, 42–45).

the flaws and virtues of *The Rough Field,* Edna Longley put the horse after the cart by observing that in *The Rough Field,* Montague "is mournfully exhuming what *Poisoned Lands* had apparently exorcised" (Longley 1975:145). That view prompts a corrective: that Montague's early poems be viewed from the vantage point that *The Rough Field* plainly provides. *The Rough Field* — ten cantos and an epilogue — is composed of sequences of poems from *Patriotic Suite* (1966) through *A New Siege* (1970) that were printed separately as chapbooks.[3] Published initially in 1972, *The Rough Field* was reissued in 1974, 1984, and 1989, and it appears in initial position in Montague's *Collected Poems.* I will focus on the fourth canto, titled "The Severed Head," which contains five short poems — "The Road's End," "A Lost Tradition," "Ulster's Pride," "The Flight of the Earls," and "A Grafted Tongue" — as well as a coda. The canto is prefaced by an illustration showing a severed head (see figure 1).

The Rough Field is distinguished by Montague's free use of gathered and sometimes researched sources — in the manner of William Carlos Williams in *Paterson* (1946–58) or of Charles Olson in *The Maximus Poems* (1960–75) — that in a postwar world prove recalcitrant by their grounding in turn-of-the-century Irish nationalist culture. Indeed, the resistance of such romantic material as Irish nationalism to postwar liberalism constitutes the very problem that Montague's early persona Peter Douglas cannot quite get a handle on in the story "The Cry" (1964; Montague 1998:59–86). Further, the archive of sources that Montague collected while composing *The Rough Field* yields a singular, illiberal image — the "severed" or "trophy" head (Coe 1989:18) — that becomes a motif and then a powerful symbol in the poem. Montague had begun to excavate that image with "fingertips of instinct" (Montague 1995:33) in early poems touching on patrimony before discovering it plain in "A Severed Head." Moved by *dindshenchas,* 'placelore', Montague's autobiographical persona stumbles on the symbol first in "A Grafted Tongue" (the fifth poem of the fourth canto) and then delves into its patrimonial ramifications in "The Fault," the fifth canto. For Montague's readers, sequence suggests consequence.

The Rough Field displays a rich range of native Irish sources, local Ulster references, and allusions to deeply rooted Gaelic matter. Although Montague (b. 1929) learned Irish at Glencull and studied it with Seán

3. Citations below are taken from the texts published in *Collected Poems* (Montague 1995).

IV

A SEVERED HEAD

And who ever heard
Such a sight unsung
As a severed head
With a grafted tongue?
Old Rhyme

Sir Thomas Phillips
made a journey
from Coleraine to
Dungannon, through
the wooded country
. . . and thereupon
wrote to Salisbury,
expressing . . . his
unfeigned astonish-
ment at the sight of
so many cattle and
such abundance of
grain . . . The hillsides
were literally covered
with cattle . . . the
valleys were clothed in
the rich garniture of
ripening barley and
oats; while the woods
swarmed with swine
. . . 20,000 of these
being easily fattened
yearly in the forest of
Glenconkeyne alone.
George Hill :
*An Historical
Account of the
Plantation of
Ulster*

Our geographers do not
forget what entertain-
ment the Irish of Tyrone
gave to a mapmaker
about the end of the
late rebellion; for, one
Barkeley being appointed
by the late Earl of
Devonshire to draw a
true and perfect map of
the north part of
Ulster . . . when he came
into Tyrone the inhabit-
ants took off his head . . .
Sir John Davies

Figure 1. Opening page of "A Severed Head" in *The Rough Field* (1972) giving a portion of plate 5 from John Derricke's *The Image of Irelande, with a Discouerie of Woodkarne* (1581). Reproduced by kind permission of Wake Forest University Press and the Gallery Press.

O'Boyle at St. Patrick's College, Armagh, in the 1940s (Montague 1989: 23), and although he translated from Irish in *A Fair House* (1974), his approach to the language is hardly academic. The traceable sources for *The Rough Field* range widely from letters and newspaper clippings to pictorial popularizations such as Proinsias Mac Cana's *Celtic Mythology* (1970) and such scholarly (if dated) tomes as George Hill's *An Historical Account of the Plantation in Ulster at the Commencement of the Seventeenth Century* (1877). In composing *The Rough Field*, Montague relied on three fundamentally nationalist works: Patrick S. Dinneen's *Irish-English Dictionary* (1927), P. W. Joyce's *The Origin and History of Irish Names of Places* (3 vols., 1869–70, 1913), and the three illustrated volumes of James Carty's *Ireland: A Documentary Record (1949–51)*. All three titles traveled with Montague's working library from Dublin to Paris and thence to Cork and Schull. From those sources and many others, Montague weaves together his own "gapped tradition" in *The Rough Field*. "A Severed Head" provides an apt symbol for the means and motive of that weaving: "*a severed head / With a grafted tongue*" (Montague 1995:30).

Montague also delineated that symbol in prose after the publication of *The Rough Field*. Just as Montague discerned in Gaelic lore one of the chief symbols of *Tides* (1970) in his essay "The Painting of Barrie Cooke" (Montague 1964),[4] so he delineated the symbol of the *tête coupée*, 'the severed head', in an essay on another Irish painter, Louis le Brocquy. Writing in 1973, Montague describes le Brocquy's "reconstructed" portrait heads so as to define the powers of the symbol of the severed head: "le Brocquy's ancestral heads draw on both Pagan and Christian tradition: they are at once commemorations and *memento mori*" (Montague 1973–74:10). Late in the same essay, Montague gives the essential "plot" of *The Rough Field* when he points out that le Brocquy's focus on the disembodied head led him back to origins and back to self. Montague refers to the three-faced head found at Corleck, County Cavan (Montague 1973–74:14), and to the heads — skulls or sculpted figures — found in France at Noves, Roqueperteuse, and Entremont, all of which were well illustrated in Mac Cana's *Celtic Mythology* (Mac Cana 1970:45, 80, 107, 134).

Writing on "the cult of the head" in *Pagan Celtic Britain*, Anne Ross

---

4. The symbol that Montague discovers in this essay on Barrie Cooke and then employs in *Tides* (1970) is the now overly popularized figure of the Síle na gCíoch, or Sheelah-na-Gig (Montague 1964:41).

observes that "the insular Celts venerated the head as a symbol of divinity and the powers of the otherworld, and regarded it as the most important bodily member, the very seat of the soul" (Ross 1967:104–9). These values are apparent in Montague's treatment of the symbol. As one would expect, the head and the skull, the act of beheading and that of veneration, all figure in early Irish literature.[5] For example, *Aided Con Culainn* (*The Death of Cú Chulainn*) is replete with references to the severed head; here the wounded Lugaid, who had taken Cú Chulainn's head, surrenders his own to Conall Cernach (Tymoczko 1981:66).[6]

Of the many signifying attributes of the tête coupée, one in particular is pertinent here: the head's ability to sing or speak with art and intelligence after having been cut from the body. Speech is the sole means by which the spirit still resident in the "severed head" may emotionally or morally affect the world of mortal men. Two Irish tales figure in this regard: *Reicne Fothaid Canainne* (*The Dirge of Fothad Canainne*) and *Cath Almaine* (*The Battle of Allen*). In *Reicne Fothaid Canainne* a Munster chieftain named Ailill Flann Bec learns of his wife's elopement with a "noble and ingenious" Connacht warrior named Fothad Canainne. Their two war-bands fight, and Fothad is slain and beheaded. Ailill's wife then carries Fothad's head to his grave, wherewith "the head of Fothad sang the *reicne* to the woman." The dirge or *reicne* that falls from the head's lips makes up an ornate lament in forty-nine couplets (Meyer 1910:10–17).[7] The example of *Cath Almaine* helps define the postmortem powers of the tête coupée: the head of a *fili*, 'a poet', or a *reacaire*, 'an entertainer', can recite or sing (Coe 1989:26). The tale portrays how the singing of a youthful minstrel's severed head, set on a pillar during a victory feast, so moved his master's enemies that they carried his severed head back to his slain body. It may have been that the youthful minstrel, Donn Bó, also sang a kind of dirge, for "all the host were weeping and sad at the piteousness and misery of the music he sang" (Stokes 1903:63).

Despite its resonance the symbol of the severed head has not been frequently explored in modern Irish poetry in English. W. B. Yeats, of

---

5. Cross 1952 lists a number of examples of the speaking head (D1610.5) and of the "self-returning head" (D1602.12).

6. In turn, this tale was well known because of W. B. Yeats's dramatization of it in *The Death of Cuchulain* (1939) and because of Oliver Sheppard's 1912 bronze in the General Post Office.

7. See also Kuno Meyer's translation of *Bruiden Atha* (Meyer 1893).

course, uses the tête coupée in *The Death of Cuchulain* (1939).[8] Writing in English after Yeats, Padraic Fallon (1905–74) based a poem of 117 lines titled "The Head" on this particular symbol. In the poem, Fallon imagines what powers may remain in the mind after death, in the head after its severing. As if to suggest that the "head alone at last" is his own, Fallon sets his imagination inside it (Fallon 1974:45). The head endures a night floating down an archetypal river and then days of sun and rain, with crows or gulls stripping its flesh away; still, "The face had dreamed / Itself right back again." It endures "no pain" until it was "bonebare and gleaming, where it floated / Down the broad vowel of the river" (46). But "its song was heard" only as one sound — "A thin / Piping" (47) — drowned in the sounds of a natural world. Fallon's theme in "The Head" is pain: the inability to feel it, to express it, to make it understood. Taken allegorically, the poem suggests that the head has been axed from the whole body of a past and from a language. Notably, Fallon's tête coupée cannot sing out its pain until too late to be articulate, too late to be heard clearly. Fallon intimates that the language found by the head may inhere in the landscape. That language may be taken as the fading Gaelic in the environs of Fallon's native Athenry; remembered by the head, the language remains lost to those who now live in the landscape. Only English is intelligible to them. Thus, the life of the head retains the language of the body it was cut from — the communal life, the past — only to go unheard because it is unintelligible. Fallon's "bonebare" skull finds its "black" tongue too late (45).

Nonetheless, by employing the tête coupée, Fallon evokes themes and experiences that John Montague and Seamus Heaney took up anew more than a generation later. In *Wintering Out* (1973) and *North* (1975), Heaney wrests much of his resonant imagery from the photographs of the garroted heads and buried bodies of P. V. Glob's *The Bog People* (1969). Likewise, Heaney is much concerned in *Preoccupations* (1980) with Anglicized and Gaelic placelore. Montague's employment of similar matter antedates Heaney's, not only *The Rough Field* but also "A Lost Tradition" (Montague 1995:33–34) and "Even English" (1995:38), both published in March 1970 in the *Irish Press*.

Montague's references in his early poems to "*a severed head / With a grafted tongue*" begin simply as images, but they gather into a single repeated motif that attains the concentration of a symbol in "A Severed

8. See the discussion in Marcus 1974.

Head." In poems antedating *The Rough Field,* the image of the head appears framed — severed — by crucial circumstances. In each poem the tête coupée is made to speak or sing its reicne. In this regard three poems are of particular interest: "Dirge of the Mad Priest," from *Forms of Exile* (1958) and *Poisoned Lands* (1961); "The Cage," from *A Chosen Light* (1967); and "To Cease," from *Tides* (1970). The most telling early deployments of the severed head emphasize the patriarchy of Irish Catholicism, and thus the consequent lament registers human inadequacy and a failure to live in *imitatio Christi.* But issues of patriotism — expressed in the thwarted republican struggle in the north during the Troubles of the 1920s — tend to supplant those of faith in Montague's later use of the motif.[9]

Montague's *Forms of Exile* opens with "Dirge of the Mad Priest," whereas *Poisoned Lands* includes this interior monologue just after "Prodigal Son." A monologue in the persona of a "Father," the "Mad Priest," the poem presents the image of the head — "God watches from the cracked mirror on the wall" (Montague 1995:198) — as an icon of the divine, but the literal face framed in the shaving mirror is the priest's own. The moment dramatized here constitutes a crisis of self-examination occasioned by a despairing sense of his having been cut off by his vocation from ordinary life. Emotionally bound in the logic of his creed and vows, the "Mad Priest" cannot recognize that the head in "the cracked mirror on the wall" is only his own reflected visage. Montague's dramatization of religious crisis by means of such an image underscores the traditional identification of the head as the seat of human spirituality, and it displays his intimacy with Irish Catholic religiosity as well. This understanding also informs a poem that follows "Dirge of the Mad Priest" in *Poisoned Lands.* "Soliloquy on a Southern Strand" (196–97) is also an interior monologue, but one spoken by the identifiable persona of the poet's uncle Thomas Montague, S.J. His name links this monologue directly to "The Bread God" (1968), which immediately precedes "A Severed Head" in *The Rough Field.* Subtitled "A Collage of Religious Misunderstandings," "The Bread God" interleaves lyrics with prose quotations from the Tyrone novelist William Carleton, Orange sectarian propaganda, and a letter dated "Christmas, Melbourne," written to Montague by his uncle late in life (23). Bitterly raised there in terms of emergent nationality and achieved class, the problem of vocation also delineates Montague's expe-

9. In his essay on le Brocquy, Montague pointedly breaks into a reflection on Bloody Sunday of 1972 and the early Ulster "Troubles" (Montague 1973–74:10).

rience in "Penal Rock / Altamuskin" (26), the fine closing sonnet of "The Bread God" (Redshaw 1982:75–78). That sonnet, in turn, makes the "Ulster Prophecy" possible, for it permits Montague's adaptation of an Ulster *amhrán bréagach,* 'a lying song', containing this line: "A severed head speaking with a grafted tongue" (Montague 1995:27).

Unlike "Soliloquy on a Southern Strand" and "Dirge of the Mad Priest," Montague's 1967 poem "The Cage" does appear in *The Rough Field.* "The Cage" too depends on the image of a head framed — this time behind the "grille / in the Clark St. I.R.T." (43–44) — a head "severed" by exile and political failure, rather than religious hysteria. The literal head here is also that of a father: "My father, the least happy / man I have known." "The Cage" offers a pensive recollection of a distant, wearisome life. What Montague's persona remembers are not the "lost years in Brooklyn" but, rather, his father's return to his "fields of Garvaghey / to see hawthorn in the summer / hedges" (44). In the son's recollection the father walks calmly with him, but the two do "not smile in / the shared complicity of a dream" (44). Now living out his own "dream," Montague's persona remembers their separate silences, and — in a Joycean moment — he comes to feel that "when / weary Odysseus returns / Telemachus should leave" (44).

Montague's persona recognizes both his father and himself in the "severed" heads of those others exiled underground by the failure of "a dream." In that recognition lies comprehended a father's dead life, an antecedent self, and a mute language of signs — in this instance "the mark of an old car / accident beating in his ghostly forehead" (44). "The Cage" closes "The Fault," the fifth canto of *The Rough Field.* The illustration accompanying that canto depicts a soldier from the Pale about to strike off the head of a kneeling "kerne" (Ir. *ceithearnach*), or Irish foot soldier. This image comes from plate 5 of John Derricke's *Image of Irelande* (1581), which also is the source of the illustration that opens "A Severed Head." In "The Fault" the three poems that precede "The Cage" ("Stele for a Northern Republican," "The Same Fault," and "The Sound of a Wound") invest the image of the head with the grim significance of a people's thwarted history, a history that "The Cage" barely hints at when printed alone in *A Chosen Light.* In "Stele for a Northern Republican," Montague's persona rehearses the father's hidden life and the Sinn Féin dream that led him into exile "underground" in Brooklyn, only to admit that his father was "right" to leave a "half-life in this / by-passed and dying place" (41). Then follows the persona's confessional identification of his patrimony in the poem "The Same Fault": "My father had the same scar / In the same place" (42). That identification of scar with scar empathetically claims the father's "severed head" as the persona's own, as if "The same fault run through / Us both; anger, impatience, / A stress born of violence." After this, the language of the head's sign finds figurative definition in "The Sound of a Wound": first as the "pastoral rhythm" of Irish traditional music; then as the lost Gaelic language of a native landscape; and finally as an irrational "bitterness" of class envy and race hatred (ibid.).

"To Cease," the third in this set of poems, continues the tête coupée imagery in the proposition "To be / a rock down / which rain pours / a granite jaw / slowly discolored" (251). As a human statement, these lines declare the wish to become monumental—to take refuge in a "dark permanence of ancient forms" (13). In this instance that is a wish to be fixed into permanence by the spare aesthetic of Samuel Beckett, to whom Montague dedicates the poem.[10] Montague's lines focus first on and return to the image of the head: "granite jaw," "your skull." His stanzas suggest that Beckett's sensibility entails the fundamentals of an Irish imagination by alluding to "a rock" like the tricephalic head found at Corleck, County Cavan; to such "a statue" as the memorial to Thomas Moore in College Green, Dublin; to "a tree" not unlike the bare, revered hawthorn of winter; and to an ancient figure flanked by animals, recalling images of the Continental figure Cernunnos.

Starting with the Corleck head, "To Cease" in its fifth stanza ends with a final image of a leaning menhir: "time bends you slowly / back to the ground" (251). Montague's free allusions to Irish placelore come into play here. The poem suggests that this same "object / honored or not" resembles a standing stone like that said to have been worshiped on the "Plain of Prostration" (Mag Slécht), below Slieve Rushen in County Cavan, until shattered by St. Patrick. A poem in The Metrical Dindshenchas describes it thus: "He was their god, the wizened Cromm ['the bent one'], hidden by many mists" (Gwynn 1924:19).[11] This stone idol—most likely invented to enhance the heroic stature of Ireland's conversion—is also known by the variant Cenn Crúaich, 'head of gore'. The town of Clogher—from clo-

10. Montague draws his understanding of Beckett's life and artistry in "To Cease" from his Nobel essay "La vie et l'oeuvre de Samuel Beckett" (Montague 1969).
11. See also Ross 1970:148–49 for a concise account of such images.

char, 'stony place' (Room 1994:38; Flanagan and Flanagan 1994:56) — in Montague's County Tyrone (Tír Eoghain) has a legend associated with it that interprets the name as meaning "the Golden Stone." The legend is perhaps first recorded in the *scholia* of the ninth-century martyrology *Félire Óengusso Céli Dé:* "a stone (*cloch*) round which was gold (*ór*), which the heathen had and worshipt. . . . and it was the chief idol of the north" (Stokes 1905:187).[12] Montague probably came to "Golden Stone" by way of P. W. Joyce's transmission of the derivation of the toponym *Clogher* from *cloch óir* (Joyce 1920:1.413–14). The design of Montague's Golden Stone pamphlets of the 1970s — *The Cave of Night* (spring 1974), *O'Riada's Farewell* (winter 1974), and *November* (spring 1977) — suggests that the symbol of the stone idol preoccupied him (see figure 2).

Stylistically severe, "To Cease" makes Beckett into a monument not unlike those "stone idols" cited above. And here, as in "Dirge of the Mad Priest" and "The Cage," the totem of the head is patriarchal. In all three poems, the heads are those of fathers — spiritual, autobiographical, artistic — while the second persons are all "sons" — the "Mad Priest," "Telemachus," the poet of "To Cease." The pattern of patrimony and patriotism here suggests that each "fatherhead" leaves the "son" an inheritance that both inhibits and informs, making the comprehension of speech or song both difficult and necessary.

Claiming that inheritance or disavowing it constitutes the nationalist or "Fenian" problem that Montague leads his persona to encounter in "A Severed Head." The subaltern question rhetorically posed in the possibly fictional Ulster "folk-rhyme" prefacing the canto proves singularly appropriate: "*And who ever heard / Such a sight unsung / As a severed head / With a grafted tongue?*" (Montague 1995:30). After that "traditional" rhyme, "A Severed Head" begins, and posed epigraphically as a folkloric image, the symbol of the tête coupée dominates the canto. One of the most problematic sequences in Montague's long poem, "A Severed Head" gives the impression that *The Rough Field* may be taken as a topographical poem.

Ascending the hills out of the Planter lowlands, Montague's persona returns to County Tyrone to find his own people. He hikes back into his name — from Montague to MacTeague to Mac Taidhg — and into the lost

12. A later generation of scholars regards the lore associated with Cenn Crúaich as contrived in order to elevate the reputation of St. Patrick. See Ó Duígeannáin 1940.

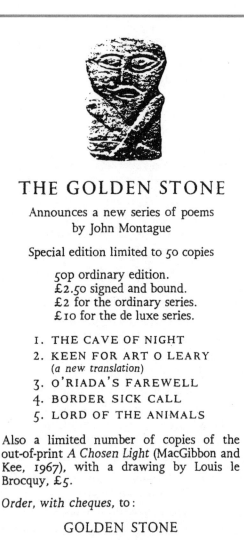

THE GOLDEN STONE

Announces a new series of poems
by John Montague

Special edition limited to 50 copies

50p ordinary edition.
£2.50 signed and bound.
£2 for the ordinary series.
£10 for the de luxe series.

1. THE CAVE OF NIGHT
2. KEEN FOR ART O LEARY
   (*a new translation*)
3. O'RIADA'S FAREWELL
4. BORDER SICK CALL
5. LORD OF THE ANIMALS

Also a limited number of copies of the
out-of-print *A Chosen Light* (MacGibbon and
Kee, 1967), with a drawing by Louis le
Brocquy, £5.

Order, with cheques, to:

GOLDEN STONE

1 Brighton Villas, Western Road,
Cork, Ireland

Figure 2. Back cover of *The Cave of Night* (spring 1974) showing the janiform stone head from Boa Island, County Fermanagh. Reproduced by kind permission of John Montague.

language of his fathers.[13] "A Severed Head" presents a quilt of allusions to the exceptional history of Ulster by quoting from George Hill's *Plantation of Ulster* (1877); from the *Annals of the Four Masters;* and from the writings of Sir George Carew, Sir Arthur Chichester, and Sir John Davies.[14] In the canto, allusions drawn from Hill's work or from Seán Ó Faoláin's *The Great O'Neill* (1942) refer also to Tyrone's history and to such writers as Sir John Harington (1561–1612), translator of *Orlando Furioso* (1591), who visited Hugh O'Neill (1540–1616), earl of Tyrone, and Ainnrias Mac Marcuis, whose poem beginning "Anocht is uaigneach Éire" ("Ireland is desolate tonight") Montague quotes later in "A New Siege," the ninth canto of *The Rough Field* (Montague 1995:71).

That welter of detail may disguise one fact of the poetry's drama: all the canto's matter — the topography of highlands or "airts" of southern Tyrone; the lore of "rock or ruin, dun or dolmen"; the history of the wars of the Elizabethan Plantation ending in the Flight of the Earls in 1607 — is mediated in the memory of Montague's autobiographical persona. His narrative of recollection opens "A Severed Head" — "my former step / Doubles mine" (31) — and closes it — "From the Glen of the Hazels / To the Golden Stone may be / The longest journey / I have ever gone" (38). Enacting the "circling failure to return" (9), Montague's persona comes gradually to comprehend the fragments of his history by repossessing the places of his past. These Wordsworthian moments help him to perceive again the loss of his language — *"Tá an Ghaeilge againn arís"* (literally 'we have Irish again', 33) — and of the inheritance it might have passed on to him.[15] Once announced, the theme of language expands directly into another conveyed by the four portraits in "Ulster's Pride" and in "Lament for the O'Neills": the collapse of the Gaelic Order of the north.[16] All three themes — the failure to return, the loss of language, the political dissolu-

---

13. The name Mac Taidg or Mhic an Taidg is a patronym meaning 'son of Tadhg' rather than a sept name; as a Christian name, "Tadhg" was taken in 1540 to mean "poet" (MacLysaght 1957:20; 1960:186).

14. Sir George Carew (1555–1629) and Sir Arthur Chichester (1563–1625), lord deputy of Ireland 1605–16), left numerous dispatches and memoranda. Sir John Davies (1569–1623), attorney general of Ireland (1606–19) is author of *Discoverie of the True Causes Why Ireland Was Never Entirely Subdued* (1612).

15. Printings of *The Rough Field* before the 1989 edition attempt to transcribe the Irish phrase as it would have been heard in Ulster: *"Tá an Ghaedilg [sic] againn arís"* (Montague 1972:30).

16. Montague's 1995 *Collected Poems* drops the title "Ulster's Pride" and retitles "Lament for the O'Neills" as "The Flight of the Earls" (34–36).

tion of a culture — are distilled in the symbol of "*a severed head / With a grafted tongue.*"

Both the persona's thoughts and "A Severed Head" close in a coda toponymically surveying Tyrone from "these airts," where "Names twining braid Scots and Irish / Like Fall Brae, [spring] native / As a whitethorn bush" (38). Here, *braid* serves as an adjective; it is Scots for *broad* and describes the confluence of two dialects of Ulster English present in a hybrid place name such as Fall Brae. *Brae,* a Scots word denoting the steep bank of a river or slope of a hillside, descends from the Old Norse word *brá,* 'brow'. That half of the place name reflects Ulster's historical links to Scotland, while the first half is an Anglicization of the Gaelic word *fál,* meaning 'hedge, wall, or walled enclosure' (cf. Joyce 1920:2.216–17; Room 1994:56). The place name Fall Brae is but one of the eighteen that stud the twenty-five lines of this last portion of "A Severed Head." Titled "Even English," this poem is a veritable digest of south Tyrone place names. Some of these names are straight Planter English, like Newtownsaville or Spur Royal, the fortified bawn built by the English campaigner Lord Ridgeway in 1615 at Augher — from the Irish *eochair,* 'border' (Room 1994:17) or 'brink' (Flanagan and Flanagan 1994:168). Other apparently English names, like Crow Hill, are actually translations, in this instance the Irish for Crow Hill being Mullach na bhFiach, 'Hill of the Ravens', also Anglicized as Mullynaveagh.

Throughout "A Severed Head" placelore prompts the ruminations of Montague's persona and sets his individual recollections of a lost country childhood in the context of a broader, longer communal history, which in turn links the words by which he discovers and reforms himself to the vernacular dialects of Ulster English and to Scottish and Irish Gaelic. Note the simile that Montague embeds in this observation from his 1973 introduction to *A Fair House: Versions of Irish Poetry:* "Like a stream driven underground, Irish language still ran under the speech and names of my childhood" (Montague 1989:51). To this drama of language and memory, "Even English" (Montague 1995:38), which ends "A Severed Head," adds a coda that echoes the persona's experiences of recollection, recognition, and communal memory, as well as the assimilation of his townland's ways of "speaking."

The painful moment of that assimilation occurs, however, in "A Grafted Tongue," the fifth and penultimate poem in "A Severed Head." In the quatrains of this poem, Montague's reader discovers that the persona's excursion, begun in "The Road's End," can hardly be a mere tour. Rather, the thwarted syntax and halting emphases at the opening of "A Grafted Tongue" reveal that these quatrains contain an intense subjective struggle. The first parenthetically incomplete, nightmarish quatrains establish the disturbed tone. Then follows a reverie-like narrative that seems to well up out of fragments of Montague's family lore remembered from childhood. The poem closes with a sign of self-comprehension measured by the lamenting vowel *o:* "To grow / a second tongue, as / harsh a humiliation / as twice to be born." After a sighing pause there follows a sibilant reaffirmation of lineage: "that child's grandchild's / speech stumbles over lost / syllables of an old order" (37). Montague lets his persona empathetically remember the schooling of his paternal grandfather, claiming it as if it had been his own, thus emphasizing his persona's inheritance of a spiritual wound, stumbling speech being its symptom. In this way "A Grafted Tongue" establishes the symbol that Montague employs next in "The Fault." There the significance of the wound—a scar on the temple—is made linguistically when the persona exclaims that he carries the liquor of a lost culture in his "bloodstream" that "rears" when he hears "a bleat of Saxon condescension" (42). That canto's leading symbol—wound, scar, fault—has its immediate genesis in the two opening quatrains of "A Grafted Tongue":

> (Dumb,
> bloodied, the severed
> head now chokes to
> speak another tongue:—
>
> As in
> a long suppressed dream,
> some stuttering garb-
> led ordeal of my own)
>
> (57)

Like the imagery, rhythms, and sounds they surround, the parentheses framing these lines suggest that their content has a source other than personal memory. Poised above the narrative of "A Grafted Tongue," this startling vision may be said to have arisen out of an impersonal body of memory, out of the mythologem of the tête coupée. The "severed / head" is human, familiar if not familial, yet it cannot be identified autobiographically. The stroke that severed it from the living body also cut it off from the body of its living language. Wounded mortally, it seems compelled to speak or sing, but Montague's persona records no lament or reicne coming from its lips. Rather than the ordinary air of language, the head "chokes" to shape its own blood into some communicable sense, and so the "grafted tongue" shapes syllables of pain and death. Epitomized in a dream image, here the history of the Plantation and Anglicization of Ireland finds compact and disturbing expression.

Montague's persona perceives these symbolic rudiments as a dream "long suppressed," and he emphatically claims this nightmare as his own by appending to the word *dream* an appositive: "some stuttering garb- / led ordeal of my own." The claim has startling force. Even so, Montague's emphasis on the words *dumb* and *stuttering* as tokens of a broken linguistic heritage is deeply traditional, as Hubert Butler's hypotheses about the settlement myths of Ireland's prehistory suggest (Butler 1949, 1950). Apocope gives a strained emphasis to these short lines. The lineation of "garb- / led" suggests, even, a pun on the Irish adjective *garbh*, 'rough', in the severed-body participle, thus also echoing Montague's title for the long poem: *The Rough Field*. Montague's public performances of his poems often contain stuttering emphases that underscore the difficulty of expression. After a pause the poet carries the poem from its inciting first image into broken narrative. Montague's persona re-creates out of family lore the nineteenth-century "education" of his grandfather, a schooling remembered in Carleton and forecast in Brian Friel's *Translations* (1980). That schoolchild's Anglicization is perceived as domestication, as Montague's neuter pronoun "it" and the animal imagery (a belled cow, a hobbled goat) make plain. Montague's simile suggests all the pathos of the child's lonely trouble. He wears a punishing "tally stick" or "hobble" to record his slips into Irish, including his own name — Mac Taidhg — rather than the Anglicized "altered syllables" of Montague. By enumeration the tally substantiates the inheritance he must betray: the more English, or *Béarla*, he learns, the more pathetically he must "stray" home to "find the turf cured width / of [his] parents' hearth / growing slowly alien" (Montague 1995:37).

As in the opening of "A Grafted Tongue," in the poem titled "The Road's End," Montague's persona claims an ancestor in this child, but the persona's tale of humiliation is the converse. As a schoolboy in Ballygawley in the 1940s, the persona had seen little virtue in the "old tongue," which he took to define only "the rural world we would soon be leaving" (Montague 1989:50). His native tongue was English; his "second tongue," Irish. But recalling his grandfather's travails leads him suddenly to phrase his realization of the worth of the "old tongue" in terms of a second birth: "To grow / a second tongue, as / harsh a humiliation / as twice to be born" (Montague 1995:37). In the halting emphases of these lines, Montague lets his persona sense that he yet suffers the wound of Anglicization, the severing of one tongue to serve the grafting of another. Just as he had claimed the vision of "the severed / head" as an ordeal of his own, so now he claims his ancestor's pain as his own in — characteristically for Montague — the "severing" of a second birth rather than a wounding and death.

The image of this schoolboy straying back to a daily more alien hearth expresses in miniature *The Rough Field*'s motif of the prodigal's return, which governs "A Severed Head," in particular. The narrative fact of return begins, as always, the mental action that constitutes the prime drama of *The Rough Field*'s ten cantos. In "A Severed Head" the reader encounters what the persona does. By allusive association the sights of the persona's upland walk in "The Road's End" prompt him to articulate consciously the recognitions and claims that come later in "A Grafted Tongue." Often, however, Montague poses allusive details in epigraphs that require more annotation. One example tells the tale: the epigraph from a letter from Sir John Davies, the English poet, author of *Orchestra* (1596), and Planter, as quoted from Hill's paraphrase in *An Historical Account of the Plantation in Ulster* (1877). Davies recounts that when an English "mapmaker" went "into Tyrone the inhabitants took off his head" (Montague 1995:30). Turning to Hill's *Account*, however, one finds it was "The Irish of Tyrconnell" who provided the "entertainment" (Hill 1970: 169). Explication of all such detail in "A Severed Head" would obscure the drama of the canto, of the persona's seizure of his inheritance. Neither Montague's persona nor his reader suspects that "The Road's End," the opening poem of the canto, will lead to the powerful recognitions and claims of "A Grafted Tongue." The persona is aware simply that he, as a child, once drove cattle between "ditches of whitethorn" with a willow — *saileach*, gen. sg. *sailí*, in Irish — switch. Now, again walking the landscape of south Tyrone, his memory becomes that "restive sally switch" (Montague 1995:31), whose smarting touch guides him between familiar fields and up into the "airts" of his childhood, the summer pasturage of Ireland's hard history (Brophy 1972:156–57).

Montague's persona lets his visual survey become an intellectual one, prompted by the allusive details of the landscape. Recalling the names of the flora, of the dead, of their habitations, he hypothesizes on their significance in "A Lost Tradition," the second poem in "A Severed Head," a poem frequently quoted owing to the prescience for other Irish writers of its formulations of Tyrone placelore: "The whole landscape a manuscript / We lost the skill to read, / A part of our past disinherited" (Montague 1995:33). It yields the metaphoric hypothesis that Brian Friel so famously adapted in *Translations*. Thinking of the place names he had once collected as "shards of a lost tradition," Montague's persona lets the idea of dindshenchas offer a metaphor that enables him to "read" the hills and fields of his native townlands, not just the top, clearly inscribed pages of personal memory but also the blotted historical ones lying underneath. That reading comes morally charged with a "but" characteristic of Yeats's rhetoric: "No rock or ruin, dun or dolmen / But showed memory defying cruelty / Through an image-encrusted name" (Montague 1995:33). And that moral perception of history eventually yields the politically charged claim of "A Grafted Tongue."

By being remembered, the landscape around Montague's persona becomes, in "A Lost Tradition," a historical anthology of tales and poems whose index would properly form a map. Whether in English or Irish, the local oral tradition bestows historical significance on places, as in the instance of the lore about Shane Barnagh, whose life as a "rapparee" (from Ir. *rápaire*, literally 'a rapier, short pike') in south Tyrone Montague paraphrases in one quatrain. Betrayed by the "Widow of Conegrah," Barnagh was assaulted by a man named McGregor, who "cut the head off him and put it in a bag and headed off to get a big lump of money for a reward from the Government" (Shaw 1931:71). Montague's persona may well have heard that legend in his childhood. "A Lost Tradition" makes it fictionally certain, however, that the persona did hear this ironic congratulation in Irish — "*Tá an Ghaeilge againn arís*," 'We have the Irish again' — in response to his stammering "school Irish" (1995:33). At this cue the persona's historical vision of the landscape comes swiftly into focus. In the imagination of the persona, the names of the land — "*Tír Eoghain*: Land of Owen, / Province of the O'Niall" — take on historical, narrative, and human substance (33). In his portrait of the O'Neills, Montague borrows much from Seán Ó Faoláin's *The Great O'Neill: A Biography of Hugh O'Neill, Earl of Tyrone, 1550–1616* (1942), including the leading epigraph from a letter by Carew written in 1595 or 1596. The troops of

Great Hugh O'Neill are envisioned marching out of Ulster, away from O'Neill's seat at Dungannon (Dún Geanainn) to assert the Gaelic Order at the Battle of Kinsale in 1601. There, in the farthest south of Ireland, in "black rain and fog," the wheel of history, hegemony, and fortune famously turned against O'Neill and "Ulster's pride, Elizabeth's foemen" (Montague 1995:33).

"The Road's End" and "A Lost Tradition," the first two poems in "The Severed Head," thus reveal how Montague's persona is prepared for the vividly detailed vision of the defeat of the Gaelic Order in Ireland. The third poem of the canto, titled "Ulster's Pride" in early printings of *The Rough Field*, gives that vision in the form of portrait vignettes of the last to hold (and lose) the title and rank of "The O'Neill," "a name worth more in price than to be called Caesar" (Ó Faoláin 1942:184). The third vignette is the metaphoric pivot of the poem, portraying Hugh O'Neill sitting in rustic state during negotiations with Robert Devereaux (1566–1601), second earl of Essex, at Dundalk in 1599. In the English party was the poet Sir John Harington, translator of *Orlando Furioso* (1591), as we have seen, who recounted that O'Neill "seemed to like [*Orlando Furioso*] so well, that he solemnly swore his boys should read all the book over to him" (Harington 1804:247–52). In O'Neill's party was Aodh Mac Aingil (1571–1626), the tutor of O'Neill's children in Ireland and later a prominent Counter Reformation theologian in Louvain and Rome (see the essays by Michael Cronin and Catherine McKenna in this volume). Mac Aingil composed an elegy for O'Neill beginning "A fhir fhéachas uait an chnáimh" ("O, you who gaze on the skull"). Aodh be Blacam's paraphrase of Mac Aingil's elegy in *Gaelic Literature Surveyed* ([1921] 1929:161) makes it plan that, exhumed, O'Neill's head speaks a reicne giving concrete Irish detail to the traditional Christian theme of the vanity of worldly and human ambitions.[17]

What both Mac Aingil and Montague commemorate is the end of the Gaelic Order. With the spectacle of the last head of Ulster's Gaelic aristocracy submitting to Mountjoy at Mellifont in 1603, the persona's vision of Ireland's subjection dissolves into an elegy keyed to his memory of the playing of a rural fiddler in "The Flight of the Earls" (Montague 1995:36–37) — the fourth poem of the canto, which once was titled "Lament for the O'Neills" — as if "to honour / a communal loss" (36). Montague's persona

17. See also Gardiner 2001:146, 159.

turns the stately air of this remembered music into a vision of "a shattered procession / of anonymous suffering" that "files through the brain" (36). The fiddler remembered here seems to be the persona's paternal uncle, an expatriate living in Brooklyn, eulogized in "The Country Fiddler" (11) for knowing "O'Neill's Lament" ("Caoineadh Uí Néill"). For Montague's persona, the motif of *ceol traidisiúnta*, 'traditional music',[18] keys perceptions of loss, discord, and change: "With an intricate / & mournful mastery / the thin bow glides & slides, / assuaging like a bardic poem, our tribal pain" (1995:37). In the first three editions of *The Rough Field*, those lines are glossed epigraphically by the Irish phrase "*Is uaigneach Eire*" [sic] 'Ireland is desolate', appearing as if parenthetically remembered in response to the phrase "our tribal pain." The Irish words come from an almost fugitive seventeenth-century lament on the Flight of the Earls composed by Ainnrias Mac Marcuis (Knott 1916:191), which does indeed close with "mournful mastery" in Robin Flower's condensed English rendering of it: "The grieving lords take ship. With these / Our very souls pass overseas" (Carty 1965:1.28). Then follows "A Grafted Tongue," the key poem in "A Severed Head," as if to suggest that its disturbed and disturbing opening parenthetical words may mark the persona's assimilation of historical sorrow and cultural trauma.

Having lost its last chief or "head"[19] and leading nobles, what remained of Ireland's Gaelic Order found itself beheaded. Lost too was the complete plenitude of that "order" or hierarchy of social and cultural understandings that, preserved in the language, had defined the traditional mores and aspirations of Ulstermen, in this instance. Generation after generation, the language came to lose its grasp on any reality but the common plight of the dispossessed Irish driven into the stony airts of a diminished life. In these first four poems of "A Severed Head," the active memory and feeling of Montague's persona supply the allusions and metaphors by which may be glimpsed the rudiments of that Gaelic culture surviving in him, prodigal as he has been. These he does come to claim as patrimony, but only after long estrangement. The sixth poem—the canto's coda beginning "Yet even English in these airts"—reiterates this claim (Montague 1995:

18. These associations are reinforced by the motif's appearance in "Patriotic Suite," the eighth canto of *The Rough Field* (Montague 1995:62).

19. From Latin *caput*, 'head', by way of Old French *chef*. The *Oxford English Dictionary*, 1971, s.v. "chief," cites a 1587 statute as the first political usage of the term: "chiefes and chiefetaines."

38). Once known in feeling ways, such remnants can never be lost to him, however much they may provoke the painful sensations of loss that the symbol of the first lines of "A Grafted Tongue" expresses so well. That speech is inextricably bound up in turn with the persona's own vision of a partisan, nationalist history—the anachronism of "Irish Ireland"—that he has until now, as Montague's manipulations of tone have revealed, tried to evade as something local and limiting.

In "A Severed Head," Montague's persona responds as if he were trying to awaken from the "nightmare" of history, to borrow Stephen Dedalus's phrase. However unanticipated, resisted, or dreaded, history's details come into real presence as if newly discovered. Having so reclaimed history, Montague's persona also claims the understanding that his native traditions have been, to a painful degree, lost to him. Thus, the canto finds its proper gravity in the symbol of the tête coupée, the power of whose psychological resonance equals the depth of its traditional significance. Further, Montague's "plotting" of "A Severed Head" also proposes that the canto's titular symbol has been adopted by his persona as an allegorical badge of his newly perceived political and poetic condition. Thus, the unifying autobiographical theme of *The Rough Field*—the persona's pursuit of consciousness—comes here to a signal focus on language. Of the ten cantos in *The Rough Field*, "A Severed Head" is the only one in which the modernist theme of the manifold difficulties of using language rises repeatedly to the explicit surface of Montague's lines.[20]

"A Severed Head" sets the use and abuse of language—Irish or Béarla, Gaeilge or English—at the heart of *The Rough Field*, just after the first three cantos' opening treatment of fatherland, family, and faith—the Joycean trinity in revised order. By doing that, rather than by translating or transposing whole works, Montague made available to modern poetry in English a rich and renewing poetic resource: the Matter of Ireland domiciled in Gaeilge, as taught from the 1890s through the 1960s. Yet by so dramatically posing that resource as a way of construing the "Troubles" in Northern Ireland, in *The Rough Field* Montague has also politicized the material in ways that unavoidably challenge other poets and other poems coming after, for the rhetorical gesture of his poetic claim can be made only once. After that the claim must be reinvented, as Ciaran Carson and

20. For other modernist elements in *The Rough Field*, see Redshaw 1974.

Seamus Heaney, in his later metaphysical poems, have done. Indeed, Montague's claim on this recalcitrant material in "A Severed Head" may have incited more poets from the South — Michael Davitt and Nuala Ní Dhomhnaill in Irish, Thomas McCarthy in English — than from the North.

Works Cited

Blacam, Aodh de. [1921] 1929. *Gaelic literature surveyed*. Reprint, Dublin: Talbot.

Brophy, James D. 1972. John Montague's "Restive sally-switch." In *Modern Irish literature: Essays in honor of William York Tindall*, ed. Raymond J. Porter and James D. Brophy, 153–69. New York: Twayne.

Butler, Hubert. 1949. The dumb and stammerers in early Irish history. *Antiquity* 23, no. 89: 20–31.

———. 1950. Who were "the stammerers"? *Journal of the Royal Society of Antiquaries in Ireland (JRSAI)* 80:228–36.

Carty, James. [1949–51] 1965. *Ireland: A documentary record*. 3 vols. 4th ed. Dublin: C. J. Fallon.

Coe, Paula Powers. 1989. The severed head in Fenian tradition. *Folklore and Mythology Studies* 13:17–41.

Cross, Tom Peete. 1952. *Motif-index of early Irish literature*. Bloomington: Indiana University Press.

Derricke, John. 1883. *The image of Irelande, with a discouerie of woodkarne*. 1581. Ed. John Small. Edinburgh: Adam and Charles Black.

Fallon, Padraic. 1974. *Poems*. Dublin: Dolmen.

Flanagan, Deirdre, and Laurence Flanagan. 1994. *Irish place names*. Dublin: Gill and Macmillan.

Gardiner, David. 2001. *"Befitting emblems of adversity": A modern Irish view of W. B. Yeats to the present*. Omaha: Creighton University Press.

Gwynn, Edward, ed. and trans. 1924. *The metrical dindshenchas*. Pt. 4. Dublin: Hodges, Figgis.

Harington, John. 1804. *Nugae antiquae, being a miscellaneous collection. . . .* Ed. Henry Harington. London: n.p.

Hartnett, Michael. 1975. *A farewell to English*. Dublin: Gallery.

Hill, George. [1877] 1970. *An historical account of the Plantation in Ulster at the commencement of the seventeenth century, 1608–1620*. Intro. John G. Barry. Shannon: Irish University Press.

Joyce, P. W. 1920. *The origin and history of Irish names of places*. 3 vols. 1869–70, 1913. Dublin: Educational Company of Ireland.

Kinsella, Thomas. 1970. The Irish writer. In *Davis, Mangan, Ferguson? Tradition and the Irish writer. Writings by W. B. Yeats and by Thomas Kinsella,* 57–70. Dublin: Dolmen.

———. 1995. *The dual tradition: An essay on poetry and politics in Ireland.* Manchester: Carcanet Press.

Knott, Eleanor. 1916. The Flight of the Earls, 1607. *Ériu* 8:191–94.

Longley, Edna. 1975. Searching the darkness: Richard Murphy, Thomas Kinsella, John Montague, and James Simmons. In *Two decades of Irish writing: A critical survey,* ed. Douglas Dunn, 118–53. Cheadle: Carcanet.

Mac Cana, Proinsias. 1970. *Celtic mythology.* London: Hamlyn.

MacLysaght, Edward. 1957. *Irish families: Their names, arms, and origins.* Dublin: Hodges Figgis.

———. 1960. *More Irish families.* Galway: O'Gorman.

Marcus, Phillip L. 1974. Yeats and the image of the singing head. *Éire-Ireland* 9, no. 4:86–93.

Meyer, Kuno, ed. and trans. 1893. Two tales about Finn. *Revue Celtique* 14:241–43.

———. 1910. *Fianaigecht: Being a collection of hitherto inedited Irish poems and tales relating to Finn and his fiana, with an English translation.* Dublin: Hodges Figgis.

Montague, John. 1964. "The painting of Barrie Cooke." *Dubliner* 3, no.1:38–41.

———. 1969. La vie et l'oeuvre de Samuel Beckett. In *Malone meurt, Oh les beaux jours,* by Samuel Beckett, 23–45. Paris: Éditions Rombaldi.

———. 1972. *The rough field.* Dublin: Dolmen.

———. 1972 [recte 1973]. *A fair house: versions of Irish poetry.* Dublin: Cuala.

———. 1973–74. Primal scream: The late le Brocquy. *Arts in Ireland* 2, no. 1:4–14.

———. 1974a. *The cave of night.* Cork: Golden Stone.

———. 1989. *"The figure in the cave" and other essays.* Ed. Antoinette Quinn. Syracuse: Syracuse University Press.

———. 1995. *Collected poems.* Winston-Salem: Wake Forest University Press.

———. 1998. *"Death of a chieftain" and other stories.* 1964. Dublin: Wolfhound.

Ó Duígeannáin, Micheál. 1940. On the medieval sources for the legend of Cenn (Crom) Cróich of Mag Slécht. *Féilsgribhinn Eóin Mhic Néill: Essays and studies presented to Professor Eóin Mac Neill on the occasion of his seventieth birthday, May 15th, 1938,* ed. John Ryan, 296–306. Dublin: At the Sign of the Three Candles.

Ó Faoláin, Seán [Sean O'Faolain]. 1942. *The Great O'Neill: A biography of Hugh O'Neill, Earl of Tyrone, 1550–1616.* New York: Duell, Sloan, and Pearce.

Redshaw, Thomas Dillon. 1974. John Montague's *The rough field:* Topos and texne. *Studies* 63:31–46.

———. 1982. That surviving sign: John Montague's *The bread god* (1968). *Éire-Ireland* 17, no. 2:56–91.

Room, Adrian. 1994. *A dictionary of Irish place-names.* 1986. Belfast: Appletree Press.

Ross, Anne. 1967. *Pagan Celtic Britain: Studies in iconography and tradition.* London: Routledge and Kegan Paul.

————. 1970. *Everyday life of the pagan Celts.* London: B. T. Batsford.

Shaw, Rose. 1931. *Carleton's country.* Dublin: Talbot.

Skelton, Robin. 1961. Review of *Poisoned lands,* by John Montague. *Critical Quarterly* 3, no. 4:375–77.

Stokes, Whitley, 1903. "The battle of Allen." *Revue Celtique* 21:41–70.

————. 1905. *Félire Óengusso Céli Dé, The martyrology of Oengus the Culdee.* London: Henry Bradshaw Society.

Tymoczko, Maria, trans. 1981. *Two death tales from the Ulster Cycle: "The death of Cu Roi" and "The death of Cu Chulainn."* Dublin: Dolmen.

John McGahern's *Amongst Women*

Whenever a world is about to disappear, a poet emerges to utter it, and through that poet it achieves a comprehensive articulation. If that world has been self-enclosed or cut off by the facts of nature from a wider society, then it often reaches such a point of artistic refinement through its own inner resources. Tomás Ó Criomhthain on the Blasket, J. M. Synge on Aran, W. B. Yeats on Anglo-Ireland, Kate O'Brien on the Victorian Catholic upper class — all these became elegists to a dying culture. In every case it was a culture that remained so separate and so sequestered as to evoke that intense form of writing that is poetic, even though it is formally offered as prose.

John McGahern was born in Dublin in 1934 but grew up in Ballinamore, County Leitrim, where his mother was a teacher. The father, a police sergeant, lived thirty miles away in the barracks at Cootehall, County Roscommon, and it was to these that the boy was moved following the death of his mother in 1945. Encouraged by a local Protestant family, the Moloneys, to enjoy the run of their library, he developed a love of reading. Yet the early experience of death and removal was crucial.

McGahern is the major contemporary inheritor of a durable mode of Irish writing: an artist of the self-enclosed world. Another name for this kind of work is "epic." In his books he attempts, like Yeats in *On Baile's Strand,* to study the fate of those heroes who survive to live in the wan afterglow of a heroic engagement. In *Amongst Women* (1990), that engagement is the Irish war of independence itself. The central character is Moran, a man who once contemplated revolution or death but who must now live through the long diminuendo of the death of his revolution. The guerrilla fighters, of whom he was a great and successful leader, have lost their old glamour and been replaced by a cunning breed of priest, politician, and doctor. Doubtless, all this was inevitable, the sad destiny of revolutions everywhere, but Moran, who had always expected to die in action, must now endure the indignities of an ignoble peace. "What was it all for?" he asks; "the whole thing was a cod" (5).[1] Only seven of the twenty-two men in his flying column lived to witness the truce, and they were in most ways the unlucky ones, doomed to live like aliens in the new land that they had brought into being.

The portrait of Moran owes something to the one truly great auto-biography to emerge from the war, Ernie O'Malley's *On Another Man's Wound* (1936). O'Malley also never expected to survive the battles and found the postheroic world quite underwhelming. In a subtle comment on O'Malley's other major book, *The Singing Flame* (1978), which treats of the civil war, McGahern has observed: "There is a pervasive and sad longing throughout for the clarity of action, as if action in itself could bring clarity to the confusion and futility of friends and former comrades fighting one another" (McGahern 1998:4).

Moran bears the name of one of the defeated, immobilized protago-nists of Samuel Beckett's trilogy, and his search, like theirs, is for a tense appropriate to a man whose life seems over, even while it still goes on. He seems to live entirely on prospects and even more on retrospects, but be can never submit to the sacrament of the present moment, being cursed always to take long views. The past is a storehouse of memories to rebuke the mediocrity of the present. The future is only what that mediocrity will become. All of McGahern's central characters have a sort of second sight by which the shape of a future life becomes discernible, but that shape is seldom consoling, and they would do far better to live without that knowledge. The trick, seldom mastered, is to realize the present, to submit to the immediate moment. This is all but impossible in a culture so de-nuded of sustaining traditions: the world of Moran has divested itself of the old folk and musical lore, but the vacuum has not been filled by a more modern version of civility or culture. Rituals of death abound in a land-scape that otherwise knows only the death of ritual. All the old institu-tional supports to human decency have been stripped away.

This state of things poses the major technical problem for McGahern. If the short story is the form appropriate to the hunted outsider figure, the novel is the one calibrated to a fixed and settled society. Yet postindepen-dence Ireland had scarcely evolved the sort of layered social fabric from which a novelist might draw some threads: this may account for the sense

---

1. All quotations from *Amongst Women* are taken from the 1990 Faber and Faber edition (McGahern 1990a).

of loneliness and isolation in McGahern's world.[2] The novel implies a sense of social amenity, shared discourse, even collective leisure, such as Ireland was beginning to settle into at the midcentury, but the very choice of that form implies a defeat for Moran's world of outlawry and heroic dissidence. *Amongst Women* may have begun as a short story about such a figure, only to turn into a novel whose real focus is on his daughters: it is with them that the narrative begins and ends.

The simple opening sentence indicates a new social order: "As he weakened, Moran became afraid of his daughters" (1). They epitomize the complexity of a modern life to which he has never fully submitted, yet they also carry its stigmata of anomie and alienation that leave them longing for "home." Even after years of married life in great cities, they will think of Great Meadow as their still center. In those cities they are but "specks of froth" against the passing scene, whereas in Great Meadow they feel themselves aristocrats of "a completed world" (2). The discrepancy is akin to that predicted by an aunt for the nine-year-old William Yeats, as he set out from Sligo for London: "Here you are somebody. There you will be nobody at all" (Yeats 1955:27). Great Meadow confers the shape and structure of a life on the Moran daughters, and they cannot allow their father to die until his life also assumes the contours of a real meaning. However obscurely, he resents their refusal to let him slip away, sensing in it a version of his own fear of death, now far deeper and more demeaning than in the days of the flying columns.

The narrative of those days requires the epic boasting of the short, self-contained anecdote. As Moran and his former lieutenant regale each other with accounts of ambushes of English forces who seemed almost to court defeat, they lament the lost splendor of that epic world. Moran notes, "For people like McQuaid and myself the war was the best part of our lives. Things were never so simple and clear again" (6). Moran was not sociable, and he was unable to make the sort of friendships that advance a peacetime career: the closest he got to any man was when he saw him through the lens of a rifle. He has not prospered in the new business order to anything like the same extent as McQuaid, a cattle dealer who drives a Mercedes. Yet even McQuaid has done his utmost to re-create his jobbing world in the image of the flying column. As exploitative as Moran of his

2. See Sampson, 1993:235. I am very indebted to Sampson's excellent chapter on *Amongst Women*.

women, he abandons his wife and home without explanation for days on end, only to burst suddenly into the house with demands for feeding and watering: "there's six men here with lorries" (13).

Their accounts of the fighting are almost Homeric in the detail accorded to passing engagements and also in the telescoping of major events: "Next we had the Treaty. Then we fought one another" (18). Moran has the gift of few words and of telling understatement, but it is a mode that seems to be ratified by the surrounding narrative, for the dialogue is never a record of how the characters speak, so much as a shorthand summary of their way of speaking. The supreme economy of McGahern's writing — which never draws attention to itself and always gives exactly the image that it receives — is achieved in the taut, telegraphed conversations. Neither the characters nor the writer would regard wordplay or manipulations of language as anything other than self-indulgence. It is as if the characters themselves have come to understand the artistic principle that the most effective utterance is that which leaves out more than it lets in.

The anecdotes told by Moran and McQuaid to the girls at the outset are really a collection of war stories. So, in a deeper sense, is the book as a whole. Its epic quality owes much to McGahern's deep immersion in Tomás Ó Criomhthain's *An tOileánach (The Islandman,* 1929), the classic account-from-within of Blasket Island life in the late nineteenth and early twentieth centuries, for the world surrounding Great Meadow is never described, since intimacy with it has already been assumed.

If every artist is to some degree a translator, in the sense of one who knows how a tradition may live in the very lament for its passing, then this is especially true of McGahern, who has always recognized that no lament is ever final. In Ireland the account of the eclipse of one dispensation may itself provide the narrative form that enables its own successor. If the novel is in many ways a domesticated version of epic, then *Amongst Women* may also be read as an attempt to assess what happens when certain epic values are "translated" into the discourse of a more modern world.

The mythic element is present in the refusal of the narrative voice to set *Amongst Women* in a very particular time or place (although references to Boyle and to Elvis Presley suggest the north midlands of the late 1950s or early 1960s). McGahern has praised this element in *An tOileánach,* that "could as easily have taken place on the shores of Brittany or Greece as on the Dingle Peninsula" (McGahern 1989:56). For him the truly great writers are characterized by the same virtues and the same abiding themes: only journalists and local colorists are seekers of difference, people who mistake variety for truth.[3] By this method, the writer manages to be utterly faithful to his immediate world of Roscommon/Leitrim, yet by keeping the references to that region vague and sparing, he can treat it as an everywhere.

The great evil to be avoided — as it was avoided by Ó Criomhthain — is to treat the events narrated as part of some portentously national narrative. All literature for McGahern, like all politics, is local: he once joked that Ireland is an island composed of thirty-two separate, self-governing republics called counties (McGahern 1993:11). It follows that the style of the narrative will be less an expression of the author's personality than a strict expression of the reality of the social world that it is asked to record. The subject, in short, determines the style, and it would be an act of near criminal egotism for an author to develop a personal signature that might then come between the reader and the reality to be presented. Which is not to imply that the author lacks personal feeling or opinion about all that he records. Yet these are expressed only seldom, and therefore to some telling effect. In that, at least, McGahern is at variance with Ó Criomhthain, who rarely offers a personal view and never one that rejects the conventional wisdom of the island.

Much of the authority of McGahern's writing derives from its combination of felt intimacy and achieved distance: he writes again and again of the power of local custom, but often having captured that power, he analyzes it with the steely language of a somewhat bemused anthropologist, convinced that there must always be some practical explanation for patently strange behavior. At times it is the sense of intimacy that is uppermost, even in the course of a cool analysis: "Moran was neither rich nor poor but his hatred and fear of poverty was as fierce as his fear of illness which meant that he would never be poor but that he and all around him would live as if they were paupers" (10). On other occasions the distance is positively interstellar, as if a Martian newly landed were reporting to people back home on the behavior patterns of civil servants in Dublin, when confronted suddenly with a runaway brother: "Such is the primacy of the idea of the family that everyone was able to leave work at once

3. John McGahern, lecture at University College Dublin, 6 March 1999. The echo of James Joyce (who said that "the ordinary is the domain of the artist; the extraordinary can safely be left to journalists"; quoted in Joyce 1992:xii) is almost certainly deliberate.

without incurring displeasure. In fact their superiors thought the sisters' involvement was admirable" (106). Yet, even in such moments (which are rare enough to be worthy of comment), there is little sense of authorial self-assertion: rather, the method recalls that of Joyce's *Dubliners,* in which "people, events, and places invariably find their true expression" because material and form are inseparable as water and a bucket (McGahern 1990b:68–69).

In *An tOileánach,* Ó Criomhthain expresses a deep, primordial fear of the day when he must draw that most modern of blandishments, a state pension: "I have only two months to go till that date—a date I have no fancy for. In my eyes it is a warning that death is coming, though there are many people who would rather be old with the pension than young without it" (quoted in McGahern 1989:58). The same fear may, at least in part, account for Moran's unwillingness to draw the Irish Republican Army (IRA) pension to which his exploits entitle him: McQuaid berates him for a false pride that denies his daughters good money that might further their education. But no Cú Chulainn ever took a state pension. Beneath the surface camaraderie of the two former soldiers lurks the old warrior desire to be top dog. Moran may be unconsciously envious of McQuaid's material success, and so the last reunion between them erupts into bitter recrimination. McQuaid notices his comrade's need to bask in the glow of perpetual attention (which he takes as a kind of cosmic ratification), and he quits the house, in terminal irritation at Moran's compulsion "to have everything on his own terms or not at all" (21). Before leaving, however, he says very simply, "some people just cannot bear to come in second" (22). It is, perhaps intentionally, as good an explanation of the causes of the civil war as has yet been given.

Thereafter, Moran senses that his doom is sealed. His long periods of withdrawal from family life, periods in which he often takes to the bed, seem to indicate a sullen revolt against the waning of his powers. He is in his way rather like those plates that his daughters broke on the kitchen floor out of sheer nervousness: "Anything broken had to be hidden until it could be replaced or forgotten" (10). And so he resigns himself to the loss of his last remaining comrade, turning to the family structure for a compensating sense of himself: "in a way he had always despised friendship; families were what mattered, more particularly that larger version of himself—*his* family" (22). This seemingly innocuous sentence may also be the best reason yet formulated for the fetishizing of family in the constitutional debates of the 1930s: it was less an assertion of the social bedrock than a flight from the very idea of society as such.

The fear of the pension is really a *timor mortis,* and to stave that off, Moran resolves to marry again. His courtship of Rose Brady is conducted in the local post office, to which he goes on a daily pilgrimage in fruitless hope of a letter from his son Luke, now in England. Only later will it transpire that Luke left following a beating by the father which took him within an inch of his life. The normally unsociable Moran must visit the family of Rose Brady: "though her mother disliked him the custom of hospitality was too strict to allow any self-expression or unpleasantness" (28–29). Rose is attracted by his sense of separateness, his superiority and self-containment. Her worried mother asks his children (whom she likes) about the rumors of beatings, but loyally they deny that these are worse than usual.

At a barn dance, where once he had been king of the night, Moran refuses to take a lesser place: "He would not take part at all" (37). Soon he no longer bothers to shave before his visits to the post office, showing that "he had gone as far towards Rose as he was prepared to go" (31). At the wedding he wears no new clothes, only his brushed brown suit, and he shames his daughters by walking the last furlong to the church in breach of a local custom that calls for a car, much as he appalls the Bradys by insisting that the wedding feast be held in their home. In years to come even the simplest gatherings of that family were held in hotels, as if to exorcise the terrible memory of that violation of social decorum, and this even though the officiating priest had praised the "outstanding simplicity" as a return to old ways (43). This is the sole reference to the priest in the novel, as if in this walk-on role he were no longer a real spiritual force in the lives of the people, whatever his social éclat. Moran, who despises priests and doctors as the illegitimate beneficiaries of his revolutionary activities, is strangely serene on his wedding day, "as if he needed this quality of attention to be fixed upon him in order to be completely silent" (45). Yet he will recur more than once to the failure of the priesthood to provide a secure prospect of eternal life. That, even more than social parasitism, is the inexcusable offense: "Strange, to this day I never met a priest who wasn't afraid to die. I could never make head or tails of that. It flew in the face of everything" (74). That fear of death was really part of their denial of life, a denial characteristic of those who had lost the tragic sense and who could never look beyond death to what comes after. In this, they contrasted utterly with Ernie OMalley, who was supremely confident that his enemies could never triumph, because dead men would help to beat them in the end.

After the marriage, Rose soon establishes the house as a place of warmth and nurturing, which it had never been under Moran. Soon the children are coconspirators, as she paints all the walls and brings plums and eggs from her old home. They can sense that the patriarchy epitomized by the father, far from being a sign of his strength, is an outward covering of his male weakness. For he is a man who feels not at all at home in the world. Under Rose's benign and loving care, even his daughters come to seem like aliens, members of another species entirely. In theory the women are mastered by this paterfamilias, but in practice "they were controlling what they were mastered by" (46). Moran lives in fear of the life instinct that they epitomize, and he comes to resent his younger son Michael's nurture of pretty flowers: "I suppose one of these days you'll be getting yourself a skirt" (65). This sentence turns out to be prophetic, in ways that Moran never intended. The flowers offend his heroic sensibility, for they have no use value, seeming redundant in their beauty; better by far, says Moran, to plant vegetables, maybe carrots. Yet already Michael has learned to view his father's brutal labors on the farmland through an alternative frame of reference, seeing them as "voluntary slavery" (65) — just what the revolution he fought for was designed to avoid. Moran's attempt to recruit his son to his own scheme of things amounts to no more than enlisting his help in the felling of trees (a war on nature initiated by the English Puritans of the seventeenth century): "this man and me are after slaughtering a few trees out there," Moran says (47). The hatred of beauty among the men of Moran's generation was attributed by McGahern to the fact that they could never fully convince themselves that they owned it.[4]

Chastened by the rebuffs, Rose increases the number of her visits to her former home, bringing apples from Great Meadow and returning laden with eggs and plums. Moran seems to notice only what she takes: his racial fear of the poorhouse is so ingrained that he panics at the thought of lost produce. Deeper than that, however, is the sense that any departure was a threat to the proud self-enclosure of his aristocratic world, an acknowledgment of social interdependence. It is probably this that leads him

4. Lecture at University College Dublin, 24 February 1999.

to deliver the third and most bitter rebuke to Rose: "we managed well enough before you ever came round the place" (69). Her grave and dignified reply—that she would not live where she was no use—is delivered with the quietness and desperate authority of someone who has discovered that "they could give up no more ground and live" (71). At this very moment, in the confusion that is as close as he will ever come to an apology, Moran realizes one of the great mysteries of his marriage: he knows less about his wife now than he did when first he met her as a stranger in the post office.

In one sense this is simply a wise recognition on Moran's part that while he may be able to categorize acquaintances, it is impossible to do so with those who share our daily lives. But in a more profound way, it is also McGahern's reminder that his characters all have depths that are hidden not just from one another but most of all from him. His duty is to honor the mystery of their being, and this is done by the eloquence of a powerful reticence that constantly reminds readers of how limited our knowledge of any person can be. *Amongst Women* is filled with vivid, rapid portraits of the main characters, such as might be made by an IRA outlaw, whose very life might depend on such powers of summation, but the book's ultimate focus is less on this or that person "than a study of the bonds that form individuals into a 'whole,' represented by 'the house'" (Sampson 1993: 217).

If *An tOileánach* is characterized by the rhythms of "a continual setting out and a returning" (McGahern 1989:56), then so is *Amongst Women*. Patrick Kavanagh claimed no less for his own aesthetic, suggesting that the truth of "going away" was matched by that of "returning" and that the latter was the ultimate in sophistication (quoted in Kennelly 1973:180). The first such return happens when Maggie comes home for Christmas, to share the story of her adventures in London and to compare them with those of Rose some years earlier in Glasgow. Moran, no longer the center of things, soon becomes listless and bored. His only interest is in news of his "lost" son Luke, who seems more vivid a presence in his troubled imagination than those loyal children by his very side. Even the reduction of London to a sort of dormitory suburb of rural Ireland holds no fascination for him. The younger girls, Sheila and Nora, are spellbound by contrast, "so poised on the edge of their own lives that they listened as if hearing about the living stream they were about to enter" (80).

The phrase that echoes Yeats's "Easter 1916" is very deliberately used, for Moran represents (as do the republican rebels of Yeats's poem) a heart with one purpose that seems "Enchanted to a stone / To trouble the living stream" (Yeats 1983:181). Yet the image is more complex than is often allowed or than Yeats may even have intended: the hearts may only "seem" enchanted to a stone, for without that stone in its fixity, no ripples could form and move around it at all.[5] By their refusal to change, the rebels have changed everything, "changed utterly," and Yeats is honest enough to admit that. McGahern's use of the image is similarly open: while it would be tempting to think of Moran as "the stone's in the midst of all" (Yeats 1983:181), a hero holding fast against a sea of troubles and seeking to arrest the living stream, the same is true of his children. They also try to hold back time, to prevent their dying father from slipping away, to prolong the vivid feelings of childhood. Yet the very structure of the book, in which there are no separate chapters but a succession of events linked seamlessly to one another, suggests just how futile is this attempt.[6] Everything in the book is somehow magically and rigorously linked to everything else: the visit to Strandhill by the elder couple is repeated by a younger couple, and the repetition of leitmotifs produces the oceanic flow and resonance of the finest music.

There are certain redeeming moments when it seems possible that the attempt to hold back time might just about succeed, and these are the occasions on which the family members seize a day out of the flow of their lives in order to save the hay. In such passages the writing expresses, even if it can never quite explain, the mystery of life as a process beyond all human comprehension and the power of nature to heal maimed lives. These moments are Hardyesque in their intense beauty, and they may owe something to that author's observation, near the close of *Far from the Madding Crowd*, that work (even more than pleasure) may bind men and women or even entire communities together. The nightly rosary, decreed by Moran, is less a religious ritual than a means of asserting family unity ("the family that prays together stays together" was an old motto), but it is out in the fields that the children discover the old Benedictine truth that to labor is to pray anyway: "They loved the sound of swishing the sheaves made as they were stooked, the clash of the tresses of hard grain against grain, the sight

5. Maud Gonne pointed this out to Yeats in a letter responding to an early version of the poem; see White and Jeffares 1992:384–85.
6. This was first pointed out by Denis Sampson in a brilliant passage in *Outstaring Nature's Eye* (1993:220–23).

of the rich ears of corn leaning delicately out on the shoulders of the stooks" (68). It is of moments like these that Moran is thinking when he says: "Alone we might be nothing. Together we can do anything" (84).

Inexorably, time's flow works to undo such hopes. Sheila and Nora achieve fine results in their examinations and leave for secure jobs in the city. At home the girls had served as a protective screen between Michael and his father; now that they are gone, the pleasure of Michael's cosseted existence is replaced by raw exposure to the old man's being. His interest in the flower garden turns out to be so flimsy that it cannot survive without their praise, and he soon embarks on a reckless love affair with an older local woman, newly returned from America. He plays truant from school and drives with her in her car across the countryside, like a motorized version of Diarmaid with his Gráinne, and eventually he leaves home rather than face the naked whipping that led Luke to flee the house. Helpless, Moran can only thank the girls for what they did for Michael in Dublin, before he went on to England. "They're all gone now" (125), he broods sadly, in the manner of Synge's old Maurya, who has lost her children to the seas of life in *Riders to the Sea*.

The echo of Synge is as deliberate and as resonant as that of Yeats. The lesson of *Riders to the Sea* is that not even the family can provide anything more than a fragile bulwark against the forces of nature. The wind and sea themselves could invade a country kitchen, proving that there is no safety in the domestic role. Not even the home was a fully secure haven, for it could not but reflect the processes at work in the outside world. The rosary as led by Moran is no more potent an answer to the superior force of the elements than was the holy water sprinkled by Maurya:

> A wind was swirling round the house, sometimes gusting in the chimney, and there was an increasing sense of fear as the trees stirred in the storm outside when the prayers ended. For the first time the house seemed a frail defence against all that beat around it.
>
> The prayers had done nothing to dispel the sense of night and stirring trees outside, the splattering of rain on the glass.   (90)

In that context, the children's feeling that within this shadow and these walls they would never die might seem to show a lack of real intelligence: as long as they sojourn in its embrace, they share in the delusion of its owner that time itself can be set at naught. That is why they try with utter futility to re-create the spirit of Monaghan Day, when the dead McQuaid last visited, but their attempt merely serves to remind their father of his losses rather than his glories.

Claude Lévi-Strauss once remarked that people often imagine in their conceit that they are the narrators of their fondest myths, whereas all the time the myths are narrating them (Levi-Strauss 1964:20). In other words, the resources of an individual are as nothing when compared with the power of the general culture: that is why self-expression can sometimes seem a crime against one's ancestors. The force of custom may become so great as to be self-sustaining, as in those Gaelic tales wherein characters act under *geasa,* some compulsion which is not explicable in terms of modern psychology but which has its own inscrutable inner logic. Ó Criomhthain never bothered to ask why people behaved as they did: "what happens is all" (quoted in McGahern 1989:57). McGahern's own texts seldom argue, judge, or assign motives, leaving such things to be inferred. This is true even of the interior monologues of his central characters: coming as they do from a culture that is rich in emotion yet poor in social and intellectual life, they might be expected to have active inner lives. Yet, with his usual discretion, McGahern often refines a Joycean interior monologue down to the merest sentence or two, as if there might be something indecent about any deeper exposure.

There is no real sense of an achieved society here, any more than there is in the world of Joyce, which may explain why the writing can often seem so close to poetry, but there is an assured implication that beneath the surface drama of the family unit (which is really the widest unit available for inspection by the writer), each character has a reasonably complex inner life that can never be fully articulated but may often be deduced or guessed at. If Ó Criomhthain had read Joyce, this is surely how he would have written. Moran's pain is that he wants to be in an epic but is entrapped in a novelistic world. He would wish to conduct his battles alone against the forces of nature but is inexorably drawn into a social network. McGahern has often quoted the classical anthropologist E. R. Dodds on the linked clash between the essentially *religious* consciousness of a Moran and the *moral* awareness of his children. "Religion," wrote Dodds in *The Greeks and the Irrational,* "grows out of man's relationship to his total environment, morals out of his relations to his fellow man" (quoted in McGahern 1989:59). The problem is that the religious and the moral sense are, despite the popular misconception, utterly opposed to each other and likely to destroy each other in the end.

Within the "moral" scheme of things, it is perfectly right for Luke and Michael to leave home and make their way in the world, but to the "religious" mind-set, their going must seem like a breach of *geasa*, an abandonment of the household gods, a denial of their own father's right to the immortality that permits a man to live all over again in his sons. This most ancient of myths speaks through Moran as surely as the land itself seeks articulation through his tiring body: "Instead of using the fields, he sometimes felt as if the fields had used him. Soon they would be using someone else in his place. It was unlikely to be either of his sons" (130).

The conflict is Oedipal but also "Cuchulanoid," and its tragic irreconcilability is summed up by Luke, who says "Either I'm crazy or he is" (146) and refuses point-blank to return home. To Moran, the quality of self-reliance and individuality that Luke felt necessary to a successful career in England appears as no more than a brutal apostasy, yet, as in Yeats's dramatic treatment of the myth, there is a strong implication that it is the women who really impel the narrative from start to finish and that it is the men's inability to live for long at peace with the feminine principle of life that leaves them at war among themselves.[7] Luke is too like his father for any rapprochement to be possible. Yet Michael is reconciled, even to the point of returning regularly to be affirmed in his frail existence by the Great Meadow.

The later stages of the book are enacted at a fast pace, with some loss of intensity in the writing, but on the understanding that the living stream is now unstoppable. Maggie returns with a hard-drinking, leather-jacketed young man, who is attracted by her "separateness" yet appalled when finally confronted with its source. Though Mark is of Irish background himself, he views the rituals of Great Meadow through the uncomprehending eyes of a rank outsider, breaking all its protocols when he asks for the loan of Moran's car and then again when he invites Moran and Rose to the pub. "That's going to be their life," observes a prescient Moran, "gather money, then a spree" (139). It is this penchant for taking the long view that prevents him from endorsing Mark's commitment to extracting

---

7. This is, for example, McGahern's reading of the symbolic meaning of Yeats's *Purgatory*, as expressed in his lecture at University College Dublin, 17 February 1999. But the same interpretation might be offered of *On Baile's Strand*.

the maximum from the present moment: he sees too deeply into the potentials of that moment for its meaning to be tolerable. Many of Synge's characters show a similar affliction and try as best they can to make the present participle real, but Moran cannot do that. For Mark, Great Meadow seems more like a war area than a home. It is an astute perception of what it is like to live in the backwash of a heroic world, where people with new information are intent on keeping it from others. The world around Great Meadow is one where people can be fully themselves only in the company of others, yet everyone is a potential enemy of everyone else, and no final privacy is possible. At home Maggie seems divested of the confidence and singularity that had so impressed Mark in London.

As he cuts the grass in the great field, Moran inadvertently supplies an image of the family's condition, cutting the legs off a hen pheasant. "I know," he apologizes breezily to Rose, "You can't see them in the grass. Anyhow the hares escaped" (159). If (as William Blake once wrote) the cut worm forgives the plow, then perhaps also the hen pheasant absolves the harvester. This is one version of the workings of tradition: that the wound of an animal will start at once to heal even as the body is dying of the shock. Another is offered by Rose to Michael just before he runs away for the last time: "He'll not change now. All you have to do is appear to give in to him and he'd do anything for you after that" (122). She alone of all the characters in the book has learned the wisdom which holds that all traditions must seem to die in order to be reborn in some newer form. As the arranger of what sweetness is to be found in the Morans' botched lives, she becomes a surrogate for the artist — and so for the workings of the creative principle.

The task of the writer, as McGahern sees it, is "to pull the image that moves us out of darkness" (McGahern 1990c:10), that darkness in which it was missing, presumed dead. To write the image is to remember it in the literal sense of that word, to recall it to consciousness, and to liberate its once despised but now real expressive potential. The process is like Walter Benjamin's redemptive time or Marcel Proust's involuntary memory: while it is vain to try too consciously to redeem the past (as the sisters do on their ill-fated Monaghan Day), it is perfectly proper to unleash old energies once trapped within a buried image.[8]

Moran's own version of Irish tradition is quite different from these. He

8. On this concept see Wolin 1982; for a good summary of the Proustian analysis, see Sampson 1993:13–20.

sees it as a state of eternal dissidence, and it is this view that leads him to identify with the local Protestant Rodden, who as a member of a beleaguered class fed Moran's own instinct for rebelliousness: "No matter how favourably the tides turned for him he would always contrive to be in permanent opposition" (163). Even as a paterfamilias, he acted as if he were never really in anything more than a temporary occupation of a safe house. Rodden, more assured, feels at home in a world that may see him as tangential, cheerfully and efficiently adjusting the harvesting machine to the actual contours of the local earth.

The scene in which the entire family (minus Luke) gather to save the hay is another Hardyesque set piece of ecstatic communal labor: timeless, seasonal, mindlessly beautiful. On this type of occasion alone does Moran learn how to live one day at a time and to redeem life's harvest. In this he might be seen as a version of Tomás Ó Criomhthain, who saw the experience of a person as "a succession of single days" not to be squandered, in McGahern's own reading of the book (McGahern 1989:56), and who knew that "there is nothing more difficult to seize than the day" (1990a: 106). Yet even in the midst of that blessedness, the family experiences what seems like a violation. Sheila's new husband, Sean Flynn, grows exhausted by the manual labor and returns to the house with his wife, and there they make love to the consternation of all the others. Even the rakish Michael feels that the true virginity of the house has been lost in their selfish absorption. It is a mark of how deathly the house has become that the simple lovemaking of newlyweds should seem like a betrayal of what it stands for.

"I suppose it'll be long before the house is ever as full again," opines Rose after the last of the children has gone (168). Moran looks as if it were unlucky to say such things, yet he himself has shown no compunction about making gloomy prognostications for the others. In *An tOileánach*, Ó Criomhthain suggests that it is best to take each day at a time, because "to plan ahead is as useless as to look back in regret" (quoted in McGahern 1989:57). Perhaps Moran, while he faces into the end, is searching for a similar wisdom. "There seems to be a superstitious fear of predicting events," says McGahern of *An tOileánach*, "as if the very human attempt itself may be enough to incur the wrath of nature" (57). It is in these circumstances that Moran achieves his miraculous epiphany. As his bodily powers wane, he grows ever more respectful of nature, even while despairing of humans.

One day he struggles out to lean on a post and survey the Great Meadow. McGahen writes, "He had never in all his life bowed in anything to a mere other. Now he wanted to escape, to escape the house, the room, their insistence that he get better, his illness" (178). Out in the fields, faced with the fresh growth and the blue tinges in the green grass, he suddenly feels himself at one with the world, even as he is about to leave it. He begins to live as he conceives of life not as an epic but as a tragedy: "To die was never to look on all this again. It would live in others' eyes but not in his. He had never realized when he was in the midst of confident life what an amazing glory he was part of. He heard his name being called frantically" (179). This scene resonates beautifully, and contrapuntally, with two preceding ones. In the first scene, Moran had shot an annoying jackdaw and the children had called out in terror to ensure that he had not killed himself, and in the second, Michael, suddenly indifferent to his garden flowers, chooses to ignore that same "glory" that now entrances his father.

That epiphany is hard won. Even on the day of his wedding to Rose, Moran had felt numb—as if his life were passing before his eyes rather than being fully lived. He had been described as walking the fields "like a man trying to see" (130). Now that he has been vouchsafed one glorious vision at the end, he can die reconciled to nature. His children, like the daughters of old Maurya in *Riders to the Sea,* have no inkling of the transformation that has overtaken their feeble parent and simply lead him away in the belief that his mind is disintegrating. In Synge's play the old woman, so long guilty of self-absorption and self-pity, managed to transcend all merely personal feeling in offering a prayer for all souls left living in the world. Here in this climactic passage, the man who slaughtered trees now learns to put himself at one with the glory all around him. Throughout his life, Moran owned but could never really see his land. Now he sees it for the first time even as he is about to lose it. The tragic trajectory had, of course, been followed long before Moran: when the Anglo-Irish governed the land in the nineteenth century, then too the owners could not see it, and the seers could never own it. Moran, for most of his days, never deeply felt the field to be his, but in that last scene of blessedness, owner and seer are briefly and wondrously one.

Which is not to say that he dies fully reconciled. The "shut up!" with which he aborts the rosary he once so studiously recited suggests that his anger with the priests is unappeased. At his funeral there is no firing party, but the tricolor is folded and removed when a little man "old and stiff enough to have fought with Finn and Oscar came out of the crowd" (183). This is the only overt reference in the novel to the world of Celtic epic, which lingered still in the countryside of McGahern's youth, "but as a whisper" (Kennedy 1984:40). Yet the epic strain in the Irish novel has never been more definitively affirmed. No sooner is that affirmation concluded than the victory of the novelistic mode is asserted, as the daughters, remarking on the return of their menfolk from the funeral, compare them to a crowd of skittish women coming home from a dance.

What is embodied in *Amongst Women* is nothing less than a total world, whole unto itself, a world that exists on its own terms and in its own style. The people are presented in their full outline, but with that same tact and discretion that would have been necessary for them to live with one another: far more is suggested that can ever or should ever be said. A kind of reticent but steely poetry allows for the same comprehensive representation of a dying culture that was achieved by Ó Criomhthain: if the energy of life is its desire for expression, here a world that remained inarticulate from the time of William Carleton becomes suddenly eloquent. Its intimate knowledge of its landscape and people confirms Synge's view that a work of art is possible only to one person at one time and at one place, yet its anthropological attitude assumes a universal readership. In that sense, it is yet another example of a radical traditionalism, because its documentation of the power of custom sits somewhat oddly with its interrogation of customs grown oppressive.

To some eyes this might seem downright eccentric, were it not for the fact that the eccentric is usually possessed of a deeper than average perception of the true nature of reality. For McGahern every civilization is constructed against the fact of death. Each person moves simultaneously in two quite contrary directions: toward emergence as a distinct individual (a process that can be painful and exhausting) and toward the dissolution of death (a moment even harder to contemplate with equanimity). Institutions such as the family (or literature itself) offer to referee and even reconcile these conflicts, affirming a margin of hope for the persistence of some personal distinction in return for a surrender to the customary demands of tradition. Yet people die anyway, despite the modern tendency to deny most evidence of human mortality.

The civilization that was rural Ireland in the mid–twentieth century had many flaws and many apologists—chief among the latter being Eamon de Valera with his vision of frugal comfort amid pastoral beauty. McGahern's account is more poised and balanced than that of most other prose writers. It captures the warm humanity of country people such as Rose Brady and the Moran children, but also the intellectual torpor of a society that regarded women doctors as exotic and even unhealthy phenomena. It recognizes the direct link between the warmth and the narrowness, because it finds a tremendous intensification of the fundamental realities of life in an enclosed and separate world. This is a world in which not just men and women seem to belong to different species but parents and children as well. All seem self-enclosed. Its children — McGahern included — would wish to feel the intensity of emotion but without the shadowside of terror and fear.

Patrick Kavanagh had made a similar attempt at distinguishing the one from the other and had gone to Dublin to write his way out of that conflict, only to conclude that a city of which he expected more than any city can give would never afford him the solid ground on which to stand while he conducted his analysis. In the end he was drawn back to a sort of late, delayed homage to the stony gray soil of Monaghan. McGahern learned the lesson well, and so he never abandoned that world, even when the provocation of censorship might have made such abandonment understandable. That censorship left him with the reputation of a dissident, yet his underlying aim was to affirm (and in affirming, examine) the values of the very society that so cruelly repressed his work. Even at an early stage, before the banning of The Dark, he enjoyed the status of an "official writer," garlanded with prestigious prizes. He has remained ever since a wonderfully ambiguous figure, a real Tory anarchist, at once a hero to the dissident intelligentsia and yet the deepest and most sympathetic recorder of a world that most members of the intelligentsia have affected to despise. He has written that world from within, with that absolute attention to detail that is in its own way a kind of prayer and might even be one of the private languages of love.

All of which is to say that McGahern's is in part a genius for translation, for translating some elements of an ancient, heroic Gaelic culture into the form of an English novel, a form often considered by some narrow-gauge nationalists as inherently inimical to that old culture. Yet, even in the act of transfer, more may have been gained than lost. For in Ireland everything must first seem to die before it can be reborn as something slightly different.

Works Cited

Joyce, James. 1992. *Ulysses.* London: Penguin.

Kennelly, Brendan. 1973. Patrick Kavanagh. In *Irish poets in English: The Thomas Davis Lectures on Anglo-Irish Poetry,* ed. Seán Lucy, 159–84. Cork: Mercier.

Kennedy, Eileen. 1984. Question and answer with John McGahern. *Irish Literary Supplement,* spring: 40–41.

Lévi-Strauss, Claude. 1964. *Le cru et le cuit.* Paris: Plon.

McGahern, John. 1989. "An tOileánach." *Irish Review* 6 (spring): 55–62.

———. 1990a. *Amongst women.* London: Faber and Faber.

———. 1990b. "Dubliners." In *James Joyce: The artist and the labyrinth,* ed. Augustine Martin, 63–72. London: Ryan Publishing.

———. 1990c. Out of the dark. *Irish Times,* 28 May, 10.

———. 1991. The solitary reader. *Canadian Journal of Irish Studies* 17, no. 1:19–23.

———. 1993. Interview with Gerry Moriarty. *Irish Press,* 6 August, 11.

———. 1998. A revolutionary mind. *Irish Times,* weekend supplement, 11 April, 4.

Ó Criomhthain, Tomás [Tomás O'Crohan]. 1929. *An tOileánach: Scéal a bheathadh féin.* Dublin: Ó Fallamhain i gcomhair le hOifig an tSoláthair.

———. 1951. *The islandman.* Trans. Robin Flower. 1934. Oxford: Oxford University Press.

O'Malley, Ernie. 1978. *The singing flame.* Tralee: Anvil.

———. 1979. *On another man's wound.* Tralee: Anvil.

Sampson, Denis. 1993. *Outstaring nature's eye: The fiction of John McGahern.* Dublin: Lilliput Press.

White, Anna MacBride, and A. Norman Jeffares, eds. 1992. *The Gonne-Yeats letters: 1893–1938.* London: Hutchinson.

Wolin, Richard. 1982. *Walter Benjamin: An aesthetic of redemption.* New York: Columbia University Press.

Yeats, W. B. 1955. *Autobiographies.* London: Macmillan.

———. 1983. *The poems: A new edition.* Ed. Richard J. Finneran. New York: Macmillan.

Notes on Contributors

MICHAEL CRONIN is director of the Centre for Translation and Textual Studies and dean of the Joint Faculty of Humanities, Dublin City University. He is a professional member and former chairperson of the Irish Translators and Interpreters Association. Author of *Translating Ireland: Translation, Languages, Cultures* (Cork University Press, 1996) and *Across the Lines: Travel, Language, Translation* (Cork University Press, 2000), he has coedited numerous volumes on travel, tourism, translation, and culture.

JOANNE FINDON is assistant professor of English at Trent University, Canada. Her work focuses on women in medieval Irish, Welsh, and English texts, and she is author of *A Woman's Words: Emer and Female Speech in the Ulster Cycle* (University of Toronto Press, 1997). She is currently working on a study of the Middle English Digby play *Mary Magdalene*.

HELEN FULTON is associate professor of English at the University of Sydney. Her principal research areas are medieval English and Celtic literatures, and she has recently published on Dafydd ap Gwilym, the Welsh romances, and Chaucer's *Shipman's Tale*. Her interest in Irish Studies is situated within her teaching areas of Middle Welsh, Old Irish, modern Welsh and Irish literatures, discourse analysis, and communication studies.

COLIN IRELAND is resident director of programs in Ireland for the Center for Education Abroad of Arcadia University, and he lectures in Old and Middle English at University College Dublin. He is editor and translator of *Old Irish Wisdom Attributed to Aldfrith of Northumbria: An Edition of "Bríathra Flainn Fhína maic Ossu"* (Arizona Center for Medieval and Renaissance Studies, 1999), and he has published in numerous journals including *Celtica, Peritia, Cambrian Medieval Celtic Studies, Neophilologus,* and *Neuphilologische Mitteilungen.*

DECLAN KIBERD is professor of Anglo-Irish literature at University College Dublin. Much of his published research has negotiated the linguistic divide between literature in English and literature in Irish. His well-known publications include *Idir Dhá Chultúr* (Coiscéim, 1993); *Inventing Ireland: The Literature of the Modern Nation* (Harvard University Press, 1995); and *Irish Classics* (Harvard University Press, 2000), which was recently awarded the prestigious Truman Capote Prize for cultural and literary criticism.

JEREMY LOWE is a lecturer in English at the University of Birmingham, where he first studied Old Irish as an undergraduate. He pursues his research interests in Old Irish alongside his work in medieval English literature. He is primarily interested in representations of violence and transgression in the Ulster Cycle and in the nature of heroism in early Irish literature. His articles have appeared in such journals as *Studia Celtica* and *Exemplaria*.

GORDON McCOY received his Ph.D. from Queen's University Belfast, with a dissertation on Protestant learners of Irish in Northern Ireland. He has published articles on the Irish-language movement and has edited *Aithne na nGael/Gaelic Identities* (Institute of Irish Studies, Queen's University Belfast, 2000). He has worked in the Civil Service and is currently development officer with ULTACH Trust, an Irish-language organization, and board member of Foras na Gaeilge, the cross-border implementation body for promoting the Irish language.

CATHERINE McKENNA is professor of English and comparative literature at Queens College and the Graduate Center of the City University of New York, and coordinator of the Medieval Studies Certificate Program of the City University of New York. She has published extensively on the poetry of the Welsh court poets of the twelfth and thirteenth centuries and is currently completing a comprehensive study of the hagiography of Saint Brigit of Kildare from the seventh through the twentieth centuries.

CAMILLE O'REILLY is a research fellow at the University of Surrey, Roehampton. Author of *The Irish Language in Northern Ireland: The Politics of Culture and Identity* (St. Martin's, 1999), she is also editor of two companion volumes, *Language, Ethnicity, and the State: Regional and Minority Languages in the European Union* (Macmillan, 2001) and *Regional and Minority Languages in Eastern Europe Post- 1989* (Macmillan, 2001). She has published various articles on Irish-language politics and is currently researching "long-haul backpacker" tourism.

CÓILÍN OWENS is associate professor of English at George Mason University. He has edited a collection of essays on Maria Edgeworth and is coeditor (with Joan N. Radner) of *Irish Drama, 1900–1980* (Catholic University of America Press, 1990). He has been active in the American Conference for Irish Studies and in the Washington, D.C., chapters of the Irish American Cultural Institute and Gaelic Language and has produced an audiotape introduction to the Irish language. His articles on James Joyce have appeared in *James Joyce Quarterly, Éire-Ireland,* and *Irish University Review.*

THOMAS DILLON REDSHAW has taught English at the University of St. Thomas since 1971 and has been director of the Center for Irish Studies there since 1996. Long-time editor of *Éire-Ireland* and current editor of *New Hibernia Review,* he is also editor of *Well Dreams: Essays on John Montague* (Creighton University Press, 2003) and is currently editing an issue of *Nua* on James Liddy. His essays have been published in journals including *Studies, Éire-Ireland, Études Irlandaises, Irish University Review, The Linen Hall Review,* and *The South Carolina Review.*

SALLY K. SOMMERS SMITH is associate professor in the College of General Studies at Boston University, where she teaches biology and physics. She holds a Ph.D. in anatomy and cellular biology from Tufts University Medical School. She fell in love with Irish traditional music in 1992 and has studied fiddle with Seamus Connolly, Laurel Martin, Kevin Burke, and Tommy Peoples. Her publications on Irish music have appeared in *Éire-Ireland, New Hibernia Review, The Recorder,* and *The Companion to Irish Traditional Music* (ed. Fintan Vallely, 1999). She reviews recordings for *Irish Music.*

MARIA TYMOCZKO is professor of comparative literature at the University of Massachusetts Amherst. Trained as a specialist in medieval Irish literature, she also publishes on Irish writing in English and on translation. She is translator of *Two Death Tales from the Ulster Cycle* (Dolmen

Press, 1981). Her book on James Joyce, *The Irish "Ulysses"* (University of California Press, 1994), and her book *Translation in a Postcolonial Context: Early Irish Literature in English Translation* (St. Jerome Publishing, 1999) have both won awards from the American Conference for Irish Studies.

Index

Abbey Theatre, 34, 62
Acta sanctorum (ed. Colgan), 146, 149–50, 152
Act of Uniformity (1650), 140 n.1
Act of Union, 14
A. E. *See* Russell, George
Aeneid (Vergil), 9
áes dána (Mod.Ir. aos dána, 'people of arts'), 96. *See also* learned classes
Aesthetes, The, 56 n.12
Afro-Celt Sound System, 114 n.13
Agreement Reached in the Multi-party Negotiations, The, 158; Belfast Agreement, 157, 158 n.2, 162, 165; cross-border implementation body, 158, 164; Good Friday Agreement, 158 n.2; north-south institutions, 158. *See also* Northern Ireland
Aided Con Culainn (*Death of Cú Chulainn,The*), 176
Ailill Flann Bec, 176. See also *Reicne Fothaid Canainne*
Ailill (king of Connacht, seer), 91. *See also* prophecy
aisling ('vision'), 32–33, 41–42. *See also* bard; bardic poetry
Alspach, Russell K., 51 n.8
alterity, 14, 18, 71
Althusser, Louis, 67 n.5
Amairgen, 43. See also *Lebor Gabála Érenn*
American Committee for Irish Studies, 6 n.7
amhrán bréagach ('lying song'), 179
Amongst Women (McGahern), 24, 195–212
An tOileánach (*The Islandman*) (Ó Criomhthain), 24, 198, 200, 203, 209
Anderson, Chester G., 28 n.1
Anderson, R. Bruce W., 129
Andersontown News (newspaper), 161 n.7
Andrews, Elmer, 62

Anglo-Irish, 14, 16, 38, 195, 210; Anglo-Irish idiom, 16. *See also* Ascendancy
Anglo-Irish idiom, 16. *See also* English language
Anglo-Norman. *See* Norman
Anglo-Saxon. *See* English language
Annála Ríoghachta Éireann (*Annals of the Kingdom of Ireland*), 8 n.12, 143–44, 147, 151
Annals of the Four Masters. See *Annála Ríoghachta Éireann*
Antrim, County, 156, 159
Antwerp, 119 n.1
Ara Caeli, 123
Aran Islands, 195
Arbois de Jubainville, Henri d', 43
archaism, 2–4, 8 n.13, 10, 32, 36. *See also* backward-looking
Armagh, County and city, 6, 123, 145, 154 n.14, 175; Book of Armagh, 152; St. Patrick's College, Armagh, 175; Tírechán of Armagh, 6
Arnold, Matthew, 11
Arthurian literature, 9
Ascendancy, 14, 23, 210. *See also* Anglo-Irish
ashplant, 36–38, 41. *See also* flesc filed
At the Hawk's Well (Yeats), 51
Auden, W. H., 172
Augher, County Tyrone (Ir. eochair, 'border, brink'), 184
augury. *See* prophecy
Augustinians, 124
aural transmission. *See* orality

Backward Look, The (O'Connor), 4 n.3
backward-looking, 4, 8 n.13, 9 n.14. *See also* archaism; Irish culture
Bacon, Francis, 145
ballad, 9, 16, 104, 159
bard, 30–35, 37, 40–42, 44, 141–42;

Note on the Cover
Boatman at Connemara by Gerard Dillon

On the cover of this volume is an oil-on-panel painting by Gerard Dillon (1916–71) titled *Boatman at Connemara*. The painting was most likely completed during Dillon's first visit to Connemara, which extended from early summer of 1939 until the outbreak of World War II, when the artist returned to Belfast. Dillon was largely self-taught. Like so many Irish artists in the first half of the twentieth century, he found in Connemara an ideal subject matter and landscape for his art. Constituting a language and iconography for representing Ireland, the images of the West served to epitomize Irish identity and tradition.

The painting is a portrait of a young Connemara boatman standing next to his currach; a bay of the sea topped by more distant mountains is in the background. With its black outlines, the painting has a primitivist feel, notable in the flattened perspective used for the currach, which both emphasizes the tarred canvas of the boat's skin and reveals the keel-less construction of the interior. The traditional boat, characteristic of the landscape of the western coasts of Ireland, is thus as much the subject matter of the painting as the boatman. The double portrait of the boatman and currach gives mute testimony to the heritage of Gaelic Ireland. Deriving from the painterly vocabulary of Dillon's contemporaries in Ireland, the artistic idiom reaches back to Gauguin and Van Gogh as well. Dillon's modernist technique is remarkable for its use of color, particularly the greens of the sky and the brilliant reds that define the boatman's hands, ears, and neck.

Here reproduced courtesy of the Dillon estate, the painting is part of the collection of the University Gallery at the University of Massachusetts Amherst. *Boatman at Connemara* was a gift to the Gallery in 1990 from Joseph Hernon, professor of history at the University of Massachusetts.

Betsy Siersma, director of the University Gallery,
Maria Tymoczko, and Colin Ireland